| *By the same author*

INDEXES AND INDEXING
BOOK COLLECTING
INFORMATION SERVICES
LIBRARY ASSISTANCE TO READERS
THE TREATMENT OF SPECIAL MATERIAL
IN LIBRARIES
DICTIONARIES OF FOREIGN LANGUAGES
BIBLIOGRAPHICAL SERVICES THROUGHOUT
THE WORLD (UNESCO)
INDEXING BOOKS
NEWNES DICTIONARY OF DATES
BRITISH BROADCASTING: A READER'S GUIDE
ENCYCLOPEDIAS, THEIR HISTORY THROUGHOUT THE AGES
MODERN BUSINESS FILING AND ARCHIVES
COMMERCIAL RECORDS STORAGE
A JORROCKS HANDBOOK

# BIBLIOGRAPHIES
Subject and National

A GUIDE TO THEIR CONTENTS
ARRANGEMENT AND USE

Robert L. Collison
*Fellow of the Library Association*

THIRD EDITION
Revised and Enlarged 1968

HAFNER PUBLISHING CO.
NEW YORK 1968

© 1962 Crosby Lockwood & Son Ltd.
26 Old Brompton Road · London · SW7

First published 1951

Second edition: revised and enlarged 1962
Third edition: revised and enlarged 1968

Published in the U.S.A. by
Hafner Publishing Co. New York 1968

*Made and printed in Great Britain by
The Aberdeen University Press*

To
JAMES E. WALKER

*The most efficient investigator, by*
*acquainting himself at the outset with previous collections of*
*material on his subject, avoids the necessity of*
*repeating operations already performed*
*by others, and spares himself the possible mortification*
*of discovering at length by accident*
*that the matter under discussion has already been*
*adequately treated and that therefore his labor has been in vain*
TOM PEETE CROSS

# Foreword

| *by* F. L. KENT, M.A.
Librarian, American University of Beirut

THE author has generously given me the opportunity of contributing a revised foreword to the new edition of this book, and this I do not only with pleasure but also with gratitude for all the benefit that I in common with large numbers of my professional colleagues have derived from the first edition and expect to derive from the second.

Few people are better qualified than Mr Collison to revise this work, or indeed to have written it in the first place. It would be difficult for anybody who had not compiled Unesco's *Bibliographical services throughout the world* for many years past to have kept pace with the immense amount of bibliographical work that has been done since 1951, or for one not possessing his technical skill and experience to have contrived to enclose all the accumulated information within reasonable limits and express it in a readable form. On completing his formidable task of revision, the author must now feel even deeper sympathy with the tribulations of Rupert Simms. One is glad to find Simms's description of his troubles retained in the introduction to this revised edition; all collectors of information suffer from them, and Mr Collison in his dealings with institutions and government agencies the world over—as well as with individuals and published works—must have long and successfully contended with them in their most frustrating form.

If librarianship be applied bibliography, as Professor Irwin assures it is, our success as librarians must be judged by our ability to apply ourselves all over again to Mr Collison's work. We must again check our bibliographical holdings and see how much we score—a humbling thought. Do we score a bonus for any important item which Mr Collison has missed? He can have left us very few chances of this; though like all true scholars he will doubtless welcome additions and suggestions for incorporation in yet another edition at some time in the future.

But what he has really achieved, once again, is to tell us not only what we ought to have, but also how to use it, and for this we are deeply indebted to him. I feel sure that the following pages will be, as were those of the first edition, in frequent and regular consultation by all students of librarianship—young and old—and by all who find their inspiration in libraries.

F. L. KENT

# Preface

I have seen and used many more bibliographies than are listed in this volume: the difficulty has been to keep the number described within reasonable limits and to avoid devoting too much space to those which, through much consultation, have become especial favourites. The question of space is also responsible for the omission of some otherwise important sections: namely, Christian denominations and sects; individual trades and professions; and individual foreign countries. A list of bibliographies of individual authors is, however, included in the chapter on Language and Literature, and from this can be judged how much the inclusion of these other items would have increased the size of this book.

One of the principal pleasures of librarianship is the mutual appreciation of the virtues of good bibliographies: it has been my good fortune to have exchanged much information of this nature, and this work has greatly benefited thereby. In particular I am indebted to Mr J. H. P. Pafford, Goldsmiths' Librarian of the University of London and to his staff for allowing me access and drawing my attention to many important items; to the late Mr K. Howard Drake, Secretary and Librarian of the Institute of Advanced Legal Studies, whose untimely death has robbed us all of an outstanding librarian; to the staff at the BBC Reference Library for informed criticism of bibliographies of all kinds; to Dr A. J. Walford for sharing with me his vast knowledge of the whole field; to the Librarian and staff of the Library at the University of California at Los Angeles for broadening my outlook in 1951–52 considerably by their enthusiastic delight in all things bibliographical; and to Madame Ravage and her successor, Mr Sándor Maller, at Unesco in Paris, for a long and thorough training in bibliographical method. To the last-mentioned I owe my introduction to many eminent bibliographers throughout the world: it is to those devoted men and women—and their predecessors—often working without encouragement or thought of reward, that we owe many of the works recorded in the following pages. Our gratitude to them for their often very remarkable achievements is best expressed by our ensuring that the next generation of bibliographers is fully trained and is fired by an equal desire and zest to serve mankind.

ROBERT COLLISON

| Contents

1. INTRODUCTION   *page* xiii

PART ONE | Subject Bibliographies

2. AUTHORSHIP | BOOK PRODUCTION | PUBLISHING | BOOKSELLING | LIBRARIANSHIP | A NOTE ON ENCYCLOPAEDIAS   3

3. PHILOSOPHY | PSYCHOLOGY | PSYCHO-ANALYSIS   8

4. THEOLOGY AND RELIGION | Bibles | The Christian Church | Non-Christian religions   13

5. THE SOCIAL SCIENCES | Statistics | International affairs | Economics | Finance | Law | Crime and criminology | Social work and welfare | Insurance | Education | Transport | Folk-lore   21

6. SCIENCE | Mathematics | Astronomy | Physics | Nuclear Sciences | Chemistry | Geology | Natural history and biology | Botany | Zoology   45

7. TECHNOLOGY AND INDUSTRY | Medicine | Engineering | Agriculture   65

8. ART | ENTERTAINMENT | AND SPORT | Architecture | Furniture | Ceramics | Numismatics | Costume | Illustrations | Painting | Engraving | Photography | Music | Broadcasting | Films | Theatre | Dancing | A note on sport   76

9. LANGUAGE AND LITERATURE | Literature in the English language: English poetry; plays; fiction; essays and speeches | Individual authors | German literature | French literature | Italian Literature | Portuguese and Spanish literature | Latin and Greek literature | Oriental classics   99

10. GEOGRAPHY | HISTORY | BIOGRAPHY | Great Britain and the Commonwealth | Archaeology | Biography and genealogy 140

## PART TWO | Universal and National Bibliographies

11. UNIVERSAL BIBIOGRAPHIES AND BIBLIOGRAPHIES OF BIBLIOGRAPHIES | Anonymous and pseudonymous works | Bibliographies of bibliographies 157

12. NATIONAL BIBLIOGRAPHIES | Great Britain | United States | France | Germany 164

13. SERIAL PUBLICATIONS 175

14. FURTHER READING 182

INDEX 185

1 | Introduction

There is something very satisfying in handling a well-constructed bibliography: the care and enthusiasm with which the bibliographer has applied himself to his task is reflected in the thoughtful annotations, the ample cross-references and the careful selection of material, so that the user is continually being directed to new and unsuspected resources, his mind stimulated by new ideas and his conception of his subject enriched by the indication of new fields as yet unexplored. The finished product, if good, reads so easily that few give thought to the arduous and exacting nature of the task that confronts every bibliographer anew: perhaps none has described the problems and the difficulties so feelingly as Rupert Simms, the handless historian, in the preface to his *Bibliotheca Staffordiensis* (Lichfield, A. C. Lomax, 1894).

'The *labour* would have been considerably lessened if those to whom application had been made for personal and literary details had obliged with *correct particulars* on such first application' wrote Simms, 'by this neglect the *labour* has been *increased* at least *three-fold*. Take one or two cases:—No. 1 received form of questions, which he filled up and returned to sender, who copied it as sent, and it was printed off. In accordance with his custom a "proof" is sent to No. 1, who corrects it so much that the whole of the paragraph has to be re-set, and great and needless loss is incurred. No. 2 is written to, when the Compiler receives a reply couched in the following terms:—"Mr. B. begs to inform Mr. S. that he cannot spare time to fill in particulars, and begs to return Mr. S. the papers sent." The best and most correct information obtainable is collected and printed off as before, and sent in "proof" to this gentleman, who returns it with: "Mr. B. begs to return Mr S. the 'proof' sent, and which he has corrected." In this case the paragraph is re-set.

'During the progress of the Work the average expense of postage has been about seven shillings per week—some weeks as much as thirty: and on an average the Compiler has received replies from about one-fourth of those to whom communications have been sent.

'The Work is not free from errors: it is not complete or perfect, either as to text or particulars. Names are omitted which ought to have been entered, and facts and dates are wanting, which, had they been included would have added to the value of the Work. These errors and omissions are the result of want of information, and not intentional. The Work is as perfect and as correct as one man can make it by hard work and continued application. Such have been the difficulties, both personal and relative, that only a person intensely in love with the work, and determined to see the book through at all hazards, could have carried out the project. Bibliography for pleasure and in kid gloves would have given up long ago.

'The Compiler repeats that the Work is as perfect and correct as a man in the lower walks of life, having to scramble and fight for the necessities of life—having oftentimes to continue the labour whilst his mind was racked with anxiety as to whence the next needs of a large family were to come from—sometimes hampered and even obliged to delay the work because he *could not find the money to pay the postage*—having more than once been on the verge of being turned out of house and home—could make it.'

The present writer can fortunately lay claim to no such hardships, and in general the work of compiling bibliographies has advanced in recognition since Rupert Simms's times. Nevertheless, there are many who even now question the value of any bibliography since it must be of necessity out of date even before it is printed.

The question must arise even more acutely in the present case, for this book is actually an informal bibliography of bibliographies—a frightening title—which seems very much out of touch with reality. Most people, however, are in the position of knowing what they want without being at all sure that it exists and, more important, where it is. Bibliographies are designed to meet this need and, although there are few completely satisfactory bibliographies, nearly all those available—both old and new—still have their uses. It is true that a bibliography is dated as soon as it is compiled, but even so the work of the scientist or research worker is lightened, since a limit is set to the amount of material which he must search for himself.

There are all kinds of bibliographies: the *Concise Oxford Dictionary* defines a bibliography as 'a list of books of any author, printer, country, subject', which indicates only the beginnings of the subject, for within the frontiers thus defined there are such refinements as selective, comprehensive, evaluative, and other varieties which all have their uses for different classes of workers. But to the student the field is much wider than this: any intelligent list, be it bookseller's catalogue, reading list, library catalogue, or auction list, is of value if it tells him what he wants to know and if, as often happens, it warns him of the existence of material he would otherwise not have known was available.

To the scientist and to the research worker of any kind today bibliographies are not only valuable—they are essential. Many a research worker has found that the task he has completed with so much effort has already been duplicated and the results published elsewhere. Disastrous waste and frustration of this kind can partly be avoided by the intelligent use of and acquaintance with bibliographies.

Introduction | xv

Bibliographies proper are of many kinds: some devote themselves entirely to books, others include periodicals, still others minutely analyse the contents of both. Some try to be comprehensive, others are carefully selective and evaluative. Some merely list items, others annotate them with varying degrees of detail. Very often the annotation, drawn from reviews or personal knowledge of the subject, can tell more about a particular item than can be gained from actual inspection.

The best bibliographies are notable for their consistency of purpose and treatment: the details are given in the same order and form throughout—which facilitates easy reference—and the contents and arrangement are based on an idea which is a real contribution to knowledge. Such bibliographies have in the past usually been the work of one man (such as the great Sonnenschein) although in recent times excellent results have been achieved by groups of bibliographers working as a team—usually under the direction and control of a general editor who really knows what he wishes to achieve.

The difficulty, however, of the one-man system is that with the death of the bibliographer the continuance of his work usually lapses and, if it is resumed later, very often takes a rather different form and changes its aims, with hampering effect on the users of the original work and its supplements.

*Pace* Mr Theodore Besterman and his admirable compilations, the day of the one-man bibliographer seems almost over: witness the case of Paetow whose bibliographical work was deemed too great to be continued by less than a large and learned committee. This is borne out by the Unesco/Library of Congress Bibliographical Survey's *Bibliographical services: their present state and possibilities of improvement* (Washington, 1950), which was 'a report prepared as a working paper for an international conference on bibliography', which stresses the need for continuity and consistency in bibliographical work.

Bibliographies are by no means infallible, although their preparation by a group of scholars usually ensures their having a greater degree of accuracy. But even so, personal opinions and taste are bound to creep in to the detriment of the bibliography itself. Moreover, there will be omissions and errors which, as Simms has shown, are not always the bibliographers' fault.

The form in which a bibliography appears materially affects its use and usefulness. Thus a bibliography arranged alphabetically by authors is quite reliable but is not as useful as one which is classified according to the development and needs of the subject. The amount of detail given is also of great importance. Where the number of pages is given or an annotation appended—quite apart from the publication details which are essential—the value is immeasurably increased. Then, indexes are absolutely essential but in a great many cases they are still not provided.

In the case of bibliographies published periodically, quite often the indexes are only given at the end of the volume which may entail a wait of six months or a year: an exasperating delay since it subjects the user to the unnecessary irritation of searching through many pages in the hope of finding material which may or may not be present, and with the added vexation of perhaps overlooking important items from time to time.

The preparation of bibliographies is always a slow and laborious business, yet their usefulness is seriously impaired if they are too long delayed. This especially applies to those published periodically which need to be punctual if they are to be relied upon. The slightest deviation too from consistency is to be deprecated, since this may also be the cause of essential items being overlooked.

International standards and rules are badly needed: in this connexion the publication of British Standard 1629: 1950 on *Bibliographical References* (Amendment PD 1186, May 1951), with all its faults, is welcome and is well worth careful study. It could certainly not have been published at a better time when the International Conference mentioned above was due to take place.

The sheer delight occasioned by a well-constructed bibliography impels the user to acquire his own personal copy. He is inclined to bore his friends with constant mention of this old standby and to quote interminably from its contents. Booksellers well understand this feeling and not a few of them have in their own homes shelves of rare and wonderful bibliographies from which they quote in their catalogues and thus tempt the well-informed bookman with the bait he best understands. Moreover, some of the best bibliographies have been the work of true booksellers who have desired to immortalize the books which pass through their hands too swiftly.

In a similar fashion, a bad bibliography is a source of constant irritation and resentment, and inaccurate references and poor comments cause the offending volume to be quickly thrown aside. Users of bibliographies are the most critical of readers and only the best will content them. The respect for good bibliographies is only exceeded by the contempt for bad. Thus it is that there are many bibliographies of the past which gather dust today and the wasted work which they represent is sure to inspire sympathy and sorrow in any bibliographer who happens to glance at them.

In this volume I have tried to draw attention to the qualities and uses of the best bibliographies. In all there are not a great many items—some four or five hundred, perhaps—but these are sufficient to put the student and the research worker on the right path. One bibliography

Introduction | xvii

will very often list and describe other available bibliographies in its own field, and through these the whole of the extant bibliographical material quickly becomes apparent, with the exception of the newest items.

New items are appearing every day, and now that peace-time conditions are gradually returning, more and more bibliographies which lapsed before or during the war are being resumed. Some of these owe their new life to the generosity of Unesco whose work in this field cannot be overpraised. These newer items warrant careful study for many of them revise and correct the contents of the older bibliographies considerably. It is possible to keep in touch with the publication of new bibliographies by a regular search of the columns of the *Times Literary Supplement* which reviews most of the more general bibliographies, and by examining the entries under the appropriate subjects in the issues of the *Bibliographical index* which is the most comprehensive record of the present time. And to these, we now have the welcome addition of Unesco's *Bibliography, documentation, terminology* (Paris, 1961 to date), which has a truly international range.

Most libraries have, as part of their basic stock, a collection of the bibliographies of most use to them, and these are freely available to their members. In the search for particular bibliographies there is, moreover, a very useful union list (published by the Greater London Division of the Association of Assistant Librarians early in 1951) which shows the whereabouts of copies of the more important bibliographies in London's libraries. But it must be admitted that librarians give inadequate support to bibliographical effort, as the sales figures for such fine pieces of work as the *Index translationum* or *Archivum* unfortunately demonstrate.

It must be remembered too that there are *living* bibliographies: that is, any good library is a current and historical bibliography of the subjects which it covers, and its catalogues and lists of accessions are invaluable bibliographical material. Notable examples of sources of this type are the libraries of the London School of Economics, the Royal Institute of British Architects, the Patent Office, the Ministry of Works, the Science Museum, and of course the British Museum.

The wealth of bibliographies today and their constant improvement makes it possible for students and research workers to tackle their work with increasing confidence, secure in the knowledge that much of the spade work which their predecessors had to do for themselves is nowadays already completed and made abundantly available. It is recommended that the student of a subject should keep his own manuscript record of general and specialist bibliographies which have been of use to him and which may help him again in the future. The form in which to keep it is naturally that which best suits his particular requirements, but perhaps it is not amiss to urge that plenty of space be left for additions and corrections to items already entered, that a loose-leaf form is preferable so that new items may be inserted without spoiling the arrangement, and that the whole be well indexed so that instant reference can be made to any particular item. The work involved is comparatively simple, and the result will more than repay the time spent in constructing a record of this kind.

# PART ONE
Subject Bibliographies

## 2 | Authorship | Book Production | Publishing | Bookselling | Librarianship

'The study and appreciation of printing is a recognition of the vital function of the graphic arts in our society and our culture', wrote Hellmut Lehmann-Haupt in 1949, and his bibliography is probably the best introduction to the whole art and industry of bookmaking and distribution obtainable today:

LEHMANN-HAUPT, HELLMUT | *One hundred books about bookmaking: a guide to the study and appreciation of printing* | 3rd edition | New York: Columbia University Press 1949

This is a series of enthusiastic appreciations of the most worthy books on writing and lettering, printing history, American developments, printing practice, printing types and decoration, illustration, bookbinding and papermaking, and periodicals on these subjects. Another useful guide is The British Federation of Master Printers' *One hundred technical books* (1963), which is a suggested nucleus for a printing works library.

On the earliest period of printing there is:

McMURTRIE, DOUGLAS CRAWFORD | *The invention of printing: a bibliography* | Chicago: The Chicago Club of Printing Club Craftsmen 1942

but the most important bibliography of printing is a much earlier work:

BIGMORE, EDWARD CLEMENTS and WYMAN, CHARLES WILLIAM HENRY | compilers | *A bibliography of printing, with notes and illustrations* | 2nd edition | 3 volumes | Quaritch, 1884-6 (reprint in 2 volumes | New York: Duschnes 1945)

which includes typefounding, stereotyping, and wood-engraving. Paper, bookbinding, copyright, and the laws regulating the press are omitted. Entries are arranged alphabetically by authors and are heavily annotated. Periodicals are included in the main sequence under that heading, but the promised section on Printers' Societies was not published.

There is also a printed catalogue of the leading institute connected with the printing trade in Great Britain:

SAINT BRIDE FOUNDATION | *Catalogue of the Technical Reference Library of works on printing and the allied trades* | 1919

4 | Authorship | Book Production | Publishing

which includes over 30,000 items, many of them from the libraries of Talbot Baines Reed, William Blades, and the London Society of Compositors. Entries are arranged alphabetically by author, with many analyticals for periodical articles and trade catalogues. Unfortunately there is no subject index.

On the production and distribution of books there is another library catalogue:

BRITISH LIBRARY OF POLITICAL AND ECONOMIC SCIENCE | *Catalogue of a collection of works on publishing and bookselling* | London School of Economics and Political Science 1936

More than 2,500 books and pamphlets are listed, with some brief annotations. British and American government publications are included. Entries are arranged alphabetically by author, and there is an analytical subject index. Since the publication of this catalogue the collection has more than trebled its size. The emphasis is rather on the economic than on the bibliographic aspects of the subjects.

Fine press books are described in the following:

*Modern private presses: a catalogue* | Johannesburg Public Library 1955

TOMKINSON, SIR GEOFFREY | *A select bibliography of the principal modern presses, public and private, in Great Britain and Ireland* | First Edition Club 1928

RANSOM, WILL | *Private presses and their books* | New York, Bowker 1929

each of which records a large proportion of the output of private presses, the first mentioned including the somewhat slim post-war effort, while the last describes a number of obscure American presses. John Ryder's *Miniature folio of private presses* (Richmond, The Miniature Press 1960) will be found helpful for contemporary items.

In addition to the bibliographies already mentioned there are several very useful items which cover a wider field. Notable among these is:

ULRICH, CAROLYN FARQUHAR, and KÜP, KARL | *Books and printing: a selected list of periodicals, 1800-1942* | Woodstock, Vt.: William E. Rudge 1943

which covers archives, palaeography, the history of printing and bookbinding, typography, paper, ink, binding, authorship, publishing, advertising, the book trade, bibliography, libraries, and collections. Entries are annotated, there are appendixes of directories, indexes, year books, associations, organizations, societies, and house organs, and a comprehensive index.

Librarianship | 5

BRITISH FEDERATION OF MASTER PRINTERS | *A selected list of graphic arts literature: books and periodicals* | Revised edition | July 1948

Entries are arranged in alphabetical order of subject and include items on administration, bookbinding, composing, design, electrotyping and stereotyping, general printing, the graphic processes, the history of printing and publishing, inks, driers and varnishes, letterpress printing, lithography, paper, periodicals both British and foreign, photographic processes, reference books, and science for the printer. There are brief annotations and a system of grading entries by symbols into elementary, more advanced and general works. Indexes of authors and publishers are also provided.

There is also the catalogue of Britain's leading society for all people connected with books:

NATIONAL BOOK LEAGUE | *Catalogue of the library ... a collection of books, pamphlets and extracts on the history and practice of authorship, libraries, printing, publishing, reviewing and reading of books* | 1944

to which a Supplement was added in 1948. Entries are arranged in alphabetical order of subjects, with an author index in each volume.

## LIBRARIANSHIP

The literature of librarianship is more extensive than might at first be supposed, and much valuable material lies buried in the back files of obscure periodicals and little-known books. The most general bibliography of the subject is:

BURTON, MARGARET and VOSBURGH, MARION E. | compilers | *A bibliography of librarianship: classified and annotated guide to the library literature of the world (excluding Slavonic and Oriental languages)* | Library Association 1934

Compiled by two students (one American and one British) at University College, the entries cover librarianship in most countries of the world. Arrangement is in classified form, the subjects covered including library history and description, special libraries, libraries for children, library practice, the library profession, law, architecture, co-operation, bibliography, the book, palaeography and archives, and the general bibliographies of librarianship. The bibliography is very heavily annotated. It is selective for bibliography, the book, and palaeography and archives: and annual reports of individual libraries, bulletins for readers and library catalogues are omitted. There is an index of authors and subjects.

6 | Librarianship

Further background material is covered in a remarkably detailed bibliography:

CANNONS, H. G. T. | *Bibliography of library economy: a classified index to the professional periodical literature in the English language/relating to library economy, printing, methods of publishing, copyright, bibliography, etc. from 1876 to 1920* | Chicago: American Library Association 1927

Cannons was an English librarian who built up the main part of this amazing list of over 32,000 references over many years. They are arranged in classified order, with very full subject schedules at the beginning, and a detailed subject index but unfortunately no author index. This was followed by:

*Library literature, 1921–1932:* a supplement to CANNONS'S *Bibliography of library economy, 1876–1920:* compiled by the Junior Members Round Table of the American Library Association, under the editorship of Lucile M. Morsch | Chicago: American Library Association 1934

This is limited almost entirely to periodicals in the English language, and includes books and pamphlets. Entries are arranged in alphabetical order of subject and author. Reviews of professional books are included, and there is an appendix of related material.

The sequence is unbroken, being continued by:

*Library literature: an annotated index to current books, pamphlets and periodical literature relating to the library profession, 1933 to date* | New York: H. W. Wilson 1933 to date

This includes author and subject entries in one alphabetical order, and abstracts are given for the more substantial foreign items. Translations of difficult titles are given. There is also a checklist of the 165 periodicals and of the books indexed. The bibliography is published quarterly cumulating into annual and three-year volumes.

*Library science abstracts 1950 to date* | Library Association 1950 to date

This is published quarterly, with an annual index of authors and subjects. It is international in scope, and covers general surveys of library services, co-operation, national and governmental libraries, university libraries, special libraries, information services, public libraries, work with children, hospital libraries, cataloguing, classification and indexing, professional education, reproduction processes, the art of the book, bibliography and bibliographies, and authors, publishers, and readers. The abstracts are very full and are signed. Attention is also drawn to the Library Association's classified *Catalogue* (1958) of its own library; and to the *Dictionary catalog* of the School of Library Science at Columbia University (7 volumes. Boston, Mass., G. K. Hall, 1967), which is based on a collection started by Melvil Dewey and, incidentally, includes an historical collection of 5,800 children's books.

From this chapter we now turn to subjects of more general interest, and readers will find that the sequence in the following pages is somewhat similar. That is to say, for each subject will be quoted, whenever they are available, the older bibliographies for historical and background material, the bibliographies of contemporary items, and the current bibliographies which continue to list items as they are published.

## A NOTE ON ENCYCLOPAEDIAS

There are two bibliographies of encyclopaedias:

ZISCHKA, GERT A. | *Index lexicorum: Bibliographie der lexikalischen Nachschlagewerke* | Hafner Publishing Company 1959

COLLISON, ROBERT L. | *Encyclopaedias: their history throughout the ages* | 2nd edition | Hafner Publishing Company 1966

The first is a classified list of encyclopaedias of both general and specialized kinds, with author index and an excellent historical introduction. The second is a bibliographical history of general encyclopaedias, written in narrative form, with an index of titles. Walford and Winchell (see pages 161–62) both have strong sections on encyclopaedias.

On modern English-language encyclopaedias, Robert L. Underbrink's *About encyclopaedias* (Jacksonville, Ill., the author, 1960) will be found useful for its annotated lists of general articles, and of reviews of individual encyclopaedias; while *General encyclopedias in print* (5th ed. New York, Bowker, 1967) carefully analyses and compares some thirty current encyclopaedias.

# 3 | Philosophy | Psychology | Psychoanalysis

'Logic, ethics and physics, psychology, theory of knowledge and metaphysics are all fused together by Plato in a semi-religious synthesis', wrote Professor Pringle-Pattison in the *Encyclopaedia Britannica*, and Benjamin Rand, the great bibliographer of philosophy, was equally comprehensive in his treatment of the subject. Rand, who came of a family which settled in Massachusetts early in the seventeenth century, was himself born and educated in Nova Scotia, but he completed his studies in Heidelberg and at Harvard and spent most of the rest of his life at the latter university. Not only was he responsible for building up the considerable collections on philosophy at Harvard but he also devoted himself to its recording, and, as the third volume to James Mark Baldwin's standard *Dictionary of philosophy and psychology* (New York: Macmillan, 1901-5), published:

RAND, BENJAMIN | *Bibliography of philosophy, psychology, and cognate subjects* | 1 volume in 2 | New York: Macmillan 1905 (reprinted 1949)

This work, which extends to well over 1,000 closely printed pages, is indispensible for the older material on the subject. The entries are arranged under the following headings: the history of philosophy, including works treating the subject in general, followed by detailed bibliographies of individual philosophers and psychologists; systematic philosophy; logic; aesthetics; the philosophy of religion; ethics; and psychology, to which more than 200 pages are devoted. An important feature of this remarkable work is the analysis of the contents of learned journals.

For the early twentieth century the bibliographical material available on philosophy is not nearly so satisfactory. Up to the Great War there was an excellent German bibliography:

*Die Philosophie der Gegenwart: eine internationale Jahresübersicht...*, *1908-1913* | Heidelberg: Weiss 1910-15

This covered books and periodicals in many languages. The first part of each volume included detailed descriptions of the chief periodicals and analysed their contents. The main part of each issue was arranged by

Philosophy | 9

subjects under which the items were not only listed but also annotated in the language of the original while, in the case of books, even chapter headings were given. For the next quarter of a century there is no similar work and one must rely on the general catalogues of books of the great national libraries and on the general subject indexes of periodicals. In 1937, however, a new start was made with:

*Bibliographie de la philosophie, 1937 to date* | Paris: Vrin 1938 to date

which is compiled by the International Institute of Philosophy and issued quarterly. It covers philosophy, metaphysics, logic, aesthetics, ethics; and the philosophy of anthropology, science, language, sociology, politics, law, history, culture, education and religion. Entries, which are limited to books, are arranged in classified order and include abstracts, often in the language of the original. Translations and reprints are included in smaller type. French translations of German, English and Italian abstracts are appended. There is an annual index of authors, titles and subjects.

Attention must also be drawn to a number of later projects. In addition to the short-lived quarterly *Philosophic abstracts* which was published in New York from 1939 to 1954 (with a cumulative index covering 1939-50) reprinted New York, Kraus, 1954, there was the *Bulletin analytique: Philosophie* which started in 1947, and became:

*Bulletin signalétique: Pt. 3—Philosophie, Sciences humaines* | Paris, Centre national de la recherche scientifique 1956- .

a classified bibliography which is issued quarterly. It includes the history of philosophy, metaphysics and general philosophy, religion, the theory of values, ethics, the philosophy of history, aesthetics and arts, logic and epistemology, scientific and technological history, psychology, education, sociology, language and ethnology. International and comprehensive in scope, it provides short abstracts of both periodical articles and book reviews, together with annual author and subject indexes. A retrospective bibliography, aiming at listing every book, periodical article and book review in most Western languages, is provided in:

*Bibliographia philosophica, 1934-1945* | Edited by G. A. de Brie | 2 volumes | Utrecht, Spectrum 1950-4

the first volume of which deals with the history of philosophy, arranged chronologically by birth-dates of philosophers, while the second covers the doctrinal aspects of philosophy, together with a name index. Translations of titles in little-known languages, and paraphrases of obscure titles are provided. It is planned to continue this very useful work.

The quarterly 'Répertoire bibliographique' which from 1934 onwards appeared in the *Revue néoscolastique de philosophie* (renamed the *Revue philosophique de Louvain* in 1946), developed into the:

*Répertoire bibliographique de la philosophie, 1949–* | Louvain, Editions de l'Institut supérieur de philosophie 1949–

which is compiled by the Société philosophique de Louvain and issued under the auspices of the International Institute of Philosophy. It covers philosophy and its history, logic, metaphysics, psychology, ethics, aesthetics; and the philosophy of law, language, religion, culture, history and education. This comprehensive classified bibliography of books and periodical articles in Western languages is issued quarterly, with annual indexes of names and reviews. *Philosophical books* (Leicester University Press), now issued three times a year, includes authoritative reviews.

Gilbert Varet's *Manuel de bibliographie philosophique* (Paris, Presses Universitaires de France, 1956, 2 volumes) is a very useful guide to outstanding books and periodical articles covering both Eastern and Western philosophers, and the Library of Congress's *Philosophical periodicals* (1952) comprises an excellent annotated world list of nearly 500 journals, including general periodicals of importance in this field.

The series of periodic pamphlets each devoted to classified treatment of a specific subject:

*Bibliographische Einführungen in das Studium der Philosophie* | Herausgegeben von I. M. Bochenski | Bern, Francke 1948–

has dealt both with various aspects of philosophy (American, Buddhist, &c.) and with individual philosophers (Aristotle, Kierkegaard, Aquinas, &c.). An index of names is appended to each issue.

A continuation of Rand's bibliography in the field of aesthetics is provided in W. A. Hammond's *A bibliography of aesthetics and of the philosophy of the fine arts*, whose revised edition (New York, Longmans, 1934) covers the period 1900–32. George F. McLean's *An annotated bibliography of Christian philosophy* (New York, Harper, 1965) covers both the classical and contemporary literature from 1900 to 1963.

## PSYCHOLOGY

In 1932 C. M. Louttit wrote: 'Psychological literature does not consist of a few hundred books but of thousands, nor of a few common journals, but of hundreds, nor of a few thousand articles but of tens of thousands ... the number of papers of psychological value may be conservatively estimated as over 100,000.' Fortunately the bibliography of the subject is rather better served than that of philosophy. For the nineteenth century and earlier there is Rand's *Bibliography of philosophy, psychology and cognate subjects* which, as Louttit points out, 'has one defect for modern psychology in that it is not at all complete for the biological and physiological literature that is now of such great importance'. This is not the case with:

*Psychological index: an annual bibliography of the literature of psychology and cognate subjects 1894-1936* | Princeton, N.J.: Psychological Review 1894-1936

which conveniently overlapped with Rand and similarly covered periodicals and books (including translations and new editions) in the more usual languages. Published annually, it consisted of a classified list of items with an index of authors but, unfortunately, no subject index. Included in the subjects were such aspects as industrial psychology, nervous and mental diseases, educational psychology, and plant and animal behaviour. During the depression in the United States a useful extension of the *Index* was prepared in the form of:

*Psychological index: abstract references . . .* 2 volumes | Columbus, Ohio: American Psychological Association 1940-1

a United States Works Projects Administration production which listed *by serial number only* those items in the *Index* for which abstracts could be found in periodicals and gave the necessary references. Since nearly half the items in the *Index* were covered in this way (for the years 1894-1928) it is a helpful aid in spite of the necessity of referring back through the original Index.

After 1936 the work of the *Psychological Index* was taken over by a service which had already been in existence for some years:

*Psychological abstracts, 1927 to date* | Lancaster, Pa.: American Psychological Association 1927 to date

Now issued bi-monthly, this has an international coverage of books, dissertations and periodical articles. There is a signed abstract of each item, and the contents are grouped under subject, sub-arranged by authors. There is an author index to each number, and, in addition, there are annual author and subject indexes, the latter indexing minor subjects to the full. The Psychology Library of Columbia University has made a photographic copy of a card file of the author entries in 42 volumes of the *Psychological index* and 33 volumes of *Psychological abstracts* and reproduced them in the *Author Index to Psychological index, 1890-1935, and Psychological abstracts, 1927-1958* (Boston, Mass.: G. K. Hall, 1960. 5 volumes). The same publishers have also issued a two-volume subject-index to *Psychological abstracts*, 1927-60.

*L'Année psychologique, 1894–* | Paris, Presses Universitaires de France 1894–

is international in scope and surveys and abstracts the outstanding books and periodical articles. It is now issued half-yearly, with annual indexes of authors and subjects. Surveys of publications in this field are also included in *The Annual review of psychology* issued, since 1950, by Annual Reviews Inc., Palo Alto. A useful introductory guide to the literature of psychology is contained in R. S. Daniel and C. M. Louttit's *Professional problems in psychology* (Prentice-Hall, 1953) which describes the more notable books and journals relating to the subject, and special attention is drawn to:

*The Harvard list of books in psychology* | 3rd edition | Cambridge, Mass., Harvard University Press, 1964

which is compiled by the University's Departments of Psychology and Social Relations and the School of Education. The 704 items are classified, with short annotations, and there is an author index.

The close links of this subject with subjects in other fields must be remembered, for much valuable supporting material will be found in bibliographies relating to such studies as sociology, biology, and education. In the present book, the special field of delinquency is treated under the heading of crime in a later chapter. Useful items may be found too in the more specialized bibliographies such as:

GRINSTEIN, ALEXANDER | *The index of psychoanalytic writings* | 5 volumes | New York, International Universities Press 1956–60

MENNINGER, KARL A. | *A guide to psychiatric books* | 2nd edition | New York and London, Grune and Stratton, 1956 | (The Menninger Clinic Monograph Series, no. 7)

of which the first supersedes John Rickman's pioneer *Index psychoanalyticus*, and will itself be continued by supplements, while the second includes suggested reading lists. Later material will be found in the general indexes of medicinal and psychological literature, notably the abstracts in the *International journal of psycho-analysis* issued by the Institute of Psychoanalysis, and the *Journal of mental science*.

In the field of psychical research useful material will be found in the catalogues of special libraries such as the *Author and title catalogues of the collection of the Society for Psychical Research* (Boston, Mass., G. K. Hall, 1964) which include the Edmund Gurney collection on hypnosis, and a comprehensive collection on witchcraft and demonology, and the *National Laboratory of Psychical Research* (compiled by Harry Price, who subsequently bequeathed the collection to the University of London Library).

# 4 | Theology and Religion

The immense amount of literature in this field is very poorly and sketchily recorded, apart from one or two subjects such as the Bible or Christian Unity. To fill the gaps reference must continually be made to the encyclopaedias, of which the chief is:

*The Encyclopaedia of religion and ethics:* edited by JAMES HASTINGS ... 13 volumes | Edinburgh: Clark 1911-26

which covers the religions of all countries, mythology, philosophy, psychology, moral practices, ethical systems and movements, folk-lore, besides anthropology, biology, economics, sociology, and people and places connected with these subjects. Very full bibliographies are appended.

The urge to compile bibliographies has, however, always proved very strong among theologians and amateurs as well. One of the most strenuous efforts in this direction was made by James Darling, an Edinburgh man who became both bookseller and publisher. Scottish Presbyterian by upbringing, he subsequently joined the Church of England. In 1839, at the suggestion of several clergymen, he founded a library for the use of theological students. It was known first as the Clerical Library, and later as the Metropolitan Library: the subscription was one guinea, and for this students were allowed to borrow any volume and to make use of the reading-room. The Library was not financially successful and at last it was sold by auction, but nevertheless it is to Darling's desire to give the users of his library as much help as possible that we owe:

DARLING, JAMES | *Cyclopaedia bibliographica* | 2 volumes in 3 | Darling 1854-9

in the preparation of the latter part of which he was helped by his son. This bibliography covers theology and cognate subjects, including Biblical criticism, commentaries, sermons, dissertations, &c.: the constitution, government, discipline, and liturgies of the Christian Church; devotional, practical and polemical divinity; ecclesiastical history and biography; the works of the Fathers of the Church and other divines, ancient and modern. The contents of collections such as the Bibliotheca Patrum of La Bigne, the Bollandine Acta Sanctorum, &c., are enumerated at length. The first volume is arranged alphabetically by authors, giving

## 14 | Theology and Religion

brief biographical details, full titles of their works and occasional annotations. Pamphlets are included. The second volume has sections on general works, and theology, but the chief part is devoted to the Holy Scriptures: 'the great aim in this volume is to point out the authors who have written in illustration of any or all of the books, chapters or verses of the Holy Scriptures. It is limited to no sect: the contributions of all denominations will be found here referred to. It is limited to no nation: English, French, Italian, German, and other nations are, in a greater or less degree, represented.' There is a selective subject index. A promised third volume was never published.

An important library catalogue which records the holdings of a collection of some 100,000 volumes is:

DR WILLIAMS'S LIBRARY | *Author catalogue of books ... to 1841*, and *Author catalogue of tracts, pamphlets, or sermons, etc. ... to 1841*, and *Author catalogue of books, pamphlets etc. ... from 1842 to 1885* to which a *Catalogue of accessions, 1900-1950* has been added, followed by annual Supplements to the present time. Unfortunately there was no printed catalogue for the period 1886-99. This library was founded in 1713 by Dr Daniel Williams, a Presbyterian minister and prominent leader among the Nonconformists of his day. The initial stock of the library was 10,000 volumes, including his own collection (mostly theology) and that of Dr William Bates. Each volume of the catalogue is arranged alphabetically by authors, with brief details of size, place of publication, and date. Since Dr Williams's day the scope of the collection has been very greatly enlarged and now covers all aspects of Christian and non-Christian religions, philosophy, ethics, and cognate subjects. An important supplement in the main volumes gives useful information on the publications of learned societies, both British and foreign, and lists a remarkable range of learned periodicals. This catalogue is especially valuable for the amount of foreign material it records.

For the older material there is:

UNION THEOLOGICAL SEMINARY, NEW YORK | *Catalogue of the McAlpine Collection of British history and theology, 1500-1700:* compiled and edited by CHARLES RIPLEY GILLETT | 5 volumes | New York 1927-30. *Alphabetical arrangement of main entries from the shelf list.* 10 volumes. Boston, Mass., G. K. Hall, 1965

This collection is named after David Hunter McAlpine of New York who originally 'agreed to meet the expenses incident to the purchase of books on English deism and kindred subjects'. The field was subsequently extended to include the writings of the divines who constituted the Westminster Assembly and other material relating to the Civil War and the Commonwealth period. It includes more than 15,000 volumes on

## Theology and Religion | 15

British history and theology printed prior to 1701, including relevant Acts of Parliament. The original catalogue is arranged chronologically, each year being subarranged by author: full titles and imprints are given, together with references to entries for similar copies in British catalogues. Of the four main volumes, three are devoted to the period 1641-1700. The fifth volume consists of a detailed index of authors, anonymous works and persons and titles alluded to in the title-pages.

Material in periodicals has only been covered for short periods. Ernest Cushing Richardson, one of the most famous librarians of his day, began as an Assistant in Amherst College Library in the late '70's, and was later appointed Librarian of Hartford Theological Seminary. 'For thirty years, 1890-1920', wrote Arundell Esdaile, 'he was Librarian of Princeton University, and Director for three more and Honorary Director and research professor for yet two more, so unwilling were the authorities to part with him.' All his life he was a scholar and especially interested in medieval theological sources, and one of his more voluminous works was:

RICHARDSON, ERNEST CUSHING | compiler | *An alphabetical subject index and index encyclopaedia to periodical articles on religion, 1890-1899* | 2 volumes | New York: Scribner 1907-11

This covered American and foreign material. The first volume was arranged alphabetically by subject, and an unusual feature which has much to recommend it was the provision of a brief authoritative definition of each subject. The second volume consisted of the same material in author order, including anonymous titles, and can be used independently since the information given is just as full. In addition, some help may be gained from a defunct German annual *Theologischer Jahresbericht, 1881-1913* (Leipzig, 1882-1916) which dealt with both books and periodicals.

For the next thirty-odd years references to items in periodicals must be sought in the general indexes to periodical literature. Since the middle of the century, however, three important indexes have remedied the situation:

*Index to religious periodical literature: an author and subject index to periodical literature, 1949–1952, including an author index to book reviews* | Chicago, American Library Association, for the American Theological Library Association 1953

This is basically Protestant in outlook, but includes selected Catholic and Jewish journals: it aims to be ecumenical on both scholarly and popular levels. It covers over thirty journals in English, French and German, none of which is indexed in the H. W. Wilson indexes; and there are some entries for 1948. Further volumes covering 1953-4 and 1957-9 were published in 1956 and 1960 respectively, and the 1955-6 volume is in preparation. In future annual volumes will be issued, with three-yearly cumulations.

## 16 | Theology and Religion

*International bibliography of the history of religions/Bibliographie internationale de l'histoire des religions, 1952–* | Leiden, Brill 1954–

is issued annually and is published (with the support of Unesco) in connection with *Numen : international review for the history of religions* under the auspices of the International Council for Philosophy and Humanistic Studies by the International Association for the History of Religions. This comprehensive international service lists books, outstanding book reviews, and articles from some four hundred journals in classified arrangement. There are no annotations.

*Répertoire général de sciences religieuses: bibliographie, 1950–* | Paris, Alsatia Colmar 1953–

whose first volume was issued in Rome, is a classified record of books and articles from about 1,000 journals. It covers the history of religions, Biblical studies, Catholic theology, theological history and Christian literature, Protestant theology and the Church, ecumenical matters, philosophy, psychology, psychoanalysis, the occult, religious sociology, Christian education, canon law, Church history, art and archaeology, religious orders, military and chivalrous orders, hagiography, biographical studies, missions, and the arts. The annual issues are provided with author indexes.

On behalf of the International Missionary Council for Theological Seminaries and Colleges in Africa, Asia, Latin America and the Southwest Pacific, an annotated bibliography has been issued:

MORRIS, RAYMOND P. | *A theological book list* | Oxford, Blackwell 1960

covering well over 5,000 items on the Christian and other religions, philosophy, ethics and psychology. On the subject of missions there is the 17-volume *Dictionary catalog of the Missionary Research Library*, New York (Boston, G. K. Hall, 1968) which records works on the history and theory of missions, non-Christian religions and ideologies, the environment of missions in the lands of the 'younger churches', and international affairs and world trends as they affect the Christian mission and its strategy.

Katherine Smith Diehl's *Religions, mythologies, folklores* (New Brunswick, N.J., The Scarecrow Press, 1956) is an annotated introduction to the literature of faith and practice in all cultures. It includes books of general and specific reference, literary and historical guides, various scriptures and their commentaries, records of institutional accomplishment, and biographies. Items are classified and annotated; the fourth section is devoted to periodicals, and there are author and title indexes. Finally, John G. Barrow's *A bibliography of bibliographies in religion* (Ann Arbor, Edwards, 1955) is an annotated list of items issued up to

Bibles | 17

1950, with an important section (pp. 330-68) devoted to bibliographies of individual theologians.

## BIBLES

There are several bibliographies of Bibles, of which the most important is:

BRITISH AND FOREIGN BIBLE SOCIETY | *Historical catalogue of the printed editions of Holy Scripture* ... compiled by T. H. DARLOW and H. F. MOULE | 2 volumes in 4 | Bible House 1903-11 (reprinted New York, Kraus, 1965)

The first volume is devoted to English Bibles, and special note should be taken of the Appendixes of (1) additional items, and (2) a list of the books of the Bible which were translated into provincial dialects of English for Prince Louis Lucien Bonaparte. The remaining three volumes describe polyglot Bibles and Bibles in foreign languages. Their contents are arranged alphabetically by language, under which there is first of all a chronological list of polyglot Bibles, followed by a chronological list of Bibles in the language concerned. Each item is heavily annotated with bibliographical and historical details, and it will be appreciated that this catalogue has its importance for the philological student as well as for theologians. There are indexes of languages and dialects, translators, editors, revisers, printers, publishers, places of printing and publication, and a general subject index. A new edition of the catalogue began publication in 1964.

Three volumes of the new *General Catalogue of printed books* of the British Museum are devoted to the Bible (1936-7). The first two volumes are arranged in the following order: editions of the complete Bible in various languages (polyglot, Greek, Latin, English, and then the remaining languages arranged alphabetically, the items being sub-arranged chronologically); selections (similarly arranged); Old Testament, Pentateuch, Historical Books, Prophets—subdivided into Greater and Minor Prophets, Hagiographa, Apocrypha, New Testament, Gospels, Epistles, Liturgical Epistles, and Gospels. New Testament Apocrypha are catalogued elsewhere under their editor or reputed author. The third volume is an Appendix and is arranged similarly.

The wealth of the numerous cathedral libraries in Britain in important editions of the Bible and in other material is not fully realized, but Miss M. S. G. Hand's[1] account of her experiences while compiling a union catalogue of their contents—in which she points out that they contain many items not listed in the *Short-title catalogue*—make one hope that nothing will prevent the eventual printing of this catalogue. In the meantime there are a number of old printed catalogues of individual cathedral

[1] 'The Cathedral Libraries Catalogue', *Library*, volume II (5th series), pp. 1-13. June 1947.

libraries which may occasionally be of use in tracing rare material, in spite of the fact that most of them give few bibliographical details.

Attention must also be drawn to the annual *Booklist* issued since 1946 by the Society for Old Testament Study which comprises long critical reviews of current literature, with an author index; to John Coolidge Hurd's annotated *A bibliography of New Testament bibliographies* (New York, Seabury Press, 1966); to *New Testament literature* (Chicago, University of Chicago Press), an annotated bibliography of books, book reviews and periodical articles, which covers in comprehensive fashion the literature issued from 1940 onwards in three-yearly volumes; and to *New Testament abstracts* (Weston, Mass., Weston College), issued three times a year since 1956. G. S. Glanzman and J. A. Fitzmyer's *An introductory bibliography for the study of Scripture* (1961) provides a useful survey of current sources, and B. M. Metzger's *Index to periodical literature on Christ and the Gospels* (Leiden, Brill, 1965) provides many references which would be difficult to trace elsewhere.

## THE CHRISTIAN CHURCH

The history of Christianity has been covered in:

CASE, SHIRLEY JACKSON | editor | *A bibliographical guide to the history of Christianity* | Chicago: University of Chicago Press 1931

which 'offers a careful selection of representative titles rather than an exhaustive bibliographical compilation ... prepared for the use of students and teachers'. It 'includes the history of Christianity in the Western Hemisphere, its career in Eastern Europe and Western Asia, and its growth in the newer fields of Africa, Asia, and the islands of the Pacific'. The contents are classified by subject, with an index of authors and subjects. Details given are brief, but periodical articles are included.

The question of the union of the Churches is dealt with in:

BRANDRETH, H. R. T. | *Union and reunion* | 2nd edition | A. & C. Black 1948

which is complementary to Senaud's bibliography[1] of international movements. Brandreth limits himself likewise to Christian union and reunion, and also deals with social, economic, &c., co-operation which Senaud omitted. Translations of foreign books are given in the place of the originals wherever possible. Items are arranged by subject and are annotated fairly fully. There are separate indexes of authors and subjects.

The recording of the literature of the individual denominations is not nearly as comprehensive as one would wish. The Baptist faith is represented by W. T. Whitley's *Baptist bibliography* (Kingsgate Press,

[1] Senaud, Auguste. *Christian unity : a bibliography.* Geneva: World's Committee of Y.M.C.A.'s 1937.

## Non-Christian Religions | 19

1916-22), a two-volume work covering the period 1526-1837, and by E. C. Starr's *A Baptist bibliography* (Philadelphia, Judson Press, 1947 onwards), which records printed material by and about Baptists, including works written against them. Congregationalism is represented by H. M. Dexter's *The Congregationalism of the last 300 years as seen in its literature* (New York, Harper, 1880); while the Society of Friends has J. A. Smith's *A descriptive catalogue of Friends' books* (J. Smith, 1867), a two-volume work which includes books written by members of the Society, with a Supplement (Hicks, 1893), and *A guide to Quaker literature* (Bannisdale Press, 1952), which is a 24-page pamphlet.

Catholic literature must be sought mainly in the bibliographies appended to the articles in the main reference works of the Church, particularly in *The Catholic encyclopedia*, the *Dictionnaire de théologie catholique*, the Vatican's *Enciclopedia cattolica*, and the notable *Catholicisme : hier, aujourd'hui, demain*, as well as the more specialized dictionaries of the *Encyclopédie des sciences ecclésiastiques*. Current literature has been covered for the period 1930-33 and from 1939 onwards by the *Catholic periodical index* (New York, H. W. Wilson, for the Catholic Library Association), a quarterly cumulative author and subject index to the main contents of some 200 Catholic journals, including book reviews.

## NON-CHRISTIAN RELIGIONS

Apart from the sections on this subject in the general bibliographies described at the beginning of this chapter, there are not many bibliographies readily available in this field. For Islam there is:

PEARSON, J. D. | compiler | *Index Islamicus, 1906-1955* | Cambridge, Heffer, 1958 (Supplement, 1956-1960 | 1962)

which is a classified catalogue of some 26,000 articles on Islamic subjects in periodicals, *Festschriften*, symposia, &c. Apart from science and technology, this remarkable bibliography covers the whole field of Islamic studies, including music, and the date 1906 has been chosen as a starting point since it saw the first publication of the *Revue du monde musulman*, the first substantial journal entirely devoted to the subject. There is an author index. Outstanding material of the past must be sought in the bibliographies appended to the articles in *The encyclopaedia of Islam*, of which a new edition has been appearing in fascicles since 1954.

Judaism is far better covered: in addition to New York Public Library's *Dictionary catalog of The Jewish Collection* (14 volumes. Boston, Mass., G. K. Hall, 1960), and the bibliographies appended to articles in *The Jewish encyclopedia*, *The Universal Jewish encyclopedia* and the uncompleted *Encyclopaedia Judaica*, there is:

BODLEIAN LIBRARY | *Catalogus librorum Hebraeorum ... digessit et notis instruxit M. Steinschneider* | 3 volumes | Berlin: Welt-Verlag, 1931 (second facsimile edition)

## 20 | Non-Christian Religions

This was first published in 1852-60: it covers the period up to 1732. The first volume describes anonymous works, the second is an author catalogue, and the third is devoted to printers, editors, &c. There are extensive bibliographical notes. On this catalogue was based:

COWLEY, A. E. | *A concise catalogue of the Hebrew printed books in the Bodleian Library* | Oxford 1929

The most recent of the great catalogues lists 175,000 books and analytical entries for 1,000 serials:

KLAU LIBRARY | Hebrew Union College | Jewish Institute of Religion | *Dictionary catalogue of the Cincinnati Library of the Hebrew Union College —Jewish Institute of Religion* | 32 volumes | Boston, Mass., G. K. Hall, 1964

This library is rich in Jewish music, material relating to Spinoza, 15th and 16th century Judaism and Hebraica, Jewish bibliography, history, and philosophy, Hebrew and Yiddish literature, Bible studies, and material on the Near East in ancient times.

For modern material on this subject in relation to Britain there is:

LEHMANN, RUTH PAULINE | *Nova bibliotheca Anglo-Judaica: a bibliographical guide to Anglo-Jewish history, 1937-1960* | Jewish Historical Society of England 1961

of which the first part is devoted to histories arranged chronologically and geographically, while the second deals with the cultural aspects of the subject—scholarship and literature, fiction with Anglo-Jewish themes, contemporary life and customs, communal organization, &c. Books and periodical articles are included, and there is an index of authors and subjects.

For Eastern religions, the reader must usually rely on the bibliographical references included in books and periodicals devoted to the study of those faiths, though the Indian sub-continent is covered in a detailed bibliography appended to J. N. Farquhar's *An outline of the religious literature of India* (Oxford University Press, 1920).

There are a number of bibliographies of Buddhism, of which the following are most useful:

HELD, HANS LUDWIG | *Deutsche Bibliographie des Buddhismus: eine übersicht über die deutschsprachliche buddhologische Literatur* | Munich: Sachs 1916

MARCH, ARTHUR C. | compiler | *A Buddhist bibliography* | The Buddhist Lodge 1935 | (Annual supplements to 1940)

The latter contains mostly English works and a few in French, German, and Dutch. The principal books on Jainism are included. Entries (for books and periodical articles) are arranged alphabetically by author, and there is an analytical subject index.

## 5 | The Social Sciences

If the literature of religion and philosophy is regarded as voluminous, the material on the social sciences must be considered vast indeed since to the wealth of material published in the past is daily added an immense quantity of books, pamphlets, and fugitive material which is nowhere recorded in full. In the British Library of Political and Economic Science we learn that

'as well as treatises and some 5,600 non-governmental periodicals (of which 2,500 are received currently) the Library contains some 400,000 controversial and other pamphlets and leaflets; rich collections of government publications from nearly all the important countries of the world, including some 3,750 serials (of which 2,200 are received currently); collections, which are probably unique, of reports of local government authorities, of banks, and of railways; much historical material; and miscellaneous manuscript and printed collections of very varied extent and kind. The total amounts to some 300,000 bound volumes, together with materials not yet bound, estimated to be the equivalent of a further 50,000 volumes.'

This quotation is taken from the introduction to:

BRITISH LIBRARY OF POLITICAL AND ECONOMIC SCIENCE | *Guide to the collections* | 1948

which is still an essential tool for any student or research worker in this field. In the space of 136 pages it summarizes and briefly describes all the important reference and bibliographical works with which it is necessary to be acquainted in the subjects of statistics, economics, commerce, finance, transport, politics, public administration, law, international affairs, colonial affairs, sociology, and anthropology. It also contains valuable sections on government publications (British and foreign), the publications of the U.S.S.R. and of international organizations.

Up-to-date and useful guides include:

LEWIS, PETER R. | *The literature of the social sciences: an introductory survey and guide* | Library Association 1960

WHITE, CARL M. | *Sources of information in the social sciences* | Paterson, N.J., Bedminster Press, 1963

The former deals generally with literature and resources available for the study of the social sciences and their history from about 1800 onwards, and concentrates particularly on the twentieth century. After a survey of the literature of the social sciences in general, there are chapters on economics, economic history and conditions, statistics, commerce and industry, political science and public administration, law, international affairs, and sociology. The latter covers the literature of economics and its history, business administration, sociology, anthropology, psychology, education, and political science. There is also Bert F. Hoselitz's *A reader's guide to the social sciences* (Glencoe, Ill., Free Press, 1959), which is helpful in this field.

The leading bibliography of the subject is:

*A London bibliography of the social sciences being the subject catalogue of the British Library of Political and Economic Science at the School of Economics, the Goldsmiths' Library of Economic Literature at the University of London, the Libraries of the Royal Statistical Society, and the Royal Anthropological Institute, and certain special collections at University College, London, and elsewhere* | Compiled under the direction of B. M. HEADICAR and C. FULLER | 4 volumes | London School of Economics and Political Science 1931-2

to which substantial Supplements (not including all the libraries mentioned above) continue to be published. The first five volumes of this catalogue cover also the libraries of the Royal Institute of International Affairs at Chatham House, and the National Institute of Industrial Psychology. Locations of material are indicated by symbols. A special feature is the wealth of British and foreign government publications indexed. Entries are arranged alphabetically by subject, sub-arranged (1) non-official works alphabetically by authors, and (2) official publications alphabetically by country sub-arranged chronologically. Every work containing a bibliography is marked with the letter 'Z'. Author indexes are given in volumes IV (for volumes I-III), V and VI, but not in later volumes. An alphabetical list of periodicals in the British Library of Political and Economic Science in 1929 is given in volume IV, and supplementary lists up to 1936 in volumes V and VI: after this they were discontinued, but it is hoped to produce a separate catalogue of periodicals. The British Library of Political and Economic Science has notified its additions since 1936 by means of monthly accessions lists arranged in classified form.

For twentieth-century material the chief bibliography is an American periodical publication:

*Public affairs information service bulletin, 1951 to date* | New York: Public Affairs Information Service 1915 to date

which is often known by its initials P.A.I.S. Compiled by a group of enthusiastic librarians, it sets a standard of bibliographical practice which has never been equalled elsewhere. It is issued weekly, cumulates frequently throughout the year, and culminates in permanent annual volumes. Unfortunately there are no multi-annual cumulations, but the tedious work of searching through its files is usually amply repaid. It includes many important foreign documents in addition to English language material, and covers the whole field of the social sciences in its broadest sense—statistics, political science, economics, law, administration, social welfare, education, transport, customs, anthropology, &c. All is grist to its mill: books, pamphlets, duplicated material, restricted items, and—in short—anything, no matter what its format, which is an original contribution to its subject. Items are arranged alphabetically by subject headings; a very few entries are also included under names where the authors are outstanding. In the preliminary pages of each volume will be found a directory of publishers, a list of periodicals covered, and another of books analysed.

There is also an important bibliography which is prepared by the International Committee for Social Sciences Documentation in co-operation with the International Sociological Association:

*International bibliography of sociology/Bibliographie internationale de sociologie, volume 1, 1951 to date* | Paris, Unesco 1952–

covering the history and organization of social studies, theories and methods of sociology, social structure, social control and communication, social evolution, social problems and social policy; and there is the:

*Bulletin analytique de documentation politique, économique et sociale contemporaine, 1946 to date* | Paris: Presses Universitaires de France 1946 to date

a monthly publication of the Fondation Nationale des Sciences Politiques. It indexes articles from more than 1,100 French and foreign periodicals, and gives abstracts of the more important of them. The material is arranged under broad subject-headings: I. General and theoretical studies, subdivided into political, economic, and social aspects; II. National problems, arranged alphabetically by countries and further subdivided by subjects—administration, national defence, intellectual and religious life, &c.; III. International relations, in two parts—international organizations and international problems, each of which is again subdivided under various aspects. Brief abstracts are given for some items, and there is an annual subject index. The *Bibliographie der Sozialwissenschaften* (1905–43, 1950 to date) indexes both books and periodicals on an international scale.

A list of current serials is subject to fairly frequent revision:

## 24 | Statistics

*World list of social science periodicals* | 2nd edition | Paris, Unesco 1957 (Documentation in the social sciences)

which records well over 1,000 journals. Arranged geographically by French name of country, there is a supplement of international organizations. There are indexes of titles, institutions and subjects.

On the question of propaganda and information there is a detailed study:

SMITH, BRUCE LANNES, and others | *Propaganda, communication, and public opinion: a comprehensive reference guide* | Princeton, N.J.: Princeton University Press 1946

This continued Lasswell's *Propaganda and promotional activities: an annotated bibliography* (University of Minnesota, 1935). It is limited in principle mainly to objective studies and analyses rather than examples of propaganda. Books, periodicals, and periodical articles for the period 1934-43 are indexed. It is continued by the Bureau of Social Science Research's *International communication and political opinion* (Princeton University Press, 1956) which covers the period 1943-1955.

## STATISTICS

The necessity for guides to the complicated and voluminous literature of statistics—much of which emanates from the governments of individual countries—has been recognized for many years past. The most useful introductory guide to the subject is contained in:

*The statesman's year-book, 1864 to date* | Macmillan 1864 to date

where the bibliography appended to the entry for each individual country indicates the main sources of reliable statistics. There is also a very useful section on this subject in Winchell's *Reference books* (q.v.). For the older statistics the following will be found useful:

MULHALL, MICHAEL GEORGE | *Dictionary of statistics* | 4th edition | Routledge 1899

WEBB, AUGUSTUS DUNCAN | *The new dictionary of statistics* | Routledge 1911

and, in addition, there is the catalogue of the leading organization in this country:

ROYAL STATISTICAL SOCIETY | *Catalogue of the library* | 1921

This work is rather amateurishly divided into three parts: I. Authors, including anonymous works; II. Official publications—arranged by town, country, &c., in one alphabetical sequence; III. Miscellaneous,

Statistics | 25

including corporate bodies. Arrangement of this kind is quite unnecessary and hampers the work of the research student: fortunately most compilers of bibliographies and catalogues today realize that the form and authorship of government and other official publications is no insurmountable barrier to including them in the main sequence. To relegate them to an appendix means too often that valuable material is overlooked.

A useful handbook, of which a post-war revision would be very welcome, is:

VERWEY, GERLOP, and RENOOIJ, D. C. | *The economist's handbook: a manual of statistical sources* | Amsterdam: *Economist's Handbook, 1934* (to which a supplement was added in 1937)

of which the first part gives information on the statistical sources available on each subject, arranged alphabetically, while the second is devoted to the statistical sources available for each country. The following guides, between them, partly fill the gap:

*Bibliography of statistical periodicals* | 7th edition | Paris, Organization for European Economic Co-operation 1957

CARTER, PHYLLIS G. | *Statistical bulletins: an annotated bibliography* | Washington, D.C., Library of Congress 1954

ELDRIDGE, HOPE TISDALE | *Materials of demography: a selected and annotated bibliography* | Paris, International Union for the Scientific Study of Population 1959

INTER-AMERICAN STATISTICAL INSTITUTE | *Bibliography of statistical textbooks and other teaching materials* | 2nd edition | Washington, D.C., Pan American Union 1960

while the Royal Statistical Society's *The sources and nature of the statistics of the United Kingdom* (2 volumes. Oliver and Boyd, 1952-7), and the Interdepartmental Committee on Social and Economic Research's series of *Guides to official sources* (H.M.S.O., 1948 to date), give additional help and detail for research into British statistics.

The first of three volumes ultimately providing about 39,000 references to articles in British and foreign periodicals:

KENDALL, MAURICE G., and DOIG, ALISON G. | *Bibliography of statistical literature, 1950–58* | Edinburgh, Oliver and Boyd, 1962

is arranged alphabetically by author. The second volume (1965) covers the years 1940–49, and the third will cover the years prior to 1940.

Current material is covered by the statistical abstracts in the *Journal* of the American Statistical Association, and by the 'International statistical bibliography' issued from time to time in the *Revue* of the International Statistical Institute. The Institute's *International journal of abstracts*,

## 26 | International Affairs

*statistical theory and methods* (Edinburgh, Oliver and Boyd, 1959 to date) attempts comprehensive coverage from the last quarter of 1958. On the specific question of population and censuses, the chief source is:

*Population index, 1935 to date* | Princeton, N.J., Princeton University, Office of Population Research and the Population Association of America 1935 to date (reprinted to 1954, New York, Johnson)

which is international in scope. It is published quarterly and is a classified bibliography of books and periodicals on all aspects of this subject. Annotations are given, and there are annual indexes of authors and countries.

## INTERNATIONAL AFFAIRS

The increasing literature on this subject is in line with the trend of the times, and no bibliography can even attempt to be comprehensive. The most complete of current efforts is, however, astonishingly detailed: this is a sequence planned and published by the Council on Foreign Relations:

*Foreign affairs bibliography: a selected and annotated list of books on international relations . . . 1919-1962* | 4 volumes | New York: Council on Foreign Relations 1933-64

These volumes are based on the bibliographies appearing in *Foreign Affairs*—an unofficial periodical whose quarterly numbers are thought throughout the world to be a fairly accurate reflection of current official opinion in the United States—and may be considered to be supplemented by the bibliographies appearing since 1962. Pamphlets, periodical articles, and government documents are omitted. Each volume is classified by subject: I. General; II. First and Second World Wars; III. Western Hemisphere; IV. Europe, Asia, Polar Regions, and Africa. There are many foreign items, and brief annotations are sometimes given. The scope includes current history, politics, economics, international law, diplomacy, and related subjects. An author index is provided. Further volumes are to be issued at ten-year intervals.

Three important current services have been established since World War II:

*International bibliography of political science/Bibliographie internationale de science politique, volume I, 1953–* | Paris, Unesco 1954– (annual, covering publications of the *previous* year)

*International political science abstracts/Documentation politique internationale, 1951–* | Oxford, Blackwell 1951– quarterly (with annual indexes of authors and subjects)

*International information service, 1963–* | Chicago, Library of International Relations, 1963–

The first is prepared by the International Committee for Social Sciences Documentation in co-operation with the International Political Science Association which, itself, is responsible—with the International Studies Conference—for the second. The *Bibliography* is a comprehensive record of books, periodical articles, and other material solely concerned with political science, systematically arranged. Many of the periodical articles in it are abstracted in the *Abstracts* which are arranged alphabetically by author's names. All abstracts are in French, apart from those for English items which are given in English. The last item is a quarterly guide to literature on geography, history, political, economic, social and cultural factors, international politics, military affairs, international law and organisation (including the UN and its agencies), atlases, yearbooks and directories.

Two other services of great use are the Union of International Associations' *Bibliographie courante des documents, comptes rendus et actes des réunions internationales/Bibliographical current list of papers, reports and proceedings of international meetings* (1961 onwards); and *International conciliation* (New York, 1907 onwards), a select bibliography of current research in international affairs by private research organizations in North America and Britain. Earlier material is listed in the World Peace Foundation's select bibliography *Documents of international organisations* (4 volumes Boston, Mass., 1947).

Helen F. Conover's annotated *A guide to bibliographic tools for research in foreign affairs* (2nd edition, Washington, D.C., Library of Congress, 1958), and Eric H. Boehm's *Bibliographies on international relations and world affairs: an annotated directory* (Santa Barbara, Calif., Clio Press for the American Bibliographical Center, 1965) provide an excellent introduction to the basic works in this field. The New York library of the United Nations issues two monthly services—*United Nations documents index* and *List of selected articles*—which cover material by and on the United Nations and its agencies, while *Ten years of United Nations publications, 1945 to 1955* (New York, United Nations, 1955) provides a complete catalogue of all the items issued by the organization during the period. A useful guide to relevant material of a previous period is given in H. Aufricht's *Guide to League of Nations publications* (New York, Columbia University Press, 1951) which covers the years 1920 to 1947 inclusive.

The narrower subject of Commonwealth affairs is fairly well documented. In the first place, the background material is contained in the catalogue of Britain's leading society in this field:

ROYAL COMMONWEALTH SOCIETY | *Subject catalogue of the library* | 5 volumes | 1930-61

Arranged by continents, subdivided by countries and aspects, this catalogue is especially valuable for the large amount of analytical material it includes from both books and periodicals which often is of considerable help on subjects to which few complete books have been devoted. Much foreign material is included, but unfortunately some of the contents of this Library were destroyed during the war and have proved irreplaceable. The arrangement is: Volume I, The British Empire in general, and Africa; II. Australasia and the Polar Regions; III. Canada, the West Indies and Colonial America; IV. The Mediterranean, India and the East. V. Biography. Attention is also drawn to the more specialized bibliographies issued by the Society; to those issued by Nuffield College; and to the quarterly *Articles on colonial and Commonwealth matters in selected periodicals*, issued by the Institute of Colonial Studies at Oxford. Mr A. R. Hewitt's *Guide to resources for Commonwealth Studies in London, Oxford and Cambridge* (Athlone Press, for the Institute of Commonwealth Studies, 1957) includes much valuable bibliographical information.

## ECONOMICS

Researches into the material on the early history of economics have been very thorough. Three important bibliographies have been published which are all devoted to this field:

McCULLOCH, J. R. | *Literature of political economy: a classified catalogue* | 1845 (reprinted by the London School of Economics in 1938)

This is a very heavily annotated list of books and pamphlets arranged under broad subjects and sub-arranged by date and then by language. The principal works are shown by titles in heavy type. There are author and catchword indexes.

HARVARD UNIVERSITY | GRADUATE SCHOOL OF BUSINESS ADMINISTRATION | BAKER LIBRARY | *The Kress Library of Business and Economics: a catalogue covering materials published through 1776 with data upon cognate items in other Harvard Libraries* | *1940*

This lists about 7,000 items chronologically by date of publication, with an alphabetical index of authors and anonymous titles.

An English bibliography covering the latter part of this field is:

HIGGS, HENRY | *Bibliography of economics, 1751–1775* | British Academy 1935

HANSON, L. W. | *Contemporary printed sources for British and Irish economic history, 1701–1750* | Cambridge University Press, 1963

Both volumes (Hanson based his work on Higgs's unpublished sequel) are

Economics | 29

chronologically arranged by year of publication, subdivided by subjects. They include foreign material and are annotated—sometimes heavily. Locations are sometimes given for 66 libraries including Cambridge University, London University, the British Museum, &c., and there are indexes of authors, subjects and anonymous titles. Further volumes covering earlier and later periods are promised.

The most comprehensive bibliography of this subject in general is of course the *London bibliography of the social sciences*, described at the beginning of this chapter. For the contemporary period there is also a number of other important bibliographies, of which two of the outstanding are:

OSAKA UNIVERSITY OF COMMERCE | INSTITUTE FOR ECONOMIC RESEARCH | *Bibliography of economic science* | Volumes 1–4 | 1934–9

PITTSBURGH UNIVERSITY | DEPARTMENT OF ECONOMICS | *Cumulative bibliography of economics books* | 2 volumes | New York, Gordon & Breach, 1965–66

of the first of which the *Guide* of the British Library of Political and Economic Science says:

'Although not completed, this is the most comprehensive bibliography of recent literature on economics, containing about 100,000 entries. The four volumes published so far are "Public finance" (1919–33), "Money and Finance", 2 parts (1919–34 and 1919–35): and "Commerce and Industry", part 1 (1919–36). Treatises as well as the more important articles in periodicals are listed. The entries are arranged in classified order, with subject and author indexes.'

BATSON, HAROLD E. | compiler | *A select bibliography of modern economic theory, 1870–1929* | Routledge 1930

does not attempt to cover descriptive economics or economic history, or money or banking. Italian economists are omitted, but American, British, French, and German publications are included. The work is divided into two parts: I. A subject bibliography arranged under broad headings such as Mathematical Method, Production, Concept of Value, &c.; II. An author bibliography, sub-arranged English and American, German and Austrian, and French. Entries are well annotated.

For British economic history the following will prove helpful:

WILLIAMS, JUDITH BLOW | *A guide to the printed materials for English social and economic history, 1750–1850* | 2 volumes | New York: Columbia University Press 1926

of which the first part is devoted to general reference works: bibliographies, catalogues, encyclopaedias, histories, local records, &c. The second part deals with special subjects: economic theory, conditions and questions; industry; social and economic conditions and movements; social and political theory and movements. Entries are heavily annotated, and there are indexes of authors and subjects.

HALL, HUBERT A. | *A select bibliography for the study, sources and literature of English mediaeval economic history* | P. S. King 1924

This is arranged in three parts: I. Introductory: the study of English medieval history—bibliographies, inventories of records and state archives, local records, provincial archives and other muniments, and catalogues of museums; II. Sources, public and local, arranged by country; III. Modern works, arranged by subject. There are appendixes of lists of the publications of learned societies, British and American periodicals, and an index of authors and subjects. This work was the co-operative effort of a group of students at the London School of Economics under the guidance of an expert in the subject, and is an excellent example of the valuable work which could be done in this direction if the writers of theses and dissertations were allowed to devote their energies instead to the many bibliographical projects which lack personnel to make them realities.

The American Economic Association's classified *Index of economic journals* (Homewood, Ill., R. D. Irwin, 1961– ) is to be completed in 5 volumes and will cover the English-language articles in some ninety major journals published during the period 1886–1959.

A number of current services have been instituted recently, notably:

*Economic abstracts: semi-monthly review of abstracts on economics, finance, trade and industry, management and labour, 1953 to date* | The Hague, Nijhoff 1953 to date | semi-monthly |

*Economic abstracts, 1951 to date* | New York University | Graduate School of Arts and Science 1952 to date | bi-monthly

*International bibliography of economics, 1952 to date* | Paris, Unesco 1955 to date | annual

*Economics Library selections: series I—New books in economics, no. 1, March 1954 to date* | Baltimore, Johns Hopkins University, Department of Political Economy 1954 to date | quarterly

*Journal of economic abstracts, 1963–* | Harvard University Press, 1963 to date | quarterly

The first is prepared by the Lib.ary of the Economic Information Service of the Netherlands Ministry of Economic Affairs in collaboration with

## Finance

the Library of the Netherlands School of Economics and the Library of the Ministry of Social Affairs. It is classified, abstracts in the language of the original document (with English summaries for the less-known languages) and has six-monthly and annual subject indexes. The second is classified, international in scope, provides all abstracts in English, but has no cumulative indexes. The third is prepared by the International Committee for Social Sciences Documentation in co-operation with the International Economic Association; it is classified, gives translated titles, and has author, subject and place indexes. The fourth is an excellent classified, selective, evaluative and annotated list. The last is arranged in alphabetical order of title of journal, has an international coverage, and provides an author index. Note should also be taken of Margaret Hall's useful *A bibliography in economics for the Honours School in Philosophy, Politics and Economics* (2nd edition. Oxford University Press, 1959), and Arthur Maltby's excellent *Economics and commerce : the sources of information and their organisation* (Bingley, 1968).

## FINANCE

The comprehensive work on this subject is:

MASUI, MITSUZO | editor | *Bibliography of finance* | Kobe: University of Commerce 1935

which covers both books and periodical articles up to the year 1933, and includes French and German as well as English-language material. The entries are arranged first by the nationality of the author, sub-arranged by subjects.

The Library of the Institute of Bankers issues a number of useful 'Where-to-look' guides on such subjects as banking and finance. There is also an important record of current material issued by the International Association for Research in Income and Wealth:

*Bibliography on income and wealth, volume I, 1937-47 to date* | Cambridge, Bowes and Bowes 1952 to date

which covers books, periodical articles, &c. Entries are classified and annotated, and there are indexes of subjects and authors' and place names.

## LAW

Those who are acquainted with the great British law libraries will realize what bibliographical problems face the research worker, especially in his search for the older material. Fortunately, much of the spadework has already been done in:

BEALE, JOSEPH HENRY | compiler | *A bibliography of early English law books* | Cambridge, Mass.: Harvard University Press 1926

ANDERSON, ROBERT BOWIE | compiler | *A supplement to Beale's bibliography* ... Cambridge, Mass.: Harvard University Press 1943

The original work is arranged under Statutes: collections and abridgements, Decisions, Treatises, and Printers, and their law books. There is an important appendix of reproductions of printers' devices not recorded in McKerrow's *Printers' and publishers' devices* . . ., and another of tables giving printer, date, locations in England and the United States, and distinguishing marks of the publications listed. Anderson is divided into two parts, the first giving additional titles with detailed descriptions, and the second giving corrections and listing variants.

The following will also prove of assistance:

FRIEND, WILLIAM LAWRENCE | *Anglo-American legal bibliographies: an annotated guide* | Washington: Library of Congress 1944

WINFIELD, PERCY HENRY | *The chief sources of English legal history* | Cambridge, Mass.: Harvard University Press 1925

HOLDSWORTH, Sir WILLIAM SEARLE | *Sources and literature of English law* | Oxford: Clarendon Press 1925

particularly the last two for their scholarly introduction to the main problems and sources which the scholar must know.

During the past hundred years several catalogues of great law libraries in Britain have been published. Most of these give few bibliographical details and are mainly of use in tracing copies of individual works. Among the more famous are:

LAW SOCIETY | *Catalogue of printed books* | 1891 (an author and subject catalogue of 47,000 volumes in one alphabetical sequence | A supplement, covering the years 1891–1906, was issued in 1906)

LINCOLN'S INN | *Catalogue of printed books* | 1859 (an author list with subject index | A supplement, covering the years 1859–90, was issued in 1890)

A more substantial and up-to-date catalogue is:

MIDDLE TEMPLE | *Catalogue of printed books* | 3 volumes | 1914

of which the first two volumes are an alphabetical author catalogue, and the third a subject index. A supplement, covering the years 1914–24, was issued in 1925. Two other outstanding catalogues which, although American, includes a great amount of British material are:

HARVARD UNIVERSITY | LAW SCHOOL | *Catalogue of the library* | 2 volumes | 1909

NEW YORK UNIVERSITY | LAW CENTER | *A catalog of the law collection . . . with selected annotations* | 1953 (and Supplements)

# Law | 33

The former lists more than 111,000 volumes. It contains only books on American and English common law. It is arranged alphabetically by authors, and has useful schedules of state laws arranged under the names of individual states. The second volume contains an appendix of collection of trials and individual trials, the latter being arranged alphabetically by the names of the accused. Much early English material is listed. A third volume, which was not published, was to have been a subject index.

*A legal bibliography of the British Commonwealth of Nations* | 2nd edition | 7 volumes | Sweet and Maxwell 1955-64

devotes its first two volumes to English law to 1954 (including Wales, the Channel Islands and the Isle of Man), volume 3 to Canadian and British-American colonial law to 1956, volume 4 to Irish law to 1956, and volume 5 to Scottish law to 1956. Volume 6 covers the law of Australia, New Zealand and their dependencies to 1958; and volume 7, the law of the British Commonwealth, excluding the United Kingdom, Australia, New Zealand, Canada, India and Pakistan.

BRITISH LIBRARY OF POLITICAL AND ECONOMIC SCIENCE | EDWARD FRY LIBRARY OF INTERNATIONAL LAW | *Catalogue of books, pamphlets, and other documents* ... compiled by B. M. HEADICAR | 1923

This contains about 3,000 volumes, 1,000 pamphlets, and many sets of periodicals. It covers public and private international law and international relations, and includes many collections of international agreements. The nucleus of the library was Professor L. Oppenheim's collection, and a selection of Sir Edward Fry's own library, and to these regular additions are made. The catalogue has a classified arrangement, with a dictionary index. A supplement, covering the years 1923-5, has been issued. Current additions to this Collection are listed in the supplements to the *London bibliography of the social sciences.*

For more than a century the Harvard Law School Library has been assembling a comprehensive collection of materials dealing with and reflecting the growth of international law throughout the world:

*Catalog of international law and relations* | 20 volumes | Dobbs Ferry, N.Y., Oceana Publications, 1965-

The private library of the Spanish diplomat, the Marquis de Olivart, formed the nucleus of this collection which has now grown to more than 100,000 volumes. It includes diplomatic history, conflict of laws, private international law, treaties, and international adjudications and arbitrations. On international law there are also the ICSSD's *Register of legal documentation in the world* (2nd edition. Paris, Unesco, 1957) which is a convenient survey of the main national sources (constitutions, legislative and administrative regulation, law reports and digests, &c.); and F. M. McA. Clifford-Vaughan's *A selective bibliography of works on international law* (the author, 1960), which lists over 700 items and gives a table of international law journals and serials.

Attention is also drawn to the accessions lists of the Palace of Peace Library at The Hague (1916 to date) covering public and private international law, comparative law, company law, national law, international relations, diplomatic science, and history.

For current law there are several excellent guides, including:

HICKS, FREDERICK CHARLES | *Materials and methods of legal research, with bibliographical manual* | 3rd edition | New York: Lawyers Co-operative Publishing Company 1942[1]

*A bibliographical guide to the law of the United Kingdom, the Channel Islands and the Isle of Man* | Institute of Advanced Legal Studies 1956

PRICE, M. O. and BITNER, H. | *Effective legal research: a practical manual of law books and their use* | New York, Prentice-Hall 1953

*Law books in print, 1957 to date* | New York, Oceana and Rothman 1957 to date

OPPENHEIM, LEONARD | *Materials on legal bibliography* | New Orleans, La.: Tulane Book Store 1948

*Where to look for your law* | 13th edition | Sweet and Maxwell 1960

LIBRARY OF CONGRESS | LAW LIBRARY | *Guides to the law and legal literature of foreign countries* | Washington 1912–31

SWEET and MAXWELL | publishers | *Guide to law reports, statutes and regnal laws &c.* | 3rd edition | Sweet and Maxwell 1959

This last is in six parts: I. Editions of the statutes; II. An alphabetical list of English, Scottish and Irish reports with period covered by each; III. Chronological list of English reports, arranged under Courts; IV. Table showing the dates of volumes and concurrent series of reports since 1809; V. Regnal years; VI. Abbreviations of titles of reports and textbooks.

BEARDSLEY, ARTHUR S. and ORMAN, OSCAR C. | *Legal bibliography and the use of law books* | 2nd edition | New York: Brooklyn Foundation Press 1947

is one of the best guides to the subject, covering law and law books, constitutional and statutory law, judicial and quasi-judicial law, reference

---

[1] Supplements to the List of Anglo-American legal periodicals are published once or twice a year in the *Law Library Journal*.

books, the search for authorities, brief making, &c. Appendixes include bibliography, state and territorial reports, parallel citations to English common-law reports, &c.

Bibliographies of law reports and legal periodicals are of course of great importance. They include:

MAXWELL, WILLIAM HAROLD and BROWN, C. R. | *A complete list of British and colonial law reports and legal periodicals: arranged in alphabetical and in chronological order with bibliographical notes: with a checklist of Canadian statutes* | 3rd edition | Toronto: Carswell Company 1937-46

INSTITUTE OF ADVANCED LEGAL STUDIES | *A survey of legal periodicals: union catalogue of holdings in British libraries* | 2nd edition | 1957

the latter being a union list of the holdings of government, law, university, and other special libraries. It covers both British and foreign serials, but omits law reports and a number of specialized periodicals on patent law. The most important current analytical indexes are:

*Index to legal periodicals, 1908 to date* | New York: H. W. Wilson 1909 to date

*Index to foreign legal periodicals, 1960 to date* | INSTITUTE OF ADVANCED LEGAL STUDIES | 1960 to date

The first (which was preceded by the *Index to legal periodical literature*, 1807-1899) is compiled by the American Association of Law Libraries, and indexes about 285 law journals published in the United States and the British Commonwealth, together with the American Bar Association reports. Issued monthly, it is cumulated annually and triennially. Each issue is arranged by subjects, with an author index, an alphabetical table of cases and—since August 1940—a book review index. The latter, compiled by the Institute of Advanced Legal Studies in collaboration with the American Association of Law Libraries, indexes about 300 journals from fifty-one countries, and is arranged by subjects, with geographical and author indexes and a list of books of which reviews, have appeared in the periodicals indexed. It is issued quarterly, with annual and five-yearly cumulations. There is also the Harvard Law School Library's *Current legal bibliography* (1961 to date) of books and periodical articles which cumulates into the *Annual legal bibliography*.

Three works of considerable help in dealing with foreign material are:

BLAUSTEIN, A. P. | *Manual on foreign legal periodicals* | Dobbs Ferry, N.Y., Oceana Publications, for the Parker School of Foreign and Comparative Law 1962

STOLLREITHER, K. | *Internationale Bibliographie der juristischen Nachschlagewerke* | Frankfurt am Main, Klostermann 1955

## 36 | Crime and Criminology

SZLADITS, CHARLES | compiler | *A bibliography on foreign and comparative law: books and articles in English* | Dobbs Ferry, N.Y., Oceana Publications, for the Parker School of Foreign and Comparative Law, 1955 and Supplements to date

to which must be added Charles Szladits's *Guide to foreign legal materials: French, German, Swiss* (Oceana Publications, 1959). Szladits has been continued by lists in the *American journal of comparative law* which will be incorporated in a supplementary volume. Unesco's *A register of legal documentation in the world* (2nd edition. Paris, 1957) provides an extensive bibliography of official government publications, legal bibliographies and periodicals and basic legal work of the various countries. The United Nations' Legislative Series (New York, 1951 to date) includes useful bibliographies in this field, and its *List of treaty collections* (New York, 1956) gives a survey of all existing treaty collections in the world.

## CRIME AND CRIMINOLOGY

This subject is—as often happens with comparatively small fields—remarkably well covered: First of all there is the catalogue of a well-known library:

HOWARD LEAGUE FOR PENAL REFORM | *Catalogue* | 1963

Another British bibliography comes from an unexpected source:

CUMMING, SIR JOHN | *A contribution towards a bibliography dealing with crime and cognate subjects* | 3rd edition | Receiver for the Metropolitan Police District 1935

The author, who had a distinguished career in the Indian Civil Service, maintains mainly a British standpoint although the scope of his bibliography is international, and limits himself mostly to the period 1885-1935. Pamphlets are generally excluded, but entries are made for the more special items from periodicals. The contents are classified by subject with extensive subdivision, and beyond this the items are chronologically arranged. Cross-references are given, and there are also a few brief annotations. There are also indexes of subjects and places, and authors. Attention is also drawn to *An international bibliography of selected police literature* (1962–new edition in preparation) compiled by the British Section of the International Police Association; to Leon Radzinowicz's *A History of English criminal law* (3 volumes. Stevens, 1948-56) with its extensive bibliographical references, and to his *Sir James FitzJames Steven, 1829-1894, and his contribution to the development of criminal law* (Selden Society Lecture, 1957) whose bibliographical references are important.

The remainder of the bibliographies on this subject are American in origin:

## Crime and Criminology | 37

KUHLMAN, AUGUSTUS FREDERICK | *A guide to material on crime and criminal justice, prepared . . . for the Committee on Survey of Research on Crime and Criminal Justice of the Social Science Research Council* | New York: H. W. Wilson 1929

This is a classified and annotated union catalogue of the contents of thirteen selected libraries published or in manuscript before 1 January 1927, including books, pamphlets, monographs, and periodical articles relating to criminology, the administration of criminal justice, criminal law, police and crime prevention, criminal procedure, punishment, institutional treatment in prisons, jails and reformatories, pardon, parole, probation and juvenile courts. The policy in determining what to include has been to be inclusive rather than selective, except in the case of periodical articles where space was not sufficient for more than a selection. In the same way, annotations are descriptive and not critical. The contents are arranged under the headings already mentioned, and classification schedules and a subject index are included, but unfortunately no index of authors. This was continued by:

CULVER, DOROTHY CAMPBELL | compiler | *Bibliography of crime and criminal justice, 1927-1937* | 2 volumes | New York: H. W. Wilson 1934-9

This covers crime and criminal statistics, administration of criminal justice, offenders, police, criminal law and procedure, judicial administration, treatment and punishment, probation, institutional treatment, pardon, parole and indeterminate sentence, and crime prevention. The more important foreign references are included, and annotations—'informative and descriptive rather than critical'—are often given. This bibliography was issued under the auspices of the University of California Bureau of Public Administration. There is an outline of the classification schedules in addition to an author and subject index.

An amateur and rather amusing bibliography with, however, much valuable material, was issued in war-time:

SPECTOR, HERMAN K. | compiler | *Bibliography on criminology-penology and allied subjects* | New York: Department of Correction 1944

This was designed primarily to provide the personnel of the Department with a guide to the literature of the subject, and to this end rhymes and even cartoons are included. Entries are arranged alphabetically by author under broad subject headings. There are many annotations, and an author index. A current service *Excerpta criminologica* (Amsterdam, 1961 to date) is issued bi-monthly and is prepared by the Excerpta Criminologica Foundation in co-operation with the National Council on Crime and Delinquency, and comprises a bibliography of recently published books on criminology, with short reviews.

Delinquency has two useful guides:

INSTITUTE FOR THE SCIENTIFIC TREATMENT OF DELINQUENCY | *Index of authors* | 2nd edition | November 1943

This is arranged in sections: Books, Pamphlets and Reports, and Journals, each sub-arranged alphabetically. Very brief details are given.

CABOT, PHILLIPPE SIDNEY DE Q. | *Juvenile delinquency: a critical annotated bibliography* | New York: H. W. Wilson 1946

covers both books and periodical articles. It is arranged alphabetically by authors, with a subject index, and covers the period 1914-44, giving a critical abstract of each item. And the International Council on Crime and Delinquency issue both an *International bibliography on crime and delinquency*, and a *Mental health book review index*.

## SOCIAL WORK AND WELFARE

The interest in social welfare which grew steadily between the wars was greatly stimulated by the years of stress after 1939. A good introductory reading list which, although partly out of date, is still of use is:

ASSOCIATION FOR EDUCATION IN CITIZENSHIP | *Bibliography of social studies: a list of books for schools and adults* | Oxford University Press 1936

Another more useful guide, which has regrettably been discontinued, included American material in the later issues:

NATIONAL COUNCIL OF SOCIAL SERVICE | *Book list* | 1944-6

These were issued annually, and listed books and periodical articles in a classified arrangement.

Since 1956 annual cumulations have been issued of:

*Bibliography of social work and administration: a classified list of articles from selected British periodicals* | *1930-52 to date* | Joint University Council for Social and Public Administration 1954 to date

which covers population, labour, social work, criminology, social psychology, leisure, and specific social services.

Two American publications are also of some help to British readers in this field.

*Social Work year book, 1929 to date* (includes bibliographies)

RUSSELL SAGE FOUNDATION | *Library bulletins, 1913 to date* (each issue is devoted to the bibliography of a particular subject)

Insurance | 39

There are also two bibliographies devoted to special but important aspects of social work:

LEIGH, CHARLES WILLIAM EDWARD | compiler | *Catalogue of the Library for Deaf Education* | Manchester: University of Manchester Press 1932 (7,000 books and periodicals in many languages)

LENDE, HELGA | *Books about the blind: a bibliographical guide to literature relating to the blind* | New York: American Foundation for the Blind 1940

The latter is selective and gives annotations. It covers such aspects as education, psychology, careers, economic and social adjustment, literature and reading, the deaf-blind, &c. The 2-volume *Dictionary catalog* (Boston, Mass., G. K. Hall, 1965) of the M. C. Migel Memorial Library of the American Foundation for the Blind records about 25,000 works, mainly in English, French, German and Spanish, covering the literature of the subject from the eighteenth century onwards.

## INSURANCE

There are two useful library catalogues on this subject:

CHARTERED INSURANCE INSTITUTE OF LONDON | *Catalogue of books in lending library* | 1936 (annual supplements)

INSTITUTE OF ACTUARIES | *Catalogue of the library* | 1935

The latter includes life assurance, pure and applied mathematics, probabilities, compound interest, health and unemployment insurance, accountancy, finance and banking, statistics, &c. Government publications of Great Britain and foreign countries are given in an appendix. The main body of the catalogue is arranged alphabetically by authors, with titles sub-arranged chronologically. Unfortunately there are no subject entries or cross-references, no analytical entries for periodicals, and no indexes. Since 1963 the Insurance Division of the Special Libraries Association has issued annually an *Insurance periodicals index* covering the contents of about thirty major insurance journals.

An additional source of information is:

*Internationale Bibliographie der Privatversicherung, 1924/25–* | Vienna 1926–

This is issued in the *Assekuranz Jahrbuch* (Vienna, Compassverlag), an annual publication, listing books, pamphlets, and periodical articles arranged in the first part in classified subject order, and in the second by country.

# EDUCATION

A comprehensive guide to the bibliographies of education was issued before the war:

MONROE, WALTER SCOTT, and SHORES, LOUIS | *Bibliographies and summaries in education: a catalogue of more than 4,000 annotated bibliographies and summaries listed under author and subject in one alphabet* | New York: H. W. Wilson 1936

and for current sources there are D. J. Foskett's *How to find out: educational research* (Oxford, Pergamon Press, 1965) and Unesco's *International guide to educational documentation* (1963), the latter including an annotated list of international sources, a list of the principal international organisations issuing educational documents, and a list of works on foreign education, followed by a series of national chapters.

There are also two library catalogues, of which a new edition of the first, together with annual supplements has now been published:

NATIONAL UNION OF TEACHERS | *Library catalogue* | 1959

LONDON COUNTY COUNCIL | EDUCATION LIBRARY | *Catalogue* | 1935

A Supplement to the latter, covering the years 1935-45, was issued in 1948. Some 76,000 volumes are listed in classified order, with brief annotations for most works, and very full for some. Analyticals are included for authors and subjects of individual chapters in books. There is an author index in each volume, and classification schedules and subject indexes are also provided. Unesco's *International directories of education: educational periodicals* (1963) lists five thousand journals currently published, part I dealing with periodicals issued by international bodies and all countries except the USA, the latter being covered in part II.

Current material is listed in a number of excellent serials, of which the best known is probably:

*Education index, 1929 to date* | New York: H. W. Wilson 1929 to date

This is a cumulative author and subject index issued nine times a year and cumulated annually and three-yearly. It indexes about 150 popular and technical periodicals and yearbooks and adds many references for pamphlets, books, analyticals in books and society transactions. Articles are generally indexed under both author and subject. Each issue includes classified checklists of the latest educational books. Educational publications of institutions, associations, and foundations are listed each month in a separate section, and many are completely analysed. Checklists of official documents are also included in each issue. Entries for all of these are also placed in the main alphabet for permanent record.

Education | 41

*British education index, 1954 to date* | Library Association 1961 to date
is a voluntary co-operative effort of the librarians of British Institutes of Education. It is a subject index to some fifty journals, few of which are covered by the previous item, and includes relevant articles from selected non-educational periodicals. Treatment is comprehensive: universities, adult education, schooling of all kinds and at all levels, psychology, and juvenile delinquency. Equal attention is given to countries outside Britain and the Commonwealth. Book reviews are not indexed unless they appear as review articles. There is an author index. The first cumulation covers the years 1954-8. There are also three international indexes:

*Education abstracts, 1949 to date* | Paris : Unesco 1949 to date
which is a monthly selective guide to books and periodical articles in many languages. Entries are classified, and there are author and subject indexes in each issue, and an annual cumulative index.

LEAGUE OF NATIONS | INTERNATIONAL INSTITUTE OF INTELLECTUAL CO-OPERATION | *International educational bibliography, 1936-1938* | Paris 1936-9

*Bulletin of the International Bureau of Education, Geneva* | Bibliographical service

This latter is a Supplement to the *Bulletin* (1927 to date) and covers material in many languages. It is issued quarterly, and is a classified list of new works with publication details and very full reviews. U.D.C. numbers and subject headings are given, and the entries are printed on one side of the page to facilitate mounting.

There are also many specialized bibliographies on various aspects of education: among the more substantial mention must be made of the following:

BARON, G. | *A bibliographical guide to the English educational system* | 2nd edition | University of London Press 1960

*Technical education abstracts, 1961 to date* | National Foundation for Educational Research 1961 to date

COLEMAN, ALGERNON | *An analytical bibliography of modern language teaching, 1927-1932:* compiled for the Committee on Modern Language Teaching | Chicago: University of Chicago Press, 1933 (Supplements, covering the years 1932-7 and 1937-42, were issued in 1938 and 1949 respectively)

CHAMPNEYS, MARY C. | *An English bibliography of examinations (1900-1932)* | Macmillan 1934

HIGSON, C. W. J. | *Sources for the history of education: a list of material contained in the libraries of the Institutes and Schools of Education* | Library Association, 1967

The last item records books on education, school textbooks and children's books from the 15th century to 1870, and government publications relating to education up to 1918. Locations are included.

## TRANSPORT

The literature of railways has been covered in greater detail than any other form of transport. Two of the best bibliographies of the subject are:

LELAND STANFORD JUNIOR UNIVERSITY | HOPKINS RAILWAY LIBRARY | *Catalogue:* by FREDERICK J. TEGGART | Palo Alto, Calif. 1895

OTTLEY, GEORGE | *A bibliography of British railway history* | Allen & Unwin, 1964

The first is international in scope, but treats the United States in greater detail. It includes economics, law, history, construction, equipment, operation, and local railways. Brief details are given together with some annotations. Entries are arranged in classified order, and there is an author index. The collection consists of some 10,000 books and pamphlets. The latter is a full classified annotated bibliography of about eight thousand monographs relating to British and Irish railway history from the earliest days to the present time. It covers the history of individual railways, government control, finance, trade unions, safety, architecture, &c. Locations are given, and there is an index of authors, titles and subjects. Another comprehensive catalogue is:

BUREAU OF RAILWAY ECONOMICS | *Railway economics: a collective catalogue of books in fourteen American libraries* | Chicago: University of Chicago Press 1912

This covers administration, construction, operation, traffic, railways of different countries, railway periodicals, and proceedings. Entries are in classified order and there is an author index.

Other useful bibliographies include:

HARVARD UNIVERSITY | GRADUATE SCHOOL OF BUSINESS ADMINISTRATION | KRESS LIBRARY OF BUSINESS AND ECONOMICS | *The pioneer period of European railroads* | Boston 1946

NATIONAL LIBERAL CLUB | GLADSTONE LIBRARY | *Early railway pamphlets, 1825–1900* | 1938 (mostly British | There are some brief annotations, and indexes of authors and railways)

PEDDIE, ROBERT ALEXANDER | *Railway literature, 1556–1830: a handlist* | Grafton 1931

The last includes books, pamphlets, and periodical articles, but not

Folk-Lore | 43

private railway bills. Some British and American locations of individual items are given. Arrangement is chronological, and there is an author index.

The following international bibliography is also of use:

EWALD, KURT | *20,000 Schriftquellen zur Eisenbahnkunde* | Kassel: Henschel 1941

Current literature is covered by the monthly *Railway engineering abstracts* (Institution of Civil Engineers, 1946 to date) which is prepared by the Institution in association with British Railways and London Transport Executive; and by the appropriate section of the *Bulletin analytique de documentation* (see page 23).

Roads are covered by the Road Research Laboratory's monthly *Road abstracts* (H.M.S.O., 1934 to date) and historically by the following:

BALLEN, DOROTHY | *Bibliography of road-making and roads in the United Kingdom* | P. S. King 1914

which attempted to be comprehensive, with the exception of Ordnance Survey maps, some guide-books, local Acts of Parliament, and annual reports of surveyors and highway committees. It is a classified list with author and subject index.

## FOLK-LORE

There are two general bibliographies, both of considerable detail:

*Bibliographie internationale des arts et traditions populaires/International folklore bibliography/Volkskundliche Bibliographie, 1917-36, 39-* | Basle, Société Suisse des Traditions Populaires, 1919-

THOMPSON, STITH | *Motif-index of folk-literature . . .* | 2nd edition | 6 volumes | Bloomington, Ind.: Indiana University 1955-58

The first, issued annually, includes periodical articles and books in many languages. Arrangement is classified, and there are author and subject indexes. The second is also classified, with a comprehensive index in the last volume. Other important sources are the *Catalogus van folklore in de Koninklijke Bibliotheek* (3 volumes in 2. 1919-22) which records the important collection in the Netherlands Royal Library at the Hague; and the two-volume *Catalog of folklore and folk songs* of the John G. White Department of Cleveland Public Library (Boston, Mass., G. K. Hall, 1965), with its 24,200 entries for folk-tales, riddles, proverbs, fables, chapbooks, romances, folk songs and ballads, superstition, magic, witchcraft, folk habits, beliefs and customs, medieval romances—and a strong collection on Robin Hood. Attention is also drawn to Eastman's *Index*, described on page 113.

T. A. Stephens, once an official of the Bank of England and a great-great-nephew of 'Kitty' Stephens, the operatic primadonna, spent the last years of his life in collecting material on proverbs, and after his death the notes he left were assembled and published by a well-known librarian:

BONSER, WILFRID | editor | *Proverb literature: a bibliography of works relating to proverbs, compiled from material left by the late T. A. Stephens* | Glaisher, for the Folk-Lore Society 1930 (reprinted, New York, Kraus, 1966)

In his preface Stephens introduces the technical name 'paremiology' and his bibliography deals with the proverbs of civilized European countries, as well as those of primitive peoples, but the bulk of European material far surpasses that of all the other continents. Material is arranged by groups of languages, and there are many annotations. Locations of material are given, and there is an author, anonymous title and subject index.

Gypsies and their customs have also been dealt with in two comprehensive bibliographies:

BLACK, GEORGE F. | *A gypsy bibliography* | Quaritch, for the Gypsy Lore Society 1914

Black, better known for his famous *Dictionary of Scottish surnames*, aimed to give a complete account of the literature relating to the Gypsies —good, bad, and indifferent. Books, pamphlets and analyticals for periodicals, transactions, &c., are included, and reviews are quoted for the more important material. Arrangement is alphabetical by author: there are many annotations, and a subject index.

MACFIE, ROBERT ANDREW SCOTT | *A catalogue of the gypsy books collected by the late Robert Andrew Scott Macfie . . .* | Liverpool: University of Liverpool 1936

This is a list arranged in alphabetical order of author with brief details and some short annotations. There is a useful appendix of songs and music.

# 6 | Science

'*Science has been well served in the past by the publications of its learned societies and academies, and by the scientific journals. But the spate of scientific publications is now such that it is becoming extremely difficult to keep abreast with events on even the most limited sector of the scientific frontier.*

'*This spate of scientific publications may, I think, be illustrated in the following way. If anyone set himself the task of merely reading—let alone trying to understand—all the journals of fundamental science published and worked solidly at his task every day for a year, he would discover that at the end of that year he was already more than 10 years behind! If the same constant reader (I think we may well call him a constant reader) had included the technical literature as well, he would find himself about 100 years behind in his work after 12 months' effort!*'

These words were spoken by Sir Edward Appleton at the Royal Society's Scientific Information Conference, 21 June to 2 July 1948. Nevertheless, the difficulties of the scientist are eased to a certain extent by the bibliographical aids now available, the chief of which will be mentioned in this chapter.

The history of science is given in:

JOHN CRERAR LIBRARY | *A list of books on the history of science* | Chicago 1911

to which Supplements were published in 1916 and 1942 onwards. International in scope, it includes the social, physical, natural, and medical sciences, but omits the applied sciences and does not cover publications on the history of learned institutions. The only bibliographies included are those having direct bearing on the position of their subjects in the history of science. The bibliography includes philosophy, metaphysics, psychology, ethics, sociology, statistics, political economy, law and education. The main volume and the first supplement are classified and annotated lists with author and subject indexes. The present supplement is being issued class by class.

Important additional material is also listed and annotated in George Sarton's highly individual *Introduction to the history of science* (3 volumes in 5, Baltimore, Md., Williams and Wilkins, for the Carnegie Institution of Washington, 1927-48), and in his *Horus: a guide to the history of science* (Waltham, Mass., Chronica Botanica, 1952), which have been supplemented from time to time in *Isis*. Another important source book is Ludwig Darmstädter's *Handbuch zur Geschichte der Naturwissenschaften und der Technik* (2nd edition, Berlin, 1908; reprinted New York, 1961) which lists about twelve thousand important scientific discoveries and inventions, including bibliographical references to the first published accounts.

Early references to the publications of learned societies are listed in J. D. Reuss's *Repertorium commentationum a societatibus litterariis editarum* [*ad 1800*] (16 volumes, Göttingen, 1801-21). This was continued by:

ROYAL SOCIETY OF LONDON | *Catalogue of scientific papers, 1800-1900* | 19 volumes | 1867-1925 (reprinted New York, Kraus, 1965)

which was an author index for the whole of the nineteenth century, covering more than 1,500 periodicals and transactions of learned societies and institutions in various languages. In the case of Russian items a French or English translation of the title is included. A *Subject index* (3 volumes in 4, 1908-14) was commenced, and the volumes covering mathematics, mechanics, and physics were issued and, owing to the amount of detail given, can be used independently of the main work, but the indexes to the remaining subjects were never published. This was continued by:

*International catalogue of scientific literature, 1st to fourteenth annual issues* | Published for the International Council by the Royal Society of London 1902-19

This listed books and periodical articles on mathematics, mechanics, chemistry, astronomy, meteorology, mineralogy, geology, mathematical and physical geography, palaeontology, general biology, botany, zoology, human anatomy, physical anthropology, physiology, and bacteriology. It was issued in separate parts, each volume containing schedules and indexes in four languages, an author catalogue and a subject catalogue, the purpose being to record the titles of all original contributions since 1 January 1901 onwards.

Current literature is covered by a number of guides:

ANTHONY, L. J. | editor | *British scientific and technical books, 1935-1952 (and) 1953-1957* | 2 volumes | Aslib 1956-60

ANTHONY, L. J. | *Select list of standard British scientific and technical books* | 6th edition | Aslib 1962

## Science | 47

*Catalogue of Lewis's medical, scientific and technical lending library* | new edition | H. K. Lewis 1957 (*Supplement, 1957–1959* 1960)

FLEMING, T. P. | *Guide to the literature of science* | 2nd edition | New York, Columbia University, School of Library Service 1957

HAWKINS, R. R. | *Standard scientific, medical and technical books published in the United States of America* | 2nd edition | New York, Bowker 1958

JOHNSON, IRMA | compiler | *Selected books and journals in science and engineering* | Cambridge, Mass.: Massachusetts Institute of Technology Press 1958

NORTHEASTERN UNIVERSITY | DODGE LIBRARY | *Selective bibliography in science and engineering* | Boston, Mass., G. K. Hall, 1965

McGRAW-HILL | *Basic bibliography of science and technology* | New York & London, McGraw-Hill, 1966

Lewis's catalogue has monthly supplements. Fleming annotates the more important items. Hawkins is a substantial work with annotations of a very high quality. The Dodge Library's *Selective bibliography* represents materials widely used for undergraduate study, and includes some items at graduate level. The 15,000 items, covering mainly the period 1953–63, are arranged by subject. The McGraw-Hill bibliography is a supporting volume to the *McGraw-Hill Encyclopedia of science and technology*. It lists books only: these are arranged alphabetically by subject, and are briefly annotated.

Current periodical literature is covered in two comprehensive services:

*Bulletin signalétique du Centre national de la recherche scientifique, 1940 to date* | Paris 1940 to date

*Referativnyi zhurnal, 1953 to date* | Moscow, Institut Nauchnoi Informatsii 1953 to date

The Centre national is part of the French Ministry of Education. Its *Bulletin* (which, from 1940 to 1955, was called the *Bulletin analytique*), comprises well over 200,000 abstracts per year, drawn from about 6,000 journals from most countries of the world. The *Bulletin* is issued in twenty-two parts: 1. Mathematics; 2. Astrophysics, Astronomy and Global Physics; 3-4. Physics; 5. Nuclear Physics; 6. Structure of Matter; 7-8. Chemistry and Chemical Engineering; 9. Engineering; 10-11. Earth Sciences; 12. Biophysics and Biochemistry; 13. Pharmacology and Toxicology; 14. Microbiology, Bacteriology and Genetics; 15. Pathology; 16-17. Biology; 18. Agriculture. These are issued monthly. Four further services are issued quarterly: 19. The Humanities; 20. Psychology and

Education; 21. Sociology and Linguistics; 22. History of Science and technology. Monthly and annual indexes of authors, and annual subject indexes are now issued for each part. The Russian abstracting service is similar in scope but smaller in coverage. It includes the following monthly services: Astronomy and Geodesy; Biology; Electrical Engineering; Physics; Geophysics; Geography; Geology; Chemistry and Chemical Engineering; Mechanical Engineering; Mathematics; and, Metallurgy. Both French and Russian services include books, documents, and other relevant material. The Russian service is especially valuable for its coverage of Asian material. In this connexion, brief mention must be made of the comprehensive English-language *Science abstracts of China* (Peking, Academia Sinica, Institute of Scientific Information, 1958 to date), each section of which is issued bi-monthly.

There are three very useful current lists of publications:

NEW YORK | PUBLIC LIBRARY | *New technical books: a selected list on industrial arts and engineering* | *1915 to date* | New York 1915 to date

*Aslib book list, October 1935 to date* | Aslib, 1935 to date

*Technical book review index* | 1917 to date

*Aslib book list*, which was formerly a quarterly but became a monthly in 1948, is a select list of recommendations of recently published scientific and technical books. The entries are partly selected by individuals and specialist organizations who are, for their own purposes, making as complete a survey as possible of the literature in their own fields and who are able to assess the relative merits of new publications. There are occasional annotations and quotations from reviews. Only books in the English language and, with a few exceptions, those published within the previous six months are included, and the regular transactions of societies are omitted. Entries are arranged under broad main headings following the order of the U.D.C. and are further classified by symbols into (A) general or elementary works, (B) intermediate works or text-books, (C) advanced or specially technical works, (D) directories, dictionaries, handbooks, lists and catalogues, encyclopaedias, year-books, and similar publications. Author and subject indexes are included in each issue and are also cumulated and issued annually. The *Technical book review index*, which is issued ten times each year, does not include so many titles, but it does give significant extracts from the earliest authoritative reviews. Although an American publication it includes a large number of British books, and quotes extensively from the more reputable British technical journals. There are annual indexes of authors and subjects, the individual issues being arranged alphabetically by author. Another very useful checklist is the *Weekly list of accessions* to the Science Museum Library.

Science | 49

Another invaluable source for books—and also periodical articles in this field—is:

POGGENDORF, JOHANN CHRISTIAN | *Biographisch-literarisches Handwörterbuch zur Geschichte der exacten Wissenschaften* ... volume 1 to date | Berlin, Akademic Verlag, 1863 to date (reprint of first 6 volumes: Ann Arbor, Mich.: Edwards Brothers 1944)

In this remarkable reference book are included scientists of all countries important in the fields of mathematics, astronomy, physics, geophysics, chemistry, crystallography, &c. The volumes covering each period (1858-63; 1858-83; 1883-1904; 1904-22; 1923-31; 1932-53) are arranged alphabetically by scientist, each entry commencing with a brief biography followed by a list of published works—first books, and then periodical articles arranged alphabetically by journal. This is an excellent source for identifying obscure references or inadequate mentions of a scientist's work.

*A world list of scientific periodicals published in the years 1900-1960* | 3 volumes | 4th edition | Butterworth 1966

is a useful complement to the Royal Society's catalogue, and is remarkably full, recording some 60,000 serials alphabetically by title. There are locations given (in about 300 British libraries), and there is also an index of the proceedings of periodic international congresses. (A notable feature is the recommended abbreviations for titles: these are slowly gaining international use and recognition.) Current periodicals are listed in the Science Museum Library's *Current periodicals* (9th edition. H.M.S.O., 1965), and in the *Index bibliographicus: volume 1: Science and technology* (The Hague, International Federation of Documentation, 1959). Another very useful guide is the Library of Congress's *Guide to U.S. indexing and abstracting services in science and technology* (Washington, D.C., 1960), which was prepared by the Library's Science and Technology Division for the National Federation of Science Abstracting and Indexing Services. It gives full details of about one thousand services.

Maureen J. Fowler's *Guides to scientific periodicals* lists, under country and subject headings, some 1,060 publications useful in selecting and searching for information on current and discontinued scientific periodicals. The National Reports Centre, set up at the National Lending Library for Science and Technology, began publication of *British research and development reports* in 1966. *Science citation index*, issued by the Institute for Scientific Information in Philadelphia, is a quarterly with annual cumulations. It lists alphabetically by author citations of named articles in 613 journals from some 30 countries.

## 50 | Mathematics

Technical dictionaries are listed in the two-volume *Bibliography of monolingual scientific and technical dictionaries* and in the fourth edition of the *Bibliography of interlingual scientific and technical dictionaries* (Paris, Unesco, 1956–59, and 1961 respectively), to which supplements are issued; and in *Foreign-language and English dictionaries in the physical sciences and engineering* (Washington, D.C., Superintendent of Documents, U.S. Government Printing Office, 1964), which lists 2,800 items, representing 47 languages, issued during the period 1952–63.

The literature of scientific instruments is listed in J. F. Smith's *Instrumentation literature and its use : a guide and source list* (Washington, D.C., National Bureau of Standards, 1953). Current literature is recorded in the British Scientific Instrument Research Association's monthly classified *Instrument abstracts* (Taylor and Francis, 1946 to date), which has an annual author and subject index.

## MATHEMATICS

On the subject of mathematics research workers are fortunate in having a very interesting and comprehensive guide which could well be used as a model for similar reference works in other fields:

PARKE, NATHAN GRIER | *Guide to the literature of mathematics and physics, including related works on engineering science* | revised edition | New York, Dover Publications 1958

of which part I is devoted to 'general considerations', including the principles of reading and study, self-directed education, literature search, and periodicals. Part II is the bibliography proper and is arranged alphabetically by subject. Each subject has a 'paragraph or two delineating the subject, suggesting related headings, and in some cases singling out titles that will prove useful as a point of departure'. The entries are truly international in scope, and there are analyticals for periodicals, encyclopaedias, &c., together with author and subject indexes. J. E. Pemberton's *How to find out in mathematics* (Oxford, Pergamon Press, 1963) covers mathematical dictionaries, encyclopaedias and theses; mathematical education; and mathematical history and biography.

The history of the subject is covered by:

MILLER, G. A. | *Historical introduction to mathematical literature* | Macmillan 1916

which includes societies and congresses, individual mathematicians, periodicals, bibliographies, &c., and gives critical annotations. Another useful guide is:

SOTHERAN, HENRY and CO | publishers | *Bibliotheca chemico-mathematica: Catalogue of works in many tongues on exact and applied science, with a subject index* | Compiled and annotated by H. ZEIT-LINGER and H. C. SOTHERAN | 2 volumes | Sotheran 1921
to which Supplements were issued in 1932, 1937, and 1952, the second being larger than the whole of the previous volumes. Though designed primarily for the collector, it is useful for checking variant editions, and for its many illuminating annotations and facsimile illustrations. The scope is wide, covering mathematics, astronomy, physics, chemistry, and allied subjects. It has a classified arrangement, and a detailed subject index.

Current literature is covered in the appropriate sections of the *Bulletin signalétique* and of the *Referativnyi zhurnal* (see page 47), and in:

*Mathematical reviews, 1940 to date* | Lancaster, Pa.: American Mathematical Society 1940 to date

This abstracting service took up the work which had previously been done by two German serials: *Jahrbuch über die Fortschritte der Mathematik* (Berlin, de Gruyter, 1868-1934), and the *Zentralblatt für Mathematik* (Berlin, Springer, 1931-41). It is a monthly publication and, like its predecessors, international in scope, with signed abstracts in various languages.

## ASTRONOMY

The background to this subject is covered by:

HOUZEAU, JEAN-CHARLES | *Bibliographie générale de l'astronomie, ou catalogue méthodique des ouvrages, des mémoires et des observations astronomiques publiés depuis l'origine de l'imprimerie jusqu'en 1880* | 2 volumes in 3 | Brussels: Havermans, 1882-9

Houzeau, who was born at Ermitage near Mons in 1820, was an astronomer who toured the world and, after a remarkable episode in the United States, became director of the Brussels Observatory. Volume I consists of printed works and manuscripts on astronomy in general, spherical astronomy, theoretical astronomy, &c., and volume II is devoted to 'mémoires et notices insérés dans les Collections académiques et les Revues'. Entries are arranged in classified order, with an author index. Section II of volume I is a bibliography of Astrology; and in volume II there is also a useful list of periodicals with dates of publications. The literature of the next forty years is recorded in the *Catalogue of the library* (3 parts, 1886-1925) of the Royal Astronomical Society.

Current literature is covered by the appropriate sections of the *Bulletin signalétique* and the *Referativnyi zhurnal* (see page 47), and in:

## 52 | Physics

*Astronomischer Jahresbericht, 1899–1900 to date* | Berlin, de Gruyter 1900 to date

*Bibliographie géodésique internationale, 1928–30 to date* | Butterworths, for the International Union of Geodesy and Geophysics 1935 to date

The first is an annual publication, the second covers three or four years in one volume. Both are comprehensive, international in scope, annotated, and adequately equipped with indexes. Attention is also drawn to the annotated (in French and English) *Bulletin trimestrial signalétique de documentation de chronométrie générale* (Besançon, Observatoire National 1931 to date).

## PHYSICS

In addition to Parke's *Guide to the literature of mathematics and physics*, 1958, mentioned above under the heading MATHEMATICS, there is:

WHITFORD, R. H. *Physics literature: a reference manual* | Washington, D.C., Scarecrow Press 1954

which covers the biographical, historical, experimental, mathematical, educational and topical aspects of the subject, in addition to its terminology.

Current literature is recorded in the appropriate sections of the *Bulletin signalétique* and of the *Referativnyi zhurnal*, as well as in:

*Die Fortschritte der Physik, 1845–1918*

*Physikalische Berichte, 1920–* | Brunswick: Vieweg, 1920– (which is a continuation of the *Fortschritte*)

*Le Journal de physique et le Radium: revue bibliographique, 1872 to date* | Paris: Société Française de Physique 1872 to date

*CPP—Current papers in physics, 1966–* | Institution of Electrical Engineers, 1966–

*Science abstracts | Section A: Physics abstracts, 1897 to date* | Institution of Electrical Engineers 1898 to date

The last is issued monthly, with annual and five-yearly author and subject indexes; it covers physics in general, chemical physics, astronomy, astrophysics, geodesy, crystallography, geophysics, biophysics, physiology, and photography, and the physical basis of electricity. *CPP*, issued twice a month, is based on the information received for *Physics abstracts*, lists in classified order the contents of more than 900 journals from all parts of the world. Attention is also drawn to *Physics express* (New York, International Physical Index, 1959 to date), which is issued nine times a year and digests current Russian literature on the subject; and to *Physics-electronics titles*, 1960 to date (Lexington, Mass., Boston Technical Publishers, 1964– ), an annual bibliography and key-words index of leading articles in about 200 journals.

## NUCLEAR SCIENCES

EURATOM, the United States Atomic Energy Commission and the United Kingdom Atomic Energy Authority have set up a common service to collect and disseminate information on translations in the field of nuclear sciences, and in particular on publications written in languages which are comparatively unfamiliar to the Western reader.

An Information Bureau, known as TRANSATOM, has been established at the EURATOM Headquarters in Brussels. In order to give the widest possible publicity to the information collected, the Bureau publishes a monthly periodical in English:

*Transatom bulletin: information on translation, covering nuclear literature, vol. 1, 1960–1 to date* | Brussels 1960 to date

This classified guide lists translations available and likely to be available, with indexes of authors and sources.

Other current sources include the United Nations' Atomic Energy Group's comprehensive *An international bibliography on atomic energy* (New York, 1949 to date), and the U.S. Atomic Energy Commission's fortnightly *Nuclear science abstracts* (Washington, D.C., Government Printing Office, 1948 to date). Additional material will be found in the *Bulletin signalétique* and the *Referativnyi zhurnal* (see page 47) and in the general abstracts listed in the section on PHYSICS above. There is also the Institute for Scientific Information's weekly *Current contents of space and physical sciences* (Philadelphia, 1961 to date). L. J. Anthony's *Sources of information on atomic energy* (Oxford, Pergamon Press, 1966) is a useful introduction to the subject.

## CHEMISTRY

There are several excellent introductory guides to the literature of chemistry. Among the chief may be mentioned:

BOTTLE, R. T. | *Use of the chemical literature* | Butterworth 1962

CRANE, EVAN JAY and others | *A guide to the literature of chemistry* | New York: Wiley 1957

DYSON, G. M. | *A short guide to chemical literature* | 2nd edition | Longmans 1958

MELLON, M. G. | *Chemical publications: their nature and use* | 4th edition | McGraw-Hill 1966

Bottle covers libraries, serials, abstracts, translations, nuclear chemistry, patents, and the history of chemistry. Crane lists and evaluates books, periodicals, patents, abstracts, theses, indexes, libraries, bibliographies, trade literature, &c. It has useful appendixes which include a bibliography of articles on chemical literature, with annotations, a bibliography of lists of periodicals, an alphabetical list of periodicals of chemical interest, and a classified select list of books on chemistry. The authority of the work is clear from the fact that the authors were editors of *Chemical abstracts*. Mellon 'pictures the progress of chemical research from the laboratory to the literature', describing the methods of searching chemical literature and distinguishing between original and secondary sources, and dealing with the rise of symposia and colloquia volumes containing original papers.

In addition to Sotheran's *Bibliotheca chemico-mathematica*, 1921-37, described under the heading MATHEMATICS in this chapter, there is another excellent guide to the earlier literature:

BOLTON, HENRY CARRINGTON | *A select bibliography of chemistry, 1492-1892* | Washington: Smithsonian Institution 1893

to which two Supplements were published, the first (1899) covering the period 1492-1897, and the second (1904) covering the period 1492-1902. This covers bibliography, dictionaries, history, biography, pure and applied chemistry, alchemy, periodicals, &c. There was also a bibliography of *Academic dissertations, 1492-1897*, published in the same series in 1901. The subjects covered by this bibliography include bibliography, dictionaries and tables, the history of chemistry, biography, chemistry pure and applied, alchemy, and periodicals.

There is also a guide to the bibliographies of chemistry:

WEST, CLARENCE J. and BEROLZHEIMER, D. D. | *Bibliography of bibliographies on chemistry and chemical technology, 1920-1924* | Washington: National Research Council 1925

to which supplements were published covering the years 1924-8 and 1929-31. This covers general reference works, abstract journals, and year books, cumulative indexes to serials, bibliographies of special subjects (the main part of the work), and bibliographies of individual chemists.

Current literature is recorded in:

*Chemical abstracts, 1907 to date* | Washington, D.C.: American Chemical Society 1907 to date (5 year cumulative indexes)

*Chemisches Zentralblatt, 1830 to date* | Berlin, Akademie-Verlag 1830 to date

*Chemical titles, 1961 to date* | Washington, D.C.: American Chemical Society 1961 to date

*Index chemicus, 1960 to date* | Philadelphia, Institute for Scientific Information 1960 to date

The first two are both comprehensive abstracting journals of international reputation, and are thoroughly classified and indexed. The American Chemical Society's *Bibliography of chemical reviews* (1961 to date) lists the reviews in *Chemical abstracts*. Published twice a month, *Chemical titles* in each issue gives approximately 3,000 titles referring to the most recent chemical research. This service provides an index of authors and key-words of selected chemical periodicals, and should bridge the gap between the initial publication and the issuing of the synopsis. These titles, which are taken from 575 periodicals dealing with pure and applied chemistry (110 of which are Russian), are classified for easy use. The first part consists of an index of key-words in alphabetical order, with part or the whole of the corresponding context. The second part comprises an alphabetical list of authors, with the titles of their articles and the corresponding periodicals. These titles are announced within two weeks of their communication to the publisher. *Index chemicus* published semi-monthly, with indexes cumulated quarterly and annually, is a register and index of articles on new chemical compounds reported in the major chemical journals of the world. The abstracts are presented graphically, enabling the chemist to quickly visualize molecular structures. It includes molecular formula and author indexes. Use of machine methods makes it possible to report articles within thirty days after publication.

Attention is also drawn to the relevant sections of the *Bulletin signalétique* and of the *Referativnyi zhurnal* (see page 47), to the Society for Analytical Chemistry's monthly *Analytical abstracts* (Cambridge, Heffer, 1954 to date), and to the Institute for Scientific Information's weekly *Current contents of chemical, pharmaco-medical and life sciences* (Philadelphia, 1961 to date).

## GEOLOGY

The record of bibliographies in this subject is extraordinarily comprehensive:

MARGERIE, EMMANUEL DE | *Catalogue des bibliographies géologiques* ... | Paris: Gauthier-Villars 1896

This covered nearly four thousand items published during the period 1726-1895, arranged in three parts: I. General bibliographies; II. Bibliographies of special subjects; III. Personal bibliographies and necrologies.

The number of references in each item were given, and there was an index of authors. This was continued by:

MATHEWS, EDWARD B. | compiler | *Catalogue of published bibliographies in geology, 1896–1920* | Washington: National Research Council, 1923

which is similarly arranged and which records about 3,700 titles. There is also an old library catalogue which is still of use in tracing background material:

MUSEUM OF PRACTICAL GEOLOGY AND GEOLOGICAL SURVEY | *Catalogue of the library* | H.M.S.O. 1878

Twenty-eight thousand volumes are listed here alphabetically by author, but there are certain subject groups which are included in the same sequence—e.g. Catalogues, Exhibitions, Journals, Maps, Museums, Reports, Statistics, &c. The 25-volume *Catalog of the U.S. Geological Survey Library* (Boston, Mass., G. K. Hall, 1965–66) indexes by author, title and subject more than half-a-million items on geology, palaeontology, petrology, mineralogy, ground and surface water, cartography, mineralogy, oceanography, and natural resources. It includes the great George F. Kuntz historical collection on gems and minerals.

There are three good guides to contemporary sources and standard works on the subject:

KAPLAN, STUART R. | *A guide to information sources on mining, minerals and geosciences*. New York & London, Interscience, 1965

MASON, B. | *The literature of geology* | New York, the author 1953

PEARL, R. M. | *Guide to geologic literature* | New York, McGraw-Hill 1951

and A. Morley Davies's *Local geology* (Murby, 1927) is still a useful aid for sources on the British Isles.

There are also several serials, including the *Bulletin signalétique* and the *Referativnyi zhurnal* (see page 47), from which information on current material may be obtained:

*Revue de géologie et des sciences connexes, 1920 to date*| Liége: Société Géologique de Belgique 1920 to date (a monthly publication, with signed abstracts of books and periodical articles and author and subject indexes)

*Annotated bibliography of economic geology, 1928 to date* | Urbana, Ill.: Econ. Geol. Publishing Co. 1929 to date (a half-yearly publication, with signed annotations | International in scope, covering books and periodical articles on ore deposits, coal, petroleum, and non-metallic products)

*Mineralogical abstracts, 1920 to date* | Mineralogical Society 1922 to date (a classified list of signed abstracts of books, periodical articles, reports, &c.)

## Geology | 57

*Bibliography and index of geology, exclusive of North America, 1933–1934 to date* | Washington: Geological Society of America 1934 to date (monthly, with annual index)

*Geomorphological abstracts, 1960 to date* | London School of Economics | Department of Geography 1960 to date (quarterly, mainly British material)

The last item is Volume A in *Geo Abstracts*, a series which includes Volume B—climatology, biogeography and cartography; Volume C—economic geography; and Volume D—social geography (see page 143).

There is also a comprehensive bibliographical card service available from the Service d'Information Géologique of the Bureau de Recherches Géologiques et Minières (Paris). Josef Lomský's *Periodica geologica, palaeontologica et mineralogica* (Prague, 1959) lists over 3,500 journals throughout the world, together with a classified index.

Specifically covering American literature and literature on North America, are:

*Bibliography of North American geology, 1919 to date* | Washington, D.C., Geological Society of America 1931 to date

*Geo Science abstracts, 1959 to date* | Washington, D.C., American Geological Institute 1959 to date

The latter replaces *Geological abstracts* (1953–58), and is attempting complete coverage of relevant items published in North America.

On meteorology there is first of all an old library catalogue:

ROYAL METEOROLOGICAL SOCIETY | *Catalogue of the library:* compiled by J. S. HARDING | Stanford 1891

This is arranged alphabetically by author. It includes periodical articles. There are appendixes of (1) anonymous works which, for some inexplicable reason, have been arranged in chronological order, (2) miscellaneous material, (3) institutions, (4) transactions, (5) journals, &c. There are also tables of subjects at the end. The same Society published a bibliography of current material in its *Quarterly Journal* from January 1917 to October 1920. This was continued by:

*Bibliography of meteorological literature, 1920–50* | Royal Meteorological Society 1922–50

*Meteorological and geoastrophysical abstracts, 1950 to date* | Boston, Md.: American Meteorogical Society 1950 to date

The latter is issued monthly. Part I of each issue comprises abstracts of current literature. Part II comprises an annotated bibliography of important references on a special subject, e.g. 'Tornado forecasting' (1959),

'Outstanding reference works' (1960), 'Upper atmosphere structure' (1961).

## NATURAL HISTORY AND BIOLOGY

Of the bibliographical works in this field, the most important is:

BRITISH MUSEUM (NATURAL HISTORY) | *Catalogue of the books, MSS., maps and drawings* . . . 8 volumes | 1903-40

The subjects covered by this magnificent and indispensable work of reference include biology, natural history, zoology, entomology, geology, palaeontology, botany, and mineralogy. The first five volumes constitute the main work, the remaining three being supplements. It is an author catalogue, but there are also some special groups of books included under the following headings in the main sequence: Atlases, Dictionaries, Encyclopaedias, Gazetteers, Societies, and Associations. Anonymous works, many separates and periodicals are included. Under the author's name his collected works are placed first, followed by individual works in chronological order, except that different editions of the same work are sometimes kept together.

ALTSHELER, BRENT | compiler | *Natural history index-guide* | 2nd edition | New York: H. W. Wilson 1940

is an index of both books and periodicals in many languages. Entries are arranged in classified order and English names, followed by their scientific equivalents, are used as headings. A system of stars indicates frequency of reference. There are also a general index of subjects and an author list of books indexed.

ELLIS MRS JESSIE CROFT | *Nature and its applications* | Boston, Mass.: Faxon 1949

has more than 200,000 references for books and periodical articles, to subjects of nature in their natural setting and form, and also to nature as used in art, sculpture, advertising, paintings, toys, and many other forms of decorative design work. It is chiefly of value for references to illustration material.

A useful introductory bibliography is:

BOTTLE, R. T. and WYATT, H. V. | *The use of biological literature* | Butterworth 1966

which includes the primary sources of information; abstracts, reviews and bibliographies; foreign serials and translations; quick-reference sources; and the literature of taxonomy, zoology, biochemistry, biophysics, anatomy, physiology, pathology, applied biology, and microbiology.

## Natural History and Biology | 59

For current material on biology readers should consult the relevant sections of the *Bulletin signalétique* and the *Referativnyi zhurnal* (see page 47), and also:

*Biological abstracts: a comprehensive abstracting and indexing journal of the world's literature in theoretical and applied biology, exclusive of clinical medicine* | Philadelphia: Union of Biological Societies 1926 to date

*International abstracts of biological sciences, 1954 to date* | Pergamon Press, for Biological and Medical Abstracts 1954 to date

*Biological abstracts* was preceded by *Botanical abstracts, 1918-1926*, and by *Abstracts of bacteriology, 1917-1925*. Attention is also drawn to the *Biological and agricultural index* (see page 74); and to the *Bibliographia biotheoretica* (Leider, E. J. Brill, 1938 to date) which deals with the publications on the logical foundations of biology, and those on mathematics and biology in the widest sense, together with the general aspects of each of the subsciences of biology, and publications that bridge the gap between two or more subsciences—such as psychology and constitution, genetics and pathology, etc.

There is also a service prepared by the International Committee for Social Sciences Documentation in co-operation with the International Congress of Anthropological and Ethnological Sciences:

*International bibliography of social and cultural anthropology, 1955 to date* | Paris, Unesco 1958 to date

This is an annual classified bibliography, with author index but lacking annotations.

## BOTANY

One of the most useful works of reference on material on this subject is the *Catalogue* of the British Museum (Natural History), described in the previous section. Another source for historical items is:

LINNEAN SOCIETY | *Catalogue of the printed books and pamphlets* | 1925

This is arranged in alphabetical order of authors, and works in Linnaeus's own library are specially marked. No manuscripts are included, a separate catalogue being available for these (publication of which is still in progress). Periodicals and proceedings are included in the main sequence. A great bibliography of the past is still of use:

PRITZEL, GEORG AUGUST | *Thesausus literaturae botanicae omnium gentium, inde a rerum botanicarum initiis ad nostra usque tempora, quindecim millia operum recensens* | New edition | Leipzig: Brockhaus 1872-7

Part I is arranged alphabetically by author, with an appendix of anonymous works. Part II is a classified catalogue with an author index. This was followed by:

JACKSON, BENJAMIN DAYDON | *Guide to the literature of botany: being a classified selection of botanical works, including nearly 6,000 titles not given in Pritzel's 'Thesaurus'* | Longmans (for the Index Society) 1881

There are two other important bibliographies:

REHDER, ALFRED | *The Bradley bibliography: a guide to the literature of the woody plants of the world published before the beginning of the twentieth century:* compiled at the Arnold Arboretum of Harvard University ... 5 volumes | Cambridge, Mass.: Riverside Press 1911–18

This deals with dendrology, arboriculture, the economic properties of woody plants, forestry, &c., and there are indexes of authors and titles, of Greek authors and titles, of Russian and Serbian authors and titles, and of subjects. The fifth volume contains additions and corrections to the preceding volumes.

BLAKE, SIDNEY FAY and ATWOOD, ALICE C. | *Geographical guide to floras of the world: an annotated list with special reference to useful plants and common plant names* | parts | Washington: U.S. Department of Agriculture 1942 to date

Part I deals with Africa, Australia, North and South America, and the islands of the Atlantic, Pacific, and Indian Oceans. This bibliography is 'an annotated selected list of floras and floristic works relating to vascular plants, including bibliographies and publications dealing with useful plants and vernacular names'. Books, pamphlets, and periodical articles up to 1939 are included. Items are annotated but not evaluated, but references are given to any critical reviews. Works which are merely popular or of historical value only are omitted. Arrangement is geographical and there are author and geographical indexes. The *Index Kewensis* provides a reference to the first description (starting from 1753) of every species of flowering plant in the world, and indicates its author and native country; while the six-volume *Gray Herbarium index* (Boston, Mass., G. K. Hall, 1966–67) comprises over a quarter-of-a-million entries giving name and literature citations, from 1886 to 1966, of newly discovered or established vascular plants of the Western Hemisphere. Three supplementary issues of card entries are made each year.

Specifically British flora is dealt with in two bibliographies:

SMART, J. and TAYLOR, G. | editors | *Bibliography of key works for the identification of the British flora and fauna* | 2nd edition | Systematics Association 1953

Botany | 61

SIMPSON, N. DOUGLAS | *A bibliographical index of the British flora* | Bournemouth, the author 1960

The latter includes floras, herbals, periodicals, societies, and references to the identification, distribution and occurrence of phanerogams, vascular cryptogams and charophytes. The information given includes plant-lore, local names, poisonous plants and weeds. The items are classified, but there is no index.

For current material there are three serials:

*Botanical abstracts: a monthly serial furnishing abstracts and citations of publications in the international field of botany in its broadest sense* | September 1918–November 1926 | 15 volumes | Baltimore 1918-26

This was a classified list of abstracts, with detailed author and subject indexes in each volume, and a cumulative index to the first ten volumes covering the period 1918-22. It was continued by *Biological abstracts* mentioned in the previous section.

*Botanisches Zentralblatt: referierendes Organ für das Gesamtgebiet der Botanik des In- und Auslandes, 1880–1919, 1922 to date* | Cassel: Association Internationale des Botanistes 1880 to date

From 1922 onwards each volume is in two parts—*Referate* and *Literatur* —each part with separate title-page and paging. Signed abstracts are given. The bibliography is international in scope. There was a cumulative index covering the years 1922-32 published in two volumes (1927-32).

*Just's botanischer Jahresbericht: systematisch geordnetes Repertorium der botanischen Literatur aller Länder, 1873 to date* | Leipzig: Borntraeger 1898 to date

Reference should also be made to the Royal Horticultural Society's *Lindley Library: catalogue*, 1927, described in the next chapter under the heading AGRICULTURE.

## ZOOLOGY

The publications of the Zoological Society are all important in this subject. First of all there is an old library catalogue:

ZOOLOGICAL SOCIETY | *Catalogue of the library* | 5th edition | 1902

This lists 11,000 works. Part I is arranged alphabetically by authors, and part II lists periodicals, journals, and transactions, arranged alphabetically by country and town. The nine-volume *Dictionary catalogue of the Blacker-Wood Library of Zoology and ornithology* (Boston, Mass.,

G. K. Hall, 1966–67) gives 140,000 entries for the bulk of the natural history holdings of McGill University, including serials, oriental MSS., the correspondence of naturalists, and a special collection on crustacea. There are two serials, each of which is invaluable:

*The zoological record... being records of zoological literature, 1864 to date* | Zoological Society of London 1865 to date

Alfred Newton was its first editor. It is a classified annual bibliography of the world's literature in the field of taxonomic zoology, and includes a preliminary section of comprehensive works, and also a list of new generic and subgeneric names, with a mathematical summary of the groups, and full bibliographic references. In this connexion the following index of material on generic names will also be found of the greatest use:

*Nomenclator zoologicus:* edited by SHEFFIELD A. NEAVE | Volume 1- | Zoological Society of London 1939 to date

There is an excellent introductory guide to the literature of the subject which, though American, is thoroughly conversant with British material:

SMITH, ROGER C. | *Guide to the literature of the zoological sciences* | 5th edition | Minneapolis, Minnesota: Burgess Publishing Company 1958

This annotated bibliography covers the use of libraries, bibliographies of the zoological sciences, abstract journals, taxonomic indexes and literature, periodicals, transactions and proceedings, &c. Ernest P. Walker's *Mammals of the world: volume 3—a classified bibliography* (Baltimore, Johns Hopkins Press, 1964) is a comprehensive and closely-classified bibliography of some 70,000 references. A 4,500-references selection from this bibliography is included in Volume 1.

A similar work has been issued covering the narrower field of entomology:

CHAMBERLIN, W. J. | *Entomological nomenclature and literature* | 3rd edition | Dubuque, Iowa, Wm. C. Brown, 1952

Most of this publication is devoted to the bibliographical aspect, including a detailed description of the publications of the United States Government and its departments, foreign serial publications, general works, catalogues, monographs, &c., together with related chemical, medical, and other works. Abstracts in this field are given in the monthly classified *Review of applied entomology* (Commonwealth Bureau of Entomology, 1913 to date) which covers agricultural, veterinary and medicinal aspects of the subject.

## Zoology | 63

ASSOCIATION FOR THE STUDY OF SYSTEMATICS IN RELATION TO GENERAL BIOLOGY | *Bibliography of key works for the identification of the British fauna and flora:* edited by JOHN SMART 1942

is international in scope. Comprehensive works are starred, and works which purport to cover all British species but which actually deal with less than half are also marked distinctively. Local fauna and flora lists are not included. Serial references are included. Entries are arranged in classified order, but there are no indexes.

A narrative history from the earliest times to 1930 of the literature of vertebrate zoology is given in the first part of:

WOOD, CASEY ALBERT | compiler | *An introduction to the literature of vertebrate zoology: based chiefly on the titles in the Blacker Library of Zoology, the Emma Shearer Wood Library of Ornithology, the Bibliotheca Osleriana, and other libraries of McGill University, Montreal* | Oxford University Press 1931

The main part of this work is devoted to a well-annotated author catalogue of the material on the subject in the libraries of McGill University. It is preceded by a classified index which gives only the most important title by any one author, the rest being discovered by referring to the entries under the author in the second part. In this index the authors are arranged chronologically under each subject, with a catchword where more than one title may be involved.

The literature of material on birds is well covered by a number of detailed bibliographies:

MULLENS, WILLIAM HERBERT and SWANN, H. KIRKE | *A bibliography of British ornithology from the earliest times to the end of 1912, including biographical accounts of the principal writers and bibliographies of their published works* | Macmillan 1917

This is arranged alphabetically by author, and the bibliographies include editions, reissues, &c. A supplement was issued in 1923 by Swann, consisting of a chronological list of British birds. The main work was quickly followed by another:

MULLENS, WILLIAM HERBERT and others | *A geographical bibliography of British ornithology from the earliest times to the end of 1918, arranged under countries: being a record of printed books, published articles, notes and records* | Witherby 1920

which is arranged by country—England and Wales, Wales, Scotland, Ireland—sub-arranged alphabetically by county, the entries being further arranged chronologically. There are no indexes. Periodical articles are included.

## 64 | Zoology

STRONG, REUBEN MYRON | *A bibliography of birds, with special reference to anatomy, behaviour, biochemistry, embryology, pathology, physiology, genetics, ecology, aviculture, economic ornithology, poultry culture, evolution, and related subjects* | 3 volumes | Chicago: Field Museum of Natural History 1939–46

This is arranged alphabetically by authors, the third volume being a 522-page subject index! Taxonomy, distribution, and palaeontology are included. Periodicals, pamphlets, and dissertations are also indexed. Periodicals primarily or entirely ornithological are marked with an asterisk in the key list of periodicals at the beginning of the first volume. Locations for rare material in American libraries are given. There is also:

IRWIN, RAYMOND | *British bird books: an index to British ornithology* | Grafton 1951

which comprises both subject and regional lists of books from 1481 to 1950. There are comprehensive indexes.

For fishes there is:

DEAN, BASHFORD | *A bibliography of fishes* | 3 volumes | New York: American Museum of Natural History 1916–23 (reprinted 1962)

which lists 35,000 titles. The first two volumes consist of an alphabetical author list, while the third is devoted to a subject index, a list of general bibliographies, voyages, periodicals, &c. The entries are fully annotated.

# 7 | Technology and Industry

'*It is perfectly possible for a scientific research worker, if he limits himself sufficiently, to be satisfied with the slow and incomplete publication service which he supplements by his own efforts, but the advance of science is absolutely dependent on the effective satisfaction of scientific workers and no system can be other than apparently efficient if it has not their full co-operation and support.*

'*Our section has the responsibility of dealing with the first stage of scientific communication, the actual form and quantity of original scientific publication. What is wrong with the present system is that the growing abundance of primary scientific publication and the confusion in which it is set out acts as a continuous brake, as an element of friction to the progress of science. We are not so much maintaining that scientific information is lost, though it may be, but that the scientific worker wastes time and effort in finding what information there is, and as a result we may be getting a far more limited and slower progress of research than we would under a better arranged system of publication.*'

In these words, spoken at the Royal Society's Scientific Information Conference in 1948 by Professor J. D. Bernal, is expressed the difficulty which confronts the scientist and technologist today. Nevertheless, the bibliographies and catalogues mentioned below are of considerable use in keeping research workers in touch with new developments as well as with background and source material in their subjects.

Material on some of the subjects covered by this chapter is included in some of the general bibliographies of science and technology described at the beginning of the previous chapter. It is suggested that the two chapters should therefore be read in conjunction with each other.

There is a detailed bibliography of the history of the subjects covered by this chapter:

JOHN CRERAR LIBRARY | *List of books on the history of industry and the industrial arts*, prepared by AKSEL S. JOSEPHSON | Chicago 1915

A series of catalogues (Boston, Mass., G. K. Hall) from the same library—*Author-title catalog* (35 volumes), *Classified subject catalog, including Subject index* (42 volumes)—cover one million volumes of current and historical research materials relating to science, technology and medicine, including 13,000 current serials. Bernard Houghton's *Technical information sources* (Bingley, 1967) is a useful guide to patents, standards and technical reports literature, and the last is also recorded in the National Lending Library for Science and Technology's *British research and development reports* (1966 to date), which includes agriculture, medicine and the social sciences.

For current periodicals there are:

*British technology index (BTI), 1962 to date* | Library Association 1962 to date

*Applied science and technology index, 1958 to date* | New York, H. W. Wilson 1958 to date

The first, covering articles published for the most part within the preceding seven weeks, is issued monthly, and indexes about 400 British journals in the fields of engineering, chemical technology, and manufacturing. It cumulates annually. The second, which was preceded by the *Industrial arts index* (1913-57), is a subject index to over 200 periodicals, and is issued monthly, cumulating throughout the year into annual volumes. The size of these individual volumes prevents multi-annual cumulation, desirable as it is. Mainly American in scope, it is nevertheless of the greatest value to any library which undertakes a serious technical service, even though the subject-headings may sometimes prove rather confusing to an English reader. Subjects covered include engineering, science (chemistry, physics, geology), industry (metallurgy, textiles, aeronautics, electronics, railways, ceramics, rubber, plastics, paper, &c.). Articles are listed only under subjects, full references being given but—unlike the *Engineering index* (described later)—no annotations. The preliminary pages of each issue contain important news of periodicals including new publications, changes of titles, &c.

## MEDICINE

The bibliography of bibliographies of medicine could itself fill a very large volume. Here it is possible only to list the most important works. On the historical side there is:

GARRISON, FIELDING HUDSON | compiler | *A medical bibliography: a check-list of texts illustrating the history of the medical sciences*, revised by LESLIE T. MORTON | 2nd edition | Grafton 1954 (reprinted Deutsch, 1965)

This attempts to list the most important contributions to the literature of medicine and ancillary sciences and to show their significance by brief annotations. It is classified (by U.D.C.) and under each subject the important works showing the development of a subject are arranged in chronological order. The histories of each subject are placed at the end of each section. The bibliography is international in scope, and full names and dates of authors are given wherever possible. There are indexes of authors and subjects.

Unquestionably the greatest library catalogue in this field is:

U.S. SURGEON-GENERAL'S OFFICE | *Index-catalogue of the library: authors and subjects* | 4 series | Washington 1880–1955

Four complete series have been published to date: I. A–Z. 16 volumes. 1880–95. II. A–Z. 21 volumes, 1896–1915. III. A–Z. 10 volumes. 1918–32. Series IV is the last and was completed in 1955. Each series consists of a dictionary catalogue of books, pamphlets, and periodicals, with many analyticals, especially of biographical and obituary articles. The annual monograph accessions have since been published as a supplement to the Library of Congress's *Catalog of printed cards* (q.v.). Two more great catalogues contribute to documentation in this field—those of the U.S. Department of Health, Education and Welfare (49 volumes), comprising author, title and subject entries for over half-a-million volumes, and the London School of Hygiene and Tropical Medicine (6 volumes), giving dictionary-catalogue entries for some 40,000 items. Both catalogues are issued by G. K. Hall of Boston.

Serial bibliographies include:

*Index medicus: a quarterly classified record of the current medical literature of the world, 1879–1926* | Washington: Carnegie Institution 1879–1926

This was the standard current bibliography of medicine. Originally a monthly publication, the first series was issued 1879–99, the second 1903–20, and the third 1921–6. It was a subject list with an annual author and subject index. It covered publications in all the principal languages, and included periodical articles and other analytical material, as well as books, pamphlets, and theses. In 1926 it merged into:

*Quarterly cumulative index medicus, 1927–59* | Chicago: American Medical Association 1927–59

which had previously been published as the *Quarterly cumulative index to current medical literature*, 1916–26—a much smaller affair covering only some 300 periodicals. The later work was an author and subject index to over 1,200 periodicals in many languages, forming practically a complete index to the periodical literature of medicine. The August and February volumes formed permanent semi-annual volumes. It included medical biography. The main index was preceded by a list of new books of which part I was arranged in alphabetical order of author, and the second was classified by subject. Another serial list was:

U.S. ARMY MEDICAL LIBRARY | *Current list of medical literature, 1941–59* | Washington 1941–59

which was a weekly classified list of articles of medical interest with a monthly subject and author index. It was international in scope.

At the beginning of 1960 the *Quarterly cumulative index medicus* and the *Current list of medical literature* were replaced by:

*Index medicus, new series, January 1960 to date* | Washington, D.C., National Library of Medicine 1960 to date

and annual cumulations of this work, which indexes articles by both subject and author, already amount to well over 100,000 items in each volume.

Other records of current literature include:

*Abstracts of world medicine, 1947 to date* | British Medical Association 1947 to date (monthly)

*Current work in the history of medicine: an international bibliography, 1954 to date* | Wellcome Historical Medical Library 1954 to date (quarterly)

*Excerpta medica, 1947 to date* | Amsterdam, Excerpta Medica Foundation 1947 to date (monthly)

*Hospital abstracts: a monthly survey of world literature, 1961 to date;* H.M.S.O. 1961 to date (monthly)

*Bibliography of medical reviews, 1955 to date* | Washington, D.C., Superintendent of Documents 1956 to date (annually)

Of these, *Excerpta medica* is by far the most comprehensive abstracting service, covering the whole field of medicine and public health, individual sections being obtainable separately. Author indexes and subject analyses are published separately for each section annually. Mention must also be made of the printed card service of abstracts of books, periodical articles and films available from the International Occupational Safety and Health Information Centre, at Geneva.

Periodicals are listed in:

*Current indexing and abstracting periodicals in the medical and biological sciences: an annotated list* | 2nd edition | 1959 | (Supplement to the World Health Organization's *Library news*)

*World medical periodicals* | 3rd edition | New York, World Medical Association 1962 (6,000 titles on medicine, pharmacy, dentistry, and veterinary medicine; indexed by subject and country).

a new edition of the first is in active preparation.

A handy reference volume for medical eponyms has been published:

KELLY, EMERSON CROSBY | *Encyclopaedia of medical sources* | Baltimore, Md.: Williams & Wilkins 1948

which is arranged alphabetically by name (including brief description and dates) with references to original sources in books and periodical articles. There is an index of subjects.

Ophthalmic literature is recorded in:

BRITISH OPTICAL ASSOCIATION | *Library and Museum catalogue* | 2 volumes | 1932-5

This is an author catalogue with many annotations and a subject index. Abstracts on this subject have been published in *Ophthalmic literature* since 1947.

Veterinary science is covered by the *Catalogue of modern works, 1900-1954* (2nd ed. 1955) in the Memorial Library of the Royal College of Veterinary Surgeons, and by the Commonwealth Bureau of Animal Health's monthly abstracting journal *The Veterinary bulletin* (1931 to date) and its *Index veterinarius* (1933 to date).

## ENGINEERING

There is a useful introductory guide of which a new edition would be welcome:

DALTON, BLANCHE H. | *Sources of engineering information* | Berkeley, Calif.: University of California Press 1949

This covers indexes to serials, abstracts, lists of serials, bibliographies, book review serials, general reference books, biography, encyclopaedias, technical dictionaries, handbooks and manuals, mathematical tables, physical tables, manufacturers' directories, and standards and specifications. It is international in scope, though naturally the emphasis is on American material. Under each of the headings entries are arranged in subject order, but there are no indexes. This can be supplemented by Sylvia Goldman's *Guide to the literature of engineering, mathematics, and the physical sciences* (2nd edition. Johns Hopkins University, for the Defense Supply Agency, U.S. Defense Center, 1964).

The most important index to current material on engineering is:

*Engineering index, 1884 to date* | New York: American Society of Mechanical Engineers 1892 to date

This is published annually. It indexes more than 1,000 current engineering periodicals, society transactions, bulletins and reports of government bureaux, research laboratories, experimental stations, and other organizations, and includes reviews of recently published books. Not every article and item is indexed, selection being based on the relative importance of material. Each entry has a brief résumé of the article, and the work is well provided with cross-references. This bibliography is truly international in scope, and British publications are well covered. There are also a list of technical publications indexed and an alphabetical index of all personal names mentioned in the entries. In addition, there is a current weekly service of entries printed on $5 \times 3$ in. cards in 295 subject divisions: readers can subscribe to these separately or in groups of subjects. Attention is also drawn to the monthly *Engineers' digest* (Engineers' Digest, 1940 to date) which is international in scope and is adequately indexed.

Current automation material is covered by three services: the *International bibliography of automatic control* (quarterly, 1962-4), and *Control abstracts* (monthly, 1966 to date) which is issued by the Institution of Electrical Engineers in collaboration with the International Federation of Automatic Control (IFAC) and includes the widest possible range of references to mechanical and pneumatic engineering as well as to electrical and electronic engineering. The Institution's monthly *Current papers on control* gives titles and references of papers to be abstracted later.

For electrical and electronic engineering, in addition to the library catalogues of the Institution of Electrical Engineers (1956) and the Central Electricity Generating Board (1957), there are three bibliographical guides.

BURKETT, JACK and PLUMB, PHILIP | *How to find out in electrical engineering* | Oxford, Pergamon Press 1967

JOHNSON, H. THAYNE | *Electronic properties of materials: a guide to the literature* | New York, Plenum Press, 1966

MOORE, C. K. and SPENCER, K. J. | *Electronics: a bibliographical guide* | 2 volumes | Macdonald 1961-66

The last item classifies about 5,600 major works issued during the period 1945 to 1964; and for current material there is the bi-monthly classified *Electronics and communication abstracts* (Brentwood, Essex, Multi-Science Publishing Co., 1961 to date); and, Section B of *Science abstracts: Electrical engineering abstracts* (Institution of Electrical Engineers, 1903 to date), covering generation and supply, machines, applications, measurements, telecommunications, radar and television, power resources, testing of materials, mechanical and civil engineering, illumination, welding, industrial technology and materials are issued monthly, with an annual index.

Engineering | 71

On marine architecture and engineering there are two library catalogues:

INSTITUTION OF NAVAL ARCHITECTS | *Library catalogue* | 1930

to which an *Addendum* was issued in June 1936. It is an author list but includes the form-heading TRANSACTIONS. Parliamentary reports are listed separately.

INSTITUTE OF MARINE ENGINEERS | *Library catalogue* | 1935

is a classified list. Journals and transactions are listed separately. There are no indexes. Abstracts on this subject have also been issued since 1946 in the *Journal of the British Shipbuilding Research Association* and, since 1938, in the *Transactions of the Institute of Marine Engineers*.

For automobile engineering there is a small library catalogue:

INSTITUTE OF THE MOTOR INDUSTRY | *Library catalogue* | 1948

This is arranged in classified order, but has no author index. The catalogue of the Automotive History Collection of the Detroit Public Library (2 volumes. Boston, Mass., G. K. Hall, 1966) analyses a unique collection of 11,000 books and serials, over 200,000 photographs, and many thousands of trade literature items covering the history of the automobile industry and individual cars and companies throughout the world. There are also two monthly abstracting services:

*Monthly summary of automobile engineering literature, 1920 to date* | Lindley, Motor Industry Research Association 1920 to date

*Bulletin mensuel de documentation, 1947 to date* | Paris: Union technique de l'Automobile, du Motorcycle et du Cycle 1947 to date

the former covering vehicles and stationary plant, fuels and lubricants, construction materials, manufacture, components, and research methods.

Much attention has been paid to the literature of aviation. For historical material there is:

BROCKETT, PAUL | *Bibliography of aeronautics* | Washington: Smithsonian Institution 1910

which is an important bibliography of more than 13,000 titles, covering the subject up to July 1909, arranged alphabetically by author, title, and subject, including books and pamphlets, and indexing articles in nearly 200 periodicals. Aeronautical patents are not included. There is an appendix of important aeronautical papers in the Bulletins of the Aerial Experiment Association. This was continued by:

## Engineering

U.S. NATIONAL ADVISORY COMMITTEE FOR AERONAUTICS | *Bibliography of aeronautics, 1909-1936* | Washington 1921-36

which was for some years compiled by Brockett. This was followed by:

U.S. WORKS PROJECTS ADMINISTRATION | *Bibliography of aeronautics* | 50 parts | Washington 1936-40

of which each part was devoted to a particular subject, including periodical articles and pamphlets.

Another excellent bibliography is:

NEW YORK | PUBLIC LIBRARY | *History of aeronautics: a selected list of references* . . . compiled by WILLIAM B. GAMBLE | 1938

The 5,000-odd entries are arranged in classified order and are well annotated. Subjects covered include balloons and airships, aeroplanes, seaplanes, gliders and gliding, parachutes, helicopters and autogiros, kites; engines and propellers, military and civil aeronautics, air mail, polar expeditions, associations and conferences, jurisprudence, photography and surveying, animal flight, and women in aeronautics. There are analytical indexes of authors and subjects.

The following is also very useful for historical material:

MAGGS BROS, LTD. | booksellers | *Bibliotheca aeronautica* 1920

to which Supplements were issued in 1942, 1930, 1936, and 1940.

Serials are covered in *Aeronautical and space serial publications: a world list*, issued in 1962 by the Science and Technology Division of the Library of Congress. This lists 4,551 titles (representing 76 countries) including yearbooks and annual reports. There is also a monthly abstract service:

*Index aeronauticus: journal of aeronautical and astronautical abstracts, 1944 to date* | Ministry of Aviation 1944 to date

which covers the mathematical, physical, chemical, medical, engineering, industrial, and other aspects of the subject. To this must be added the 'Aeronautical reviews' in *Aerospace engineering;* and the *International aerospace abstracts* (New York, Institute of the Aerospace Sciences, 1961 to date) a monthly journal sponsored by the National Science Foundation and the Air Force Office of Scientific Research. For space research there is also Bernard M. Fry and Foster E. Mohrhardt's *A guide to information sources in space science and technology* (Interscience 1963), with annual supplements. The basic volume covers the period 1958 to January 1962 and classifies about 4,000 entries under 19 subject sections.

# AGRICULTURE

The history of agriculture is covered by:

ROTHAMSTED EXPERIMENTAL STATION, HARPENDEN | *Library catalogue of printed books and pamphlets on agriculture, published between 1471 and 1840* | 2nd edition | 1940 (Supplement 1949)

This is arranged in sections—English authors; foreign authors and translations; historical and geographical list of foreign authors and translations, subdivided alphabetically by country; incunabula. There are also two well-illustrated narrative histories (with indexes of authors and titles) of outstanding items:

FUSSELL, G. E. | *The Old English Farming Books from Fitzherbert to Tull, 1523 to 1730* | Crosby Lockwood 1947

FUSSELL, G. E. | *More Old English Farming Books from Tull to the Board of Agriculture, 1731 to 1793* | Crosby Lockwood 1950

Another interesting bibliography of historical material is:

PERKINS, W. FRANK | compiler | *British and Irish writers on agriculture* | 3rd edition | Lymington: Charles T. King 1939

This lists books and serials up to 1900. It has the following sections: author list; county reports; anonymous works; serials; and a subject index.

A good modern introduction to the subject is:

BLANCHARD, J. RICHARD, and OSTVOLD, HAROLD | *The literature of agricultural research* | Berkeley: University of California Press 1958

which is annotated, and includes plant sciences, food and nutrition, and the economic aspects of agriculture.

The great catalogue of agricultural material is the *Dictionary catalog of the National Agricultural Library, 1862–1965* (68 volumes. New York, Rowman & Littlefield, 1966) which provides one-and-a-half million entries for agriculture, animal science, forestry, pest control, plant science, rural life, soils, fertilisers, and soil conservation. This is supplemented by a monthly classified *National Agricultural Library catalog* with author and translations indexes. In addition, the *Dictionary catalog* (37 volumes. Boston, Mass., G. K. Hall, 1966–67) of the Library of the U.S. Department of the Interior gives 670,000 entries for published and unpublished material on natural resources, land management, mines and mineral resources, wildlife, fish and fisheries, and a special collection of 19th and 20th century ornithological books. For current material there is a comprehensive index (formerly, until 1964, known as the *Agricultural index*):

*Biological and agricultural index*, 1916 to date | New York: H. W. Wilson, 1919 to date

which is issued monthly, with annual cumulations. It is a detailed alphabetical subject index of the contents of 78 biological and 68 agricultural periodicals, covering agriculture, animal husbandry, biology, botany, dairying, ecology, entomology, feeding stuffs, forestry, genetics, horticulture, microbiology, mycology, nutrition, physiology, plant science, poultry, soil science, veterinary medicine, and zoology.

U.S. DEPARTMENT OF AGRICULTURE | *Bibliography of agriculture, 1941 to date* | Washington 1942 to date

This is a monthly publication with annual cumulated author and subject indexes. It covers agricultural economics and rural sociology, agricultural engineering, entomology, plant science, forestry, food processing and distribution, human nutrition, and animal industry. There is also the quarterly classified *World agricultural economics and rural sociology abstracts* (Amsterdam, North-Holland Publishing Co., 1959 to date), which is prepared by the International Association of Agricultural Librarians and Documentalists in collaboration with the International Conference of Agricultural Economists.

There is also a more specialized index of current material in an important field of agriculture:

IMPERIAL BUREAU OF SOIL SCIENCE | *Bibliography of soil science, fertilisers and general agronomy, 1931 to date*

This is international in scope, and is classified by U.D.C. It covers books, periodicals, pamphlets, &c. The sections consist of: An index to new classification numbers; the main bibliography, in classified order; a geographical bibliography; a list of periodicals; and author and subject indexes. Note should also be taken of the series of abstracts published by the appropriate bureaux of the Commonwealth Agricultural Bureaux on applied entomology, applied mycology, medical and veterinary mycology, nutrition, animal breeding, veterinary science, dairy science, forestry, helminthology, horticulture, herbage, field crops, plant breeding, soils and fertilisers, weeds, agricultural economics and rural sociology (see the *Publications list* of the Commonwealth Agricultural Bureaux, Farnham Royal, Buckinghamshire).

On horticulture there is an important library catalogue:

ROYAL HORTICULTURAL SOCIETY | *The Lindley Library: catalogue of books, pamphlets, manuscripts and drawings* | 1927

Agriculture | 75

which is arranged in alphabetical order of author, and includes books, periodicals, official publications, pamphlets, transactions, proceedings, &c.

The main library catalogue of forestery is:

YALE UNIVERSITY | FORESTRY LIBRARY | *Dictionary catalogue* | 12 volumes | Boston, Mass. : G. K. Hall 1962 to date

which covers some 90,000 works on forestry and related subjects. The *Basic library list for forestry*, edited by E. F. Hemmings and issued by the Commonwealth Forestry Institute (4th edition. Oxford, 1967) is an excellent aid in this field.

On food there is:

BAKER, E. ALAN and FOSKETT, D. J. | *Bibliography of food: a select international bibliography of nutrition, food and beverage technology and distribution, 1936–1956* | Butterworths 1958

which is a classified list of books and outstanding periodical articles, with indexes of authors and subjects.

# 8 | Art | Entertainment | and Sport

The Victoria and Albert Museum has the best library on art in Great Britain, and some of it—for instance, its special collections of books and periodicals on such subjects as furniture, jewellery, &c.—is without equal. Unfortunately, there is no complete printed catalogue of its resources, although a number of lists on special subjects were issued at the turn of the century, and this is unfortunately true of the smaller collections at the Ashmolean, and the Courtauld. For the work of individual artists, however, there are very good bibliographies in:

THIEME, ULRICH and BECKER, FELIX | *Allgemeines Lexikon der bildenden Künstler von der Antike bis zur Gegenwart* ... | 37 volumes | Leipzig: Seemann 1907-50

which is the outstanding reference book on artists of all times. It has been continued for the present century by Hans Vollmer's *Allgemeines Lexikon der bildenden Künstler des XX Jahrhunderts* (Leipzig, Seemann, 1953-61, 5 volumes). There are also four catalogues of fairly large art collections:

KUNSTHISTORISCHES INSTITUT IN FLORENZ | *Katalog* | 9 volumes | Boston, Mass.: G. K. Hall 1965

This Library specializes in the history of Italian art from Early Christian times to the present day. Its nucleus is a fairly complete collection on Italian artists and monuments; this is supplemented by sections on history, literature, etc., where they are relevant to the study of the history of art. The arts of other nations are represented wherever they show evidence of contacts with Italy. The catalogue includes some 70,000 entries for books and serials arranged by authors.

LONDON UNIVERSITY | PREEDY MEMORIAL LIBRARY | *Catalogue of books on archaeology and art and cognate works belonging to the Preedy Memorial Library and other collections* ... | 1935-7

The first section is devoted to archaeology and early art, the second to art, and the third to indexes of subjects, authors, and artists. The main arrangement of the first section is under the earliest civilizations of the classical east, followed by the continental divisions and their various national areas. The second section commences with general and historical works, and contains divisions for the various forms of art with appropriate subdivisions. A small Supplement was issued in 1937.

NEWCASTLE-UPON-TYNE | PUBLIC LIBRARIES | *Fine arts catalogue* | 2nd edition | 1934

contains a number of illustrations from notable works, and covers the following subjects: gardening and town planning, architecture, sculpture, carving, numismatics, pottery, art metalwork, drawing and decoration, painting, engraving and photography, &c. Only brief details are given. Entries are arranged in classified order, and there is an index of authors and subjects.

LIVERPOOL | PUBLIC LIBRARIES | HORNBY LIBRARY | *Ex bibliotheca Hugh Frederick Hornby: catalogue* ... | 1906

This private collection which so greatly enriched Liverpool's resources was designed to illustrate the history and progress of the graphic arts from early times to the present day. It contains a number of special collections including an important section of French illustrated books of the eighteenth century, another on the great English designers and artists of the early nineteenth century—notably Cruikshank, Bewick and his pupils and imitators. It also includes bookbindings, examples of modern illustration processes, autographs, and prints. Authors and subjects are included in one alphabetical sequence. There are many annotations, and an index of artists and engravers.

Attention must also be drawn to the catalogues of the great European libraries of art such as the Rijksmuseum at Amsterdam, the Académie Royale des Beaux-Arts at Brussels, the Österreichisches Museum für Kunst und Industrie at Vienna, &c.; and to the Metropolitan Museum of Art's *Library catalog* (Boston, Mass., G. K. Hall, 1960, 25 volumes). These catalogues are rarely seen in the libraries of the English-speaking world, but they are fully described in a major bibliography:

CHAMBERLIN, MARY W. | *Guide to art reference books* | Chicago: American Library Association 1959

which lists some 2,500 books and periodicals and provides detailed annotations. The guide covers the literature of architecture, painting, sculpture, prints and engravings, drawings, and the applied arts, but omits numismatics, interior decoration (apart from furniture and textiles), and the theatre. Contents are classified and there is an index of authors and subjects.

A very useful little introductory guide to the bibliography of art is:

LUCAS, EDNA LOUISE | *The Harvard list of books on art* | Cambridge, Mass.: Harvard University Press 1952

to which must be added its companion volume, Benjamin Rowland's *The Harvard outline and reading lists for Oriental art*, issued in the same year; and, Neville Carrick's *How to find out about the arts* (Oxford, Pergamon Press, 1965).

Literature of modern art is covered in:

KARPEL, BENJAMIN | *Arts of the 20th century: a selective guide to the literature of the modern arts, 1900-1950* | New York: Wittenborn 1960

which gives a classified list of about two thousand items. And on the philosophical aspects of art there is W. A. Hammond's *A bibliography of aesthetics and of the philosophy of the fine arts from 1900 to 1932*, of which a revised edition was issued in 1934.

For current material there are several comprehensive serials:

*Art index: a cumulative author and subject index to a selected list of fine arts periodicals, and museum bulletins, 1929 to date* | New York: H. W. Wilson 1929 to date

This covers articles in 113 English-language and foreign journals on archaeology, arts and crafts, graphic arts, industrial design, interior decoration, landscape architecture, architecture, ceramics, decoration and ornament, painting, and sculpture. A useful feature is the inclusion of titles of works of art (up to ten) accompanying the text of an article in a note, unless they appear in the title or are not descriptive—in which case the number is given. Book reviews are included under both author and subject, and exhibitions under the names of the artists. Illustrations without text are also listed. This publication is issued quarterly, cumulating throughout the year into annual and two-yearly volumes. It is international in scope, and covers the chief British periodicals.

*Répertoire d'art et d'archéologie, 1910-* | Paris: Morancé 1914-

is an annual publication of the Bibliothèque d'Art et d'Archéologie de l'Université de Paris. It covers books, pamphlets, and periodical articles, and the annotated entries are arranged under the following headings: General—covering history, iconography, aesthetics and criticism, bibliography and periodicals, education, technique, museums and collections, exhibitions and sales, topography, &c.; France; other countries, arranged first by period, subdivided by countries. There are indexes of authors and artists in each issue. It is international in scope.

*Annuario bibliografico di storia dell'arte, 1952-* | Modena: Società Tipografica Editrice Modenese 1954-

deals with the history of art, and is prepared by the Library of the Istituto

Nazionale d'Archeologia e Storia dell'Arte. It is a classified and annotated list of books and periodical articles, with a name index. This Library also issued a *Catalogo dei periodici* in 1947, supplemented by a list of its current serials, *Indice dei periodici attivi*, issued in 1956.

*Bibliography of the history of British art, 1934 to date* | Courtauld Institute of Art | 1936 to date

lists books and periodical articles on the history of British art, excluding Roman but including Celtic and Viking art, and covering architecture, painting, sculpture, the graphic and applied arts. Writings on British private collections and museums have been noted even though the arts discussed may not be British: also, writings on foreign artists working in Great Britain. The bibliography is primarily historical, but modern art and living artists are included together with contemporary criticism. The periodicals indexed are chiefly British, but include a number of important foreign journals. From 1937 onwards, heraldry, costume, &c., are omitted as they are included in *Writings on British history* (q.v.).

One of the most helpful guides to current books on art is:

VICTORIA AND ALBERT MUSEUM | *Library accessions*

This is particularly important for the large amount of foreign material included—owing to the Museum's wide contacts abroad sometimes the first mention of an outstanding publication is contained in these lists. There is also a section devoted to the recataloguing of items, and this is of great value since the entries are the result of careful and detailed research. Entries are duplicated on one side of the paper only to facilitate mounting. Another international index which covered a wide range of books and periodicals was the *Internationale Bibliographie der Kunstwissenschaft, 1902-1917/18*, (Berlin: Behr, 1902-20).

## ARCHITECTURE

On this subject it will have been noted that the general catalogues and indexes listed above—the *Art index*, the *Bibliography of the history of British art*, &c.—cover the more general material to a certain extent. The Royal Institute of British Architects is world-famous for its library, and its catalogue is of the greatest importance:

ROYAL INSTITUTE OF BRITISH ARCHITECTS | *Catalogue* | 2 volumes | 1937

Volume I is arranged alphabetically by authors, and volume II consists of a classified index and alphabetical subject index of books and manuscripts. This catalogue is especially noted for its large proportion of

## 80 | Architecture

analytical entries for periodicals. It is kept up to date by means of monthly duplicated accessions lists, and lists of periodical articles. The library also issues a large number of highly specialized bibliographies on such subjects as Observatories, &c., and, from 1965, an *Annual review of periodical articles* in classified order with subject index.

The Avery Architectural Library at Columbia University, with its great collection of books, periodicals and architectural drawings, has issued a new edition of its own and other resources within the University:

**Catalogue of the Avery Memorial Architectural Library of Columbia University** | 2nd edition | 12 volumes | Boston, Mass.: G. K. Hall 1967

**Avery index to architectural periodicals** | 12 volumes | Boston, Mass.: G. K. Hall, 1964

covering architecture, archaeology, town planning, the decorative arts, sculpture, painting, etc. Dennis Sharp's *Sources of modern architecture: a bibliography* (New York: Wittenborn, 1966) is a useful biographical and subject bibliography with geographical analysis of items.

Town planning is included in the catalogues listed above and current material can also be found in:

MINISTRY OF HOUSING AND LOCAL GOVERNMENT | *Classified accessions list and index to periodical articles*

which is published bi-monthly, and in the Ministry's specialized bibliographies. Useful material on this subject is also contained in the accessions lists of the Ministry of Health, and of the Ministry of Public Building and Works.

### FURNITURE

There are two good library catalogues on this subject:

SHOREDITCH | PUBLIC LIBRARIES | *Furniture and allied trades: a catalogue of the books in the special collection . . . 1950*

This is in three sections: I. Timber—types, diseases, seasoning, preservation, measurement; II. Woodworking—carpentry, cabinet making, decoration, upholstery; III. Furniture—English, German, French, Italian, Spanish, Portuguese, American, Oriental, modern, and ecclesiastical. Brief details are given, and there is an author index.

GRAND RAPIDS, MICH. | PUBLIC LIBRARY | *List of books on furniture, with descriptive notes* | 1927 (Supplement 1954)

is an alphabetical author list, with a subject index. The bibliographies issued by the Timber Development Association will also be found useful for this subject.

# Ceramics and Glass | 81

On the special subject of clocks there is:

BAILLIE, GRANVILLE HUGH | *Clocks and watches: an historical bibliography* | N.A.G. Press 1951

which deals with mechanical timepieces during the period 1344 to 1800. Items are arranged chronologically, with annotations. There are name and subject indexes. There is an older but still useful work:

CLOCKMAKERS' COMPANY | *Catalogue of the Library . . .* | 2nd edition | Blades 1898

which is arranged in three parts: I. Books, which includes periodical articles, and which has entries for authors and subjects in one alphabetical sequence; II. Manuscripts; III. Prints, drawings, paintings, engravings, &c.

A weekly abstract journal is available:

*Industrial design abstracts, 1947 to date* | Council of Industrial Design 1947 to date

which covers interior decoration, furniture, tableware, household and garden equipment, manufacture and marketing, dress and accessories. There is an index every six months.

## CERAMICS AND GLASS

The outstanding bibliography of ceramics is that of the great collector Solon:

SOLON, LOUIS MARC EMMANUEL | compiler | *Ceramic literature: an analytical index to the works published in all languages on the history and technology of the ceramic art: also to the catalogues of public museums, private collections, and of auction sales in which the descriptions of ceramic objects occupy an important place: and to the most important price-lists of the ancient and modern manufactories of pottery and porcelain* | Griffin 1910 | (Supplement 1911)

The main body of this bibliography consists of an author list (heavily and often lengthily annotated) covering technology, history, classical, oriental, and European ceramics, decorative tiles, ancient stoneware, acoustic pottery, terra sigillata, buccaros, stoves, architectural terra-cotta, biographies, bibliography, marks and monograms, theory, collecting and collectors, fiction, museums and collections, and exhibitions. Solon is outspoken in his criticism and unsparing of shoddy material. Periodical articles are included. English translations of foreign titles are given. There is also a shorter classified list at the end of the volume. This collection is now in the keeping of the North Staffordshire Technical College which has issued its own catalogue:

NORTH STAFFORDSHIRE TECHNICAL COLLEGE | *Catalogue of the Ceramic Library* | 1925

to which a Supplement was added in 1930. This library includes not only the Solon Library, but also the collections of the Ceramic Society, the British Refractories Research Association, and other bodies.

Abstracts for twentieth-century material are available in:

*British Ceramic Research Association abstracts, 1900 to date* | Hanley 1900 to date

which covers ceramic raw materials, manufacturing processes, fuels, kilns and firing, and finished products. There is an annual index.

The literature of glass is covered by:

DUNCAN, G. S. | *A bibliography of glass* | Dawson, for the Society of Glass Technology 1960 (Supplement 1965)

INTERNATIONAL COMMISSION ON GLASS | *Bibliography of glass literature* | Charleroi 1966

The latter lists current books and serials relating to glass and ceramics, and journals that occasionally publish articles on glass. There is a subject index.

## NUMISMATICS

Since the war a useful new serial bibliography has commenced publication:

*Numismatic literature, 1947 to date* | The American Numismatic Society 1947 to date

This is issued quarterly. The first issue in 1947, and no. 1A of 1949 covered the years 1940–5. The subjects covered include Greek, Roman, Byzantine, medieval and modern European, British, North and South American, and Asian coins; tokens; medals; decorations; seals; paper money; and other minor subjects. There are also a book review index, brief obituaries, and a list of coin trade catalogues in each issue. Most books and articles are given a short description, but some have long signed reviews. An author index to the issues for 1947–9 was published in 1949.

There is a useful introduction to the literature of the subject: Philip Grierson's *Coins and medals: a select bibliography* (George Philip, for the Historical Association, 1954); and G. K. Hall of Boston issued the 7-volume *Dictionary and auction catalogue* of the American Numismatic Society in 1962–63.

# COSTUME

The best bibliography of costume is a French publication:

COLAS, RENÉ | *Bibliographie générale du costume et de la mode* | 2 volumes | Paris: René Colas 1933 (reprinted New York: Hacker 1966)

which is international in scope, and covers both books and periodicals. Subjects covered include civil, military, and religious costume, fashions, hair styles, accessories, &c. The main body of the work is arranged alphabetically by authors with full bibliographical details. In the case of important books full lists of the plates and illustrations are given. Starred items indicate that the compiler has not been able to examine them satisfactorily. There is also a classified list of books, and indexes of authors and anonymous titles are given. The reprinting in 1964 of the famous *Katalog der Freiherrlich von Lipperheideschen Kostumbibliothek* (Berlin, 1896–1905) affords a new opportunity to study the largest collection of costume books ever formed.

The celebrated Hiler Library of Costume, which is now the property of the Queens Borough Public Library in New York, is listed in:

HARZBERG, HILER | *Catalogue of the Hiler Costume Library* | Paris: Lecram Press 1927

Based primarily on this library is an important annotated index:

HILER, HILAIRE and HILER, MEYER | *Bibliography of costume* | New York: H. W. Wilson 1939 (reprinted Bronx, N.Y.: Benjamin Blom 1966)

This indexes more than 8,000 books and periodicals on the subject, and covers works in many languages. Subjects included are dress, jewellery, and decoration of the body, in general and for special occasions, of all countries, times, and peoples: also items on such subjects as reform of dress (sumptuary laws are, however, omitted), psychology of dress, art of dress: and needlework and its branches. General museum guides, books on coats of arms, laundering, and books on textiles which do not show actual dress have been omitted. Entries (sometimes annotated but mostly referenced to Colas's and Lipperheide's works) for authors, titles, subjects, editors, illustrators, engravers, &c., are arranged in one alphabetical sequence. Another index was issued a little before:

MONRO, ISABEL and COOK, DOROTHY E. | *Costume index: a subject index to plates and to illustrated text* | New York: H. W. Wilson 1937

This is a subject index of national and local costume, the indexing being as specific as possible. Medals, badges, arms, and armour are not covered, nor have stage costumes or pictures of Biblical characters been included.

European costume after 1800 has been entered under the heading 'Nineteenth century' because of the slight differences in dress found in various countries after that period. Very little material on religious dress is included, and the only periodical indexed is the *National geographic magazine*. Individual items of dress are only indexed when they appear by themselves and not as part of a complete costume. Arrangement is alphabetical by subject, and there is a list of books indexed. A Supplement was issued in 1957.

## ILLUSTRATIONS

One of the largest classes of illustrations—those of portraits of famous people—is covered by a noteworthy index:

*A.L.A. portrait index: index to portraits contained in printed books and periodicals*, edited by WILSON COOLIDGE LANE and NINA E. BROWNE | Washington: Library of Congress 1906 (reprinted New York: Burt Franklin 1965—in 3 volumes)

This indexes more than 1,100 books and sets of periodicals published up to the end of 1904, and about 120,000 portraits of some 40,000 people are recorded. Dates are included, and the type of illustration indicated. Photographical reproductions are noted by means of asterisks. Portraits of an author prefixed to editions of his works are omitted except when the volumes have been indexed for the other portraits they contain. Genealogical works and local histories are in general omitted, and so are a few large collections of engravings.

Other important indexes of portraits are less familiar in the libraries of the English-speaking world, and include the *Allgemeiner Porträt-Katalog* of the firm of Hans Dietrich von Diepenbroick-Grüter (Hamburg, 1931), W. E. Drugulin's *Allgemeiner Portrait-Katalog* (Leipzig, Kunst-Comptoir, 1859-60), Erwin Heinzel's *Lexikon historischer Ereignisse und Personen* . . . (Vienna, Hollinek, 1956), and H. W. Singer's *Allgemeiner Bildniskatalog* and his *Neuer Bildniskatalog* (Leipzig, Hiersemann, 1930-6 and 1937-8 respectively), all of which are described in detail in Mary W. Chamberlin's *Guide to art reference books* (q.v.).

For reproductions of paintings, including portraits, there are four important indexes:

MONRO, ISABEL STEVENSON and MONRO, KATE M. | *Index to reproductions of European paintings* | New York: H. W. Wilson 1956

MONRO, ISABEL STEVENSON and MONRO, KATE M. | *Index to reproductions of American paintings* | New York: H. W. Wilson 1948 (Supplement 1964)

Illustrations | 85

which both index illustrations in books and catalogues of exhibitions, and both of which comprise entries under artists, titles and some subjects, in one alphabetical order, locations (where ascertainable) being indicated by symbols.

*Catalogue of colour reproductions of paintings prior to 1860* | 3rd edition | Paris: Unesco 1955

*Catalogue of colour reproductions of paintings—1860 to 1963* | Paris: Unesco 1963

are both arranged alphabetically by artists' names and include small half-tone illustrations of the paintings listed.

For other subjects there are:

ELLIS, MRS JESSIE CROFT | compiler | *Travel through pictures: references to pictures, in books and periodicals, of interesting sites all over the world* | Boston, Mass.: Faxon 1935

which is a smaller work: much of the material mentioned is essentially American and therefore not easily available in Britain, but it is still of use on many occasions. It is arranged alphabetically by country, subdivided alphabetically by place. There is an index of cross-references of places.

ELLIS, MRS JESSIE CROFT | compiler | *General index to illustrations: 22,000 selected references in all fields exclusive of nature* | Boston: Faxon 1931

covers all subjects, but is especially strong in art, architecture, history, literature, including pictures of artists, sculptors, authors, and people prominent in governmental affairs, &c. (both living and dead), as well as references to their work. Entries are arranged alphabetically by subjects, and there is a list of books and periodicals indexed. Another work which is useful for illustrations is Mrs Ellis's *Nature and its applications*, 1949, which is described in the chapter on SCIENCE. There are also Lucile E. Vance's *Illustration index* (New York, Scarecrow Press, 1957), and the wealth of references in the cumulative indexes to the *National geographic magazine* (1899-1946 and 1947-63) plus the annual supplements.

## PAINTING

Owing to the very small amount of bibliography especially devoted to this subject, the reader would have difficulty in tracing much of the material he requires were it not for the excellent bibliographies in Thieme and Becker's *Allgemeines Lexikon der bildenden Künstler*, already mentioned at the beginning of this chapter. In addition there is a specific index:

McCOLVIN, ERIC RAYMOND | *Painting: a guide to the best books, with special reference to the requirements of public libraries* | Grafton 1934

## 86 | Engraving

This covers theory and practice, art galleries, the general history of painting, schools of painting, and includes books on drawing and on the drawings of old and modern masters, but not material on illuminated manuscripts. Books of most general value are marked with an asterisk, and there are recommended selections for very small libraries and for children's libraries. Occasional annotations are given, and there are indexes of subjects, schools, artists, and authors.

## ENGRAVING

In addition to the *Catalogue* of the Hornby Library mentioned at the beginning of this chapter there is the bibliography given in:

HIND, ARTHUR MAYGER | *A history of engraving and etching from the fifteenth century to the year 1914* | Constable 1923

which helps to support the small number of general bibliographies on this subject. There are two comprehensive bibliographies:

LEVIS, HOWARD C. | *A descriptive bibliography of the most important books in the English language relating to the art and history of engraving and the collecting of prints* | Ellis 1912

to which a Supplement and Index of authors and subjects was issued in 1913. This is a classified list with numerous detailed annotations. Levis is selective and critical of the works he lists. The 17-page Addenda in the main volume, and the short Errata list in the Supplement should be noted.

COLIN PAUL | *La gravure et les graveurs* | 2 volumes | Brussels: van Oest 1916–18

lists well over 3,000 items: the first volume covers general works, arranged in classified order, with an author index; the second is devoted to monographs, arranged alphabetically by name of artist, with an author index.

## PHOTOGRAPHY

The main bibliography of this subject is represented by:

ROYAL PHOTOGRAPHIC SOCIETY OF GREAT BRITAIN | *Library catalogue* | 3rd edition | 2 parts | 1939–52 (Supplements 1953)

of which the first part is an author catalogue of some 7,000 works, and the second is a classified subject catalogue with an alphabetical index of subjects. The supplements are arranged in a similar fashion. The Society also issues:

*Photographic abstracts, volume 1, 1921 to date* | 1921 to date

which is prepared under the auspices of the Society's Scientific and Technical Group, and is now issued twice a month. These abstracts are classified, and subject coverage includes kinematography, stereoscopy, and scientific, medical and X-ray aspects of the field. Increasing attention is being paid to foreign-language material, and all abstracts are in English, annual author and decennial subject indexes are issued. The American counterpart, Eastman Kodak's *Monthly abstract bulletin* (Rochester, N.Y., 1914 to date), should also be noted.

BONI, ALBERT | *Photographic literature* | New York & London: R. R. Bowker 1962

is an international bibliography of some 12,000 basic books, journals, articles, technical papers, patents, &c., covering photography from the earliest times. Items are analysed under at least 1200 subject headings, including techniques, theory, processes, chemistry, physics, apparatus, materials, industry, history, biography, aesthetics, &c.

## MUSIC

For the general basic material the bibliographies appended to the articles in the latest edition of Sir George Grove's *Dictionary of music and musicians* (Macmillan) will give the reader the outstanding items on particular subjects and composers and instruments. Similarly Willi Apel's *Harvard dictionary of music* indicates the more important material, including periodical articles. The bibliographies in *Die Musik in Geschichte und Gegenwart: allgemeine Enzyklopädie der Musik* (Kassel, Bärenreiter, 1949 to date) are especially important. A useful introductory bibliography is:

DUCKLES, VINCENT | *Music reference and research materials* | Glencoe Free Press 1964

an annotated list of nearly 1200 dictionaries, encyclopaedias, bibliographies, catalogues of music libraries and collections, discographies, and yearbooks. In addition:

DARRELL, R. D. | *Schirmer's guide to books on music and musicians: a practical bibliography* | New York: Schirmer, London, Chappell 1951

DAVIES, J. H. | *Musicalia: sources of information in music* | Pergamon Press, & J. Curwen 1966

have a wider coverage and provide helpful notes.

Eitner's great *Biographisch-bibliographisches Quellen-Lexikon der Musiker und Musikgelehrten der christlichen Zeitrechnung bis zur Mitte des neunzehnten Jahrhunderts.* (10 volumes, Leipzig: Breitkopf, 1900–4) is now being slowly replaced by:

*Répertoire international des sources musicales* | volume 1– | Munich-Duisberg: Henle; London, Novello 1960 to date

which is being compiled by the International Association of Music Libraries in collaboration with the International Musicological Society. The first volume of the first series, *Recueils imprimés XVIe:–XVIIIe siècles* (1960) demonstrates fully the care which the compilers are taking to ensure that this vast work will be as comprehensive as possible in its recording of research material. The recent reprint (12 volumes. Hilversum, Knuf, 1967) of F. Pazdirek's *Universal-Handbuch der Musikliteratur aller Zeiten und Völker* (originally published Vienna, 1904–10)—especially valuable for 19th century publications—should be noted.

The reference guide to the world's largest collection of performing editions:

DAVIES, J. H. | *BBC Music Library catalogues* | 9 volumes | The BBC 1965–67

comprises over a quarter-of-a-million entries for Chamber Music, Piano and Organ Music (2 volumes), Songs: Composers, and Titles (4 volumes), and Vocal Scores including Opera (2 volumes). Another important catalogue:

NEW YORK | PUBLIC LIBRARY | *Dictionary catalog of the Music Collection* | 33 volumes | Boston, Mass., G. K. Hall, 1965–66

is comprehensive and its half-a-million entries are especially strong in the fields of folk song, 18th and 19th century libretti, full scores of operas, complete works, historical editions, Beethoven, Americana, American music, vocal music, record catalogues, manuscripts, Festschriften, yearbooks, &c.

Current literature is recorded in the accessions lists of the national libraries and of the great music libraries, in addition to:

*Bibliographie des Musikschrifttums, 1936–41, 1950 to date* | Frankfurt-am-Main: Hofmeister 1936–41, 1954 to date

which is issued under the auspices of the Institut für deutsche Musikforschung. This outstanding bibliography covers both books and periodical articles in many languages, and is now issued biennially. Attention is also drawn to *The music index* (Detroit, Information Service, 1949 to date) which is issued monthly, with annual cumulations. This indexes about 200 journals, with emphasis on English-language materials, and includes reviews of books, music, performances and recordings.

Music itself is listed in the accessions lists of the national copyright libraries and in those of the great music libraries. In addition, there is the:

*British catalogue of music, 1957 to date* | Council of the British National Bibliography 1957 to date

which is a quarterly national bibliography of music scores and books about music, with annual cumulations. For the moment, modern dance music and some popular music items are excluded. A printed card service is also provided. In 1958 the Composers' Guild of Great Britain issued the first volume of its *Catalogue of members' compositions*. This listed orchestral works; further volumes covering vocal, choral, instrumental and chamber music are promised.

For early music, there is a surprising number of great and comprehensive catalogues. Among the most famous must be mentioned:

BRITISH MUSEUM | DEPARTMENT OF PRINTED BOOKS *Catalogue of printed music published between 1487 and 1800* ..., by W. BARCLAY SQUIRE | 2 volumes | 1912

The first Supplement was included in volume II. A second Supplement was published in 1940. This bibliography is international in scope, and items in periodicals (especially songs) are included. It is arranged alphabetically by composer and by title in one sequence. The supplements include some items published before 1487.

BRITISH MUSEUM | DEPARTMENT OF MANUSCRIPTS | *Catalogue of MS. music* ..., by AUGUSTUS HUGHES-HUGHES | 3 volumes | 1906-9

Volume I is devoted to sacred vocal music, volume II to secular vocal music, and volume III to instrumental music, treatises, &c. Each volume arranges its entries in classified order, with author, subject, and title indexes.

BRITISH MUSEUM | *Catalogue of the King's Music Library* | 3 volumes | 1927-9

Part I is devoted to the Handel manuscripts—autographs, copies, and adaptations. Part II to miscellaneous manuscripts—separate works, anonymous works, and collections. Part III to printed music and musical literature. All are sub-arranged alphabetically by composer, author, or title.

Parallel with the British Museum's catalogue are:

SCHNAPPER, EDITH B. | *British union-catalogue of early music printed before the year 1801* | 2 volumes | Butterworth 1957

U.S. LIBRARY OF CONGRESS | *Catalogue of early books on music (before 1800)* | Washington 1913 (Supplement 1944)

The first is arranged by composers and records more than fifty thousand works held in over one hundred British libraries. A vocal index lists some ten thousand titles. The latter is arranged alphabetically by composers, and the Supplement is similarly arranged, with an appendix of books on Asiatic music. There is an index of anonymous works. Wyn K. Ford's *Music in England before 1800* (Library Association 1967) is an annotated select bibliography, with indexes of authors and sources. Howard Mayer Brown's *Instrumental music printed before 1600* (Harvard University Press, 1965) is a bibliography which also lists modern editions of collections and individual compositions.

Mention must be made of the famous Hirsch collection which after many unhappy vicissitudes has at last found a permanent home in the British Museum. This collection is rich in manuscripts, first and early editions of the classics. A finely produced and illustrated catalogue of the more important items has been published:

HIRSCH, PAUL | *Katalog der Musik Bibliothek Paul Hirsch* | 4 volumes | Berlin: Breslauer, 1928-30 (volumes I and II): Frankfurt-am-Main, 1936 (volume III): Cambridge University Press 1947 (volume IV)

Four other items are of use in tracing entries for important material:

BOSTON | PUBLIC LIBRARY | *Catalogue of the Allen A. Brown collection of music* | 4 volumes | 1908-16 (a dictionary catalogue, which analyses many songs included in collections | The fourth is a supplementary volume)

BACKUS, EDYTHE N. | *Catalogue of music in the Huntington Library printed before 1801* | San Marino, Calif.: Huntington Library 1949 (contains large and important analytical index to songs)

PHILADELPHIA FREE LIBRARY | *The Edwin A. Fleischer collection of orchestral music ... : a descriptive catalogue* | 2 volumes | 1933-45

Music | 91

HEYER, ANNA HARRIET | *Historical sets, collected editions and monuments of music: a guide to their contents* | Chicago: American Library Association 1957 (Supplements from time to time)

The literature of opera is very well covered. In the first place there is the remarkable:

LOEWENBERG, ALFRED | *Annals of the opera, compiled from the original sources* | 2nd edition | 2 volumes | Geneva: Societas Bibliographica 1955

which contains entries for 3,000 to 4,000 operas arranged chronologically by dates of first performances. Titles are given in the languages of the original libretti, but translations are provided for the less familiar languages. Librettists are named. The bibliography is well annotated, and there are indexes of titles, composers (including dates), librettists, and miscellaneous items.

LIBRARY OF CONGRESS | *Catalogue of opera librettos printed before 1800*, prepared by O. G. T. SONNECK | 2 volumes | Washington 1914 (reprinted, 2 volumes in 4. New York, Burt Franklin, 1965)

Volume I is a title catalogue arranged by original title, but entries include alternative titles and translations, and very full annotations concerning details of first performances and notes concerning publication and history. The second volume is devoted to indexes of authors, composers, and arias. There is also a companion volume by the same author:

LIBRARY OF CONGRESS | *Dramatic music: catalogue of full scores* | compiled by O. G. T. SONNECK | Washington 1908

and further information on this subject can sometimes be obtained from the catalogues of gramophone records.

The earlier songs are indexed in some of the general bibliographies described at the beginning of this chapter. In addition, there is:

DAY, CYRUS LAWRENCE and MURRIE, ELEANORE BOSWELL | *English song-books, 1651-1702: a bibliography with a first-line index of songs* | Bibliographical Society 1940

which lists 250 collections for England and Scotland. Some books published later than 1702 are included, but manuscript music, collections of songs without music, song-tunes without words, sacred songs, and so-called single-songs are omitted. Entries are chronologically arranged with locations, full bibliographical descriptions, and some illustrations. There are indexes of over 4,000 songs, 200 composers, 250 authors, and of singers and actors, printers, publishers and booksellers, and ballad-tunes. Attention is also drawn to M. Dean-Smith's *A guide to English folk-song collections, 1822-1952* (Liverpool University Press, 1954), which was published in association with the English Folk Dance and Song Society. It is arranged by song titles, and includes historical annotations.

SEARS, MINNIE EARL | editor | *Song index: an index to more than 12,000 songs in 177 song collections comprising 262 volumes* | New York: H. W. Wilson 1926 (Supplement 1934) (reprinted in one volume. Shoe String Press, 1967)

excludes collections of individual composers, hymn books, collections of folk dances and singing games, collections published in foreign countries (except Great Britain), and collections with words only or without instrumental setting. The main work consists of one alphabetical sequence of titles, composers, authors, first lines, and references. Attributions are given in cases of doubt, and voice is included wherever possible. There are also a classified list of collections indexed, and a directory of publishers. The *Stecheson classified song directory* (Hollywood, Calif.: Music Industry Press, 1961) indexes some 100,000 popular songs under 400 subjects. Desirée de Charms and Paul F. Breed's *Songs in collections* (Detroit, Information Service, 1965) indexes by titles and first lines over 9,000 songs in some 400 collections published between 1940 and 1957. Nat Shapiro's *Popular music* (2 volumes. New York, Adrian Press, 1964-66) indexes, with annotations, American popular songs of the period 1940 to 1959; further volumes are in preparation.

There is also a special index of children's songs:

CUSHING, HELEN GRANT | *Children's song index* | New York: H. W. Wilson 1936

This slightly overlaps with Sears's *Song index*, but includes 178 collections not covered by that work. It also has the additional advantage of subject-entries which are included in the main alphabetical sequence of authors, titles, and composers.

Orchestral music has several good bibliographies: among them are:

SALTONSTALL, CECILIA DRINKER and SMITH, HANNAH COFFIN | compilers | *Catalogue of music for small orchestra* | Washington: Music Library Association 1947

This is arranged alphabetically by composer, and lists for each composition the movements, time, instruments, publisher, and date. There are indexes of titles and wind.

ALTMANN, WILHELM | compiler | *Kammermusik-Katalog: ein Verzeichnis von seit 1841 veröffentlichten Kammermusikwerken* | 5th edition | Leipzig: Hofmeister 1942 is in classified order and covers chamber music for string and wind instruments, chamber music with pianos, sonatas for harp and other instruments, works for the guitar and other instruments, and vocal music. There are indexes of publishers and of names of composers. Other useful works are:

FARISH, MARGARET K. | *String music in print* | New York & London, Bowker 1965

U.S. LIBRARY OF CONGRESS | *Orchestral music ... catalogue: scores* | Washington 1912

Farish is arranged by number of instruments required, and covers 18,000 items including solo music, chamber music, study scores, and study material.

For gramophone records the main works are:

*Archives of recorded music* | Paris: Unesco 1949 to date

CLOUGH, F. F. and CUMING, G. J. | *The world's encyclopaedia of recorded music* | Sidgwick & Jackson 1952 *(Supplement, 1953-55, 1957)*

GREENFIELD, EDWARD and others | *Stereo record guide* | Blackpool: Long Playing Record Library 1960 (two-yearly Supplements)

*L.P.R.L. Selective classical catalogue and handbook* | 2nd edition | Blackpool: Long Playing Record Library 1966

The Unesco volumes, some of which are issued by other publishers, are in three series: *A*–Western music; *B*–Oriental music; *C*–Ethnographical and folk music. Clough and Cuming is a comprehensive and detailed list. The fourth of the supplementary volumes to Greenfield brings the complete work up to date, acting as an index to the other volumes and including mono as well as stereo catalogue numbers. Another useful list is the new edition of *The Penguin guide to bargain records*.

## BROADCASTING

Radio and television are comprehensively covered in two works:

U.S. DEPARTMENT OF HEALTH, EDUCATION AND WELFARE | Office of Education | *Radio and television: a selected bibliography* | Revised edition | Washington, D.C.: Government Printing Office 1960 (Bulletin 1960, no. 25)

HARWOOD, KENNETH | 'A world bibliography of selected periodicals on broadcasting' | *Journal of broadcasting*, Summer 1961 pp. 251–78

The first is a classified and annotated guide with an index of titles. The second is arranged by countries.

British broadcasting is dealt with in more detail in:

*British broadcasting* | 3rd edition | British Broadcasting Corporation 1958 (*Supplement 1958-60*)

COLLISON, ROBERT L. | *Broadcasting in Britain* | National Book League 1961 (Reader's guides, 4th series, no. 9)

both of which are fully annotated, the first being a comprehensive list especially notable for its coverage of official documents, while the latter lists the hundred outstanding works. Both are indexed.

## FILMS

The best bibliography of this subject was a project of the W.P.A. Unfortunately, only one volume was published:

*Film index: a bibliography* | Volume I—the film as art | New York : H. W. Wilson 1941

This lists books and periodical articles in the English language only. The first part is devoted to history and technique, and the second to types of films. Under these headings entries are arranged in classified order. There are digests and annotations for all entries, and an author and title index. This is supplemented to a certain extent by:

BRITISH FILM INSTITUTE | *Library catalogue* | 1961

BRITISH FILM INSTITUTE | *A select bibliography of books on the cinema* | 1953 (Supplement, 1955)

LIBRARY OF CONGRESS | DIVISION OF BIBLIOGRAPHY | *Moving pictures in the United States and foreign countries: a selected list of recent writings* | 1936 (Supplement, 1940)

With the assistance of the Belgian National Commission for Unesco and the International Federation of Film Archives, the Cinémathèque Belge has published the second edition of the *Répertoire mondial des périodiques cinématographiques/World List of Film Periodicals and Serials* (Brussels, La Cinémathèque, 1960). This work lists periodicals proper, appearing regularly, yearbooks (even if they do not appear every year) and works brought up to date periodically. It does not include publications which are not concerned primarily with the cinema, publications issued by industrial or commercial cinema firms and containing only their own news, or bulletins of film societies concerned only with internal matters and liaison with members.

Films themselves are recorded in:

*The British national film catalogue, 1963 to date* | British National Film Catalogue, 1964 to date

which is issued six times a year with annual cumulations. Each issue is divided into three parts: 1—classified and annotated catalogue of non-fiction films; 2—alphabetical title list of fiction films, with summaries; 3—a production index of sponsors, production companies, producers, directors, cameramen, writers, commentators, editors, composers, &c., and there is also a title and subject index for non-fiction films. From 1966 8 mm. cassette films have been separately listed.

Other useful lists include:

*Motion pictures, 1894-1959* | 4 volumes | Washington, D.C.: Library of Congress 1953-59

NATIONAL FILM ARCHIVE | *Silent news films, 1895-1933* | British Film Institute 1951

NATIONAL FILM ARCHIVE | *Silent non-fiction films, 1895-1934* | British Film Institute 1960

and those which are based on books or plays are listed in A. G. S. Enser's *Filmed books and plays, 1928 to date* (Grafton, 1951 to date), annual supplements being published in the *Library world*. H. P. Manz's *Internationale Filmbibliographie, 1952-62* (Zürich, Hans Rohr, 1963) is an annotated bibliography of nearly three thousand publications on the cinema, films, and the film industry. Annual supplements keep it up to date.

## THEATRE, MUSIC HALL AND CIRCUS

This section should be read in conjunction with the section on PLAYS in the next chapter, for many of the play indexes also contain material on the history and technique of the theatre (notably the *Players' Library*). For historical material there are:

ARNOTT, JAMES FULLARTON and ROBINSON, JOHN WILLIAM | *English theatrical literature, 1559-1900: a bibliography* | The Society for Theatre Research, 1967

BOSTON, MASS | PUBLIC LIBRARY | *Catalogue of the Allen A. Brown collection of books relating to the stage* | 1919

The first incorporates Robert William Lowe's classic *A bibliographical account of English theatrical literature* (Nimmo, 1888), and lists 5,000 British pamphlets, books, broadsides, and serials, with notes on overseas editions. Items are classified, and there are author and title indexes.

## Theatre, Music Hall and Circus

In the Reference Department of the New York Public Library the word 'theatre' is interpreted in its broadest sense and includes the stage, cinema, radio, television, carnivals, nightclub performances, the circus, and magic. The *Catalog of the theatre and drama collections* (Boston, Mass.: G. K. Hall, 1967–68) is a record of an outstanding library on this subject, comprising the Drama Collection (6 volumes) of more than 120,000 plays in western languages, with a six-volume 'author listing'; and the Theatre Collection (9 volumes), covering books and serials on stage history, production techniques, acting, theatre criticism, biography and material on individual theatres throughout the world.

A useful selective guide in narrative form with full critical annotations written by the former editor of *Theatre Arts* is still of use:

GILDER, ROSAMOND | *A theatre library: a bibliography of one hundred books relating to the stage* | New York: National Theatre Conference 1932 (well annotated)

But the most comprehensive work on the subject is:

BAKER, BLANCH M.| compiler | *Theatre and allied arts* | 2nd edition | New York: H. W. Wilson 1952 (reprinted Bronx, N.Y.: Blom 1966)

This is an excellently annotated classified list of 6,000 books on the history and criticism of the drama and stage, and on the allied arts of the theatre. It is limited to books in English or translations—except in the case of costume. Entries are arranged alphabetically by title under subsection headings. There are author and analytical subject indexes. The last work of the author of *Annals of the opera* was the culmination of years of research on the Continent and in his adopted country, and helps to fill a considerable gap in British theatrical bibliography:

LOEWENBERG, ALFRED | compiler | *The theatre of the British Isles, excluding London: a bibliography* | The Society for Theatre Research 1950

which lists about 1,500 items on theatres and performances of all kinds with a selection of entries for the better-known amateur theatres. After a general section, entries are arranged alphabetically by names of towns and countries, sub-arranged chronologically. Periodical articles, collections of manuscripts, news clippings, play-bills, and programmes are included, and there is an index of personal names.

For current material there is only one specialized bibliography of note, though much useful material is contained in the general indexes such as the *Reader's guide*, the *International index*, &c.

*Dramatic index: covering articles and illustrations concerning the stage and its players in the periodicals of America and England: with a record of books of the drama and of texts of plays, 1909–49* | Boston, Mass.: Faxon 1910–52 (cumulated edition, 1909–49, in 2 volumes: Boston, Mass., G. K. Hall, 1965)

This was published annually, and is kept up to date by quarterly Supplements in the *Bulletin of bibliography*. Material is taken mainly from thirty-seven British and American periodicals. Entries for critical material are arranged alphabetically by subjects and names of persons (including descriptions and dates) in one sequence. There are also appendixes of (1) an author list of English books on drama published during the year, (2) a title list of English plays (excluding Shakespeare) published during the year.

Circuses are covered in great detail in:

STOTT, RAYMOND TOOLE | *A bibliography of circus books in English* | Derby: Harper 1964

STOTT, RAYMOND TOOLE | *Circus and allied arts: a world bibliography* | 3 volumes | Derby: Harper 1958–63

The first lists about 1,100 monographs issued from 1773 to 1964. The latter includes conjuring, equitation, marionettes, toy theatres, Buffalo Bill, dime novels, &c., from 1500 to the present day. Locations for copies in the British Museum, the Library of Congress, and the Bibliothèque Nationale, are given.

## DANCING

There are four bibliographies of dancing:

*A bibliography of the dance collection of Doris Niles and Serge Leslie* | 2 volumes | Dancing Times 1966–67

BEAUMONT, CYRIL W. | *A bibliography of dancing* | Dancing Times 1929 (reprinted Holland Press, 1964)

MAGRIEL, PAUL DAVID | *A bibliography of dancing* | New York: H. W. Wilson 1936 (Supplement, 1941) (reprinted Bronx, N.Y.: Blom 1965)

MINNEAPOLIS PUBLIC LIBRARY | *An index to folk dances and singing games* | Chicago: American Library Association 1936 (Supplement, 1949)

Magriel includes dance music, ballet, décor, costume, masques, mime and pantomime, &c. It is classified, and books dealing with many aspects are entered under the appropriate headings. There are many brief annotations, and an author, subject, and analytical index.

Current literature is indexed in:

BELKNAP, S. YANCEY | compiler | *Guide to the performing arts, 1957 to date* | New York: Scarecrow Press 1960 to date

This is an annual publication which continues *Guide to dance periodicals* (1931–56). Its scope is international and it includes entries for illustrations The main section is followed by a television supplement, both of which are arranged in dictionary form.

English ballet, from its origins to the present day, is recorded in:

FORRESTER, F. S. | *Ballet in England: a bibliography and survey, c. 1700–June 1966* | The Library Association, 1968

which covers ballets, ballet companies, choreographers, dancers, technique and notation, design, music, costume, film and television.

## A NOTE ON SPORT

The bibliography of sport has yet to be undertaken on a comprehensive scale. Perhaps this is partly due to the fact that there is no library devoted to sport as a whole. There are several good small libraries on such subjects as cricket, mountaineering, football, and so on—similarly there are a number of bibliographies on single aspects of sport, including:

*Cricket: a catalogue of an exhibition of books, manuscripts and pictorial records, presented by the National Book League with the co-operation of the Marylebone Cricket Club* | Cambridge University Press 1950

HAMPTON, J. FITZGERALD | *Modern angling bibliography: books published on angling, fisheries, fish culture, from 1881 to 1945* | Herbert Jenkins 1947

*Library of mountaineering and exploration and travel* | Chicago: Edward C. Porter 1959

MAGRIEL PAUL | *Bibliography of boxing: a chronological check list of books in English published before 1900* | New York Public Library 1948

In 1958 the late R. Wylie Lloyd bequeathed to the National Library of Scotland his collection of Alpine material. The *Shelf-catalogue of the Lloyd Alpine Collection* (Boston, Mass.: G. K. Hall 1965) lists some 2,000 items of Alpine and other mountaineering literature in several languages, mostly issued in the 19th and early 20th centuries, but with some material published in the three preceding centuries.

# 9 | Language and Literature

One of the most useful guides to this subject is:

EPPELSHEIMER, HANNS WILHELM | *Handbuch der Weltliteratur, von den Anfängen bis zur Gegenwart* | 3rd edition| Frankfurt-am-Main: Klostermann 1960

which is truly international and includes, in its bibliographies of individual writers, translations as well as guides and references to criticism and evaluation.

There is also a similar guide to a narrower subject:

PALFREY, THOMAS ROSSMAN | compiler | *A bibliographical guide to the Romance languages and literatures* | 3rd edition | Evanstown, Ill.: Chandler 1947

which was compiled on behalf of the Department of Romance Languages, Northwestern University. The bibliography of individual authors is omitted. Entries are classified—General; French; Italian; Portuguese and Brazilian; Spanish, Catalan and Spanish-American; Romanian. The first two sections—General and French—are subdivided by period. All are subdivided in the following way: (*a*) bibliographies, (*b*) linguistics, (*c*) literature, (*d*) periodicals, (*e*) history. There are no indexes.

Another introductory guide to the early history of the subject is:

EDWARDES, MARION | *Summary of the literatures of modern Europe (England, France, Germany, Italy, Spain) from the origins to 1400* | Dent 1907

This is selective and is arranged by countries subdivided chronologically. The principal writers for each century are given, together with brief biographical details, works, notes about works and bibliographical references to editions, translations, and critical works and articles.

The following supporting material may also be found of use from time to time:

KELLER, HELEN REX | *The reader's digest of books* | Allen & Unwin, 1947 (covers the outstanding books of the world, giving a critical summary of each | Items are arranged alphabetically by title or catchword, with references from alternative titles | There is a detailed index)

## Language and Literature

KUNITZ, STANLEY JASSPON and HAYCRAFT, HOWARD | *Twentieth century authors: a biographical dictionary of modern literature* | New York: H. W. Wilson 1942 (Supplement 1955)

*Literary and library prizes* | 5th edition | New York: Bowker 1963 (Nobel, American, British Commonwealth, Continental and Latin-American | Details of contests and fellowships open are also included)

CLAPP, JANE | *International dictionary of literary awards* | New York: Scarecrow Press, 1963

*Sequels: incorporating Aldred and Parker's 'Sequel stories':* Edited by FRANK M. GARDNER | 5th edition | Association of Assistant Librarians, 1967 (Variant American titles are given where known | no indexes)

KERR, ELIZABETH | *Bibliography of the sequence novel* | Minneapolis, Minn.: University of Minnesota Press 1950 (includes 3,173 separate novels, and 999 sequences; especially useful for foreign novels)

For translations in general—those of particular literatures will be covered under the appropriate sections—there is:

FARRAR, CLARISSA PALMER and EVANS, AUSTIN PATTERSON | *Bibliography of English translations from medieval sources* | New York: Columbia University Press 1946

This aims to include English translations of important literary sources produced during the period from Constantine the Great to the year 1500 within an area roughly inclusive of Europe, northern Africa, and western Asia. Books and periodical articles up to 1942 are included. Entries are heavily annotated with descriptions, details of contents, notes of editions, &c. It is arranged alphabetically by author (but some subject-headings are included), collections being placed first, followed by single works arranged alphabetically by original title. There is an index of authors, titles, translators, and subjects.

Language has several useful bibliographies. For dictionaries there are three general guides:

COLLISON, ROBERT L. | *Dictionaries of foreign languages* | New York and London: Hafner Publishing Co. 1955

*Foreign language-English dictionaries* | Washington, D.C.: Library of Congress 1955 | 2 volumes

WALFORD, A. J. | *A guide to foreign language grammars and dictionaries* | Library Association 1964

ZAUNMÜLLER, WOLFRAM | *Bibliographisches Handbuch der Sprachwörterbücher* | New York and London: Hafner Publishing Co.; Stuttgart, Hiersemann 1958

## Language and Literature | 101

The first is a bibliography, in narrative form, of some 1,400 general and specialized dictionaries of about 250 languages and dialects, with historical, explanatory and evaluative notes. The Library of Congress bibliography devotes volume I to Special subject dictionaries, with emphasis on science and technology, while volume II covers General language dictionaries. Walford annotates items in the French, Italian, Spanish, German, Portuguese, Russian and Scandinavian languages, and includes commercial and technical dictionaries, and notes on language records. Zaunmüller lists about 5,600 dictionaries issued since the introduction of printing into Europe and covers some 500 languages and dialects, both general and specialized dictionaries being included, and preference being given to works published since 1850.

Current historical and critical studies are covered in the annual issues of the Modern Language Association of America's *Research in progress in the modern languages and literatures*, which appeared from 1948 to 1961; and in:

*Year's work in modern language studies:* edited for the Modern Humanities Research Association, 1929-30 to date | Oxford University Press 1931 to date

This is a classified bibliography of books and periodicals, with an author index. It is international in scope covering medieval Latin, Italian, French, Provençal, Hispanic, Romanian, Germanic and Celtic studies, Slavonic and international languages. For current literature there is also:

*Linguistic bibliography, 1939-1947 to date* | Cambridge: Heffer 1950 to date

of which the first issue, covering the war years, is in two volumes. This includes articles in periodicals, and is international in its field. The subject of language teaching is referred to under the section on EDUCATION.

## LITERATURE IN THE ENGLISH LANGUAGE

This rather cumbrous heading is used in order to include the literatures of the Commonwealth and the United States. The bibliography of Tom Peete Cross (from the Introduction of which the quotation at the beginning of this book is taken) has been revised since his death in 1951, and now appears as:

BOND, DONALD F. | *A reference guide to English studies* | Chicago: University of Chicago Press 1962

This is selective and covers general bibliographies and related subjects in addition to those specifically relating to literature. Entries are arranged in classified order under the following main headings: bibliographies covering literature exclusive of literature in America, history and biography, anonymous and pseudonymous literature, auxiliary subjects—Celtic, chronology, folk-lore, economic and political science, education, fine arts, music, philosophy and psychology, prohibited books, science, religion, palaeography, American literature, and a preliminary section on general bibliographies, periodicals, learned societies, dissertations, encyclopaedias, dictionaries, &c. There are many brief annotations and indexes of authors, titles, and subjects.

Other useful guides are:

ALTICK, RICHARD D. and WRIGHT, ANDREW | *Selective bibliography for the study of English and American literature* | 3rd edition | 1967

NORTHUP, CLARK SUTHERLAND | *A register of bibliographies of the English language and literature* | New Haven, Conn.: Yale University Press 1925 (reprinted 1962)

the latter 'attempts to supply a full though not a complete list of the bibliographies of the language and literature of the English-speaking peoples' to 1 October 1922. The main work consists of a well-annotated alphabetical list of authors and topics. There is also a short list of general bibliographies. The additions and corrections on pp. 419–49 should be noted. There is a detailed index. It was followed by:

VAN PATTEN, NATHAN | *An index to bibliographies and bibliographical contributions relating to the work of American and British authors, 1923–1932* | Stanford, Calif.: Stanford University Press 1934

which covers books and periodicals. Contributions relating to collected works precede those relating to individual items. Full names and dates of birth and death are given. There are an appendix of general works, and an index of compilers of bibliographies. Specifically relating to the English language are:

ALSTON, R. C. | *A bibliography of the English language from the invention of printing to the year 1800* | volumes | E. J. Arnold, for the author 1965 to date

KENNEDY, ARTHUR GARFIELD | *A bibliography of writings on the English language from the beginnings of printing to the end of 1922* | Cambridge, Mass.: Harvard University Press 1927

Kennedy deals rather with the scientific than with the artistic study of English. It omits works on literary style and the art of expression in general, and also omits Rhetoric and textbooks of composition after 1800 and all

## Literature in the English Language | 103

studies of versification. It is international in scope and includes bibliographies. Entries are arranged in classified order. There are indexes of (1) authors, reviewers, &c.; (2) subjects; (3) three indexes of special studies of individual words—Anglo-Saxon, Middle English, and Modern English. There is also a later and shorter bibliography:

KENNEDY, ARTHUR GARFIELD and SANDS, DONALD B. | *A concise bibliography for students of English* | 4th edition | Stanford, Calif.: Stanford University Press 1960

The great general bibliography of English literature is:

*The Cambridge bibliography of English literature:* edited by F. W. BATESON | 4 volumes | Cambridge University Press 1940 (Supplement, 1957)

This includes some Commonwealth but no American literature. It is arranged chronologically, subdivided by literary forms. Under each author the arrangement is: bibliographies, collected editions, separate works with date of first edition and subsequent editions within the first fifty years, with reference to important later editions, and a selection of biographical and critical works. The fourth volume consists of an index of subjects, titles, and authors. The *Supplement* lists additional material up to the end of 1954, and an additional volume will cover writers of the first half of the twentieth century. The *Concise Cambridge bibliography of English literature* (1958) anticipates this coverage by dealing with the whole period from the beginnings to 1950. Other useful guides are:

*Annals of English literature, 1475–1950: the principal publications of each year, together with an alphabetical index of authors with their works* | 2nd edition | Oxford: Clarendon Press 1961

BATESON, F. W. | *A guide to English literature* | Cambridge University Press | 1964

*English literature from the sixteenth century to the present: a select list of editions* | 2nd edition | Longmans, Green, for the British Council 1965

the purpose of the first is to give at a glance the main literary output of any year or series of years; to show what books people were likely to be reading at any time, and with what rivals a candidate for literary fame had to reckon. All the books of major and a selection of those of minor writers have been included. In the side-column are recorded the births and deaths of authors, the publication of newspapers, periodicals, translations, editions, and other compilations not to be classed as original literature, together with a selection of foreign events which have a bearing on the course of English literature. Special attention is paid to Commonwealth authors. Form—prose, verse, tragedy, comedy, drama—is indicated, and there is a full author index. It should also be remembered that the bibliographies at the end of the entries in the *Dictionary of national biography* are very useful sources for English authors, and that the similar works for various parts of the Commonwealth very often supply the only material on authors with purely local reputations. The last item is an excellent chronological list of anthologies and collections, general critical material, and biographies and criticisms of individual authors.

For older material there is a very important work:

WELLS, JOHN EDWIN | *A manual of the writings in Middle English, 1050–1400:* published under the auspices of the Connecticut Academy of Arts and Sciences | New Haven: Conn., Yale University Press 1926

to which a number of Supplements have since been added, 'At times, as with the Romances, the Legends, and the drama, a desire for greater completeness has led to the inclusion of pieces later than 1400.' There is a classified arrangement of romances, tales, chronicles, works, dealing with contemporary conditions, homilies and legends, works of religious information and instruction, proverbs and precepts, translations and paraphrases of the Bible, dialogues, debates, catechisms, science, information documents, Richard Rolle and William Wycliffe and their followers, lyrical and dramatic pieces, Gower and Chaucer. Entries are heavily annotated.

Two very useful sources for more modern works are:

KUNITZ, STANLEY JASSPON and HAYCRAFT, HOWARD | compilers | *British authors before 1800* | New York: H. W. Wilson 1952

KUNITZ, STANLEY JASSPON and HAYCRAFT, HOWARD | compilers | *British authors of the nineteenth century* | New York: H. W. Wilson 1936

which include Commonwealth authors. Biographies are given, and portraits and pseudonyms wherever possible. The more important works of each author are mentioned *passim*.

Another useful bibliography in the field is:

EASTWOOD, W. and GOOD, J. T. | *Signposts: a guide to modern English literature* | Cambridge University Press, for the National Book League 1960

which gives well over 700 references to various aspects of English literature in the twentieth century.

American literature has its own guides, chief of which are:

BLANCK, JACOB | compiler | *Bibliography of American literature* | New Haven: Yale University Press 1955–   |   volumes

## Literature in the English Language | 105

GOHDES, CLARENCE | *Bibliographical guide to the study of the literature of the U.S.A.* | Durham, N.C.: Duke University Press 1959

JONES, HOWARD MUMFORD and LUDWIG, RICHARD M. | *A guide to American literature and its backgrounds since 1890* | 3rd edition | Harvard University Press 1964

the first being arranged alphabetically by authors, and devoted to the first editions of some 300 writers who died before 1930. Gohdes's guide includes nearly 800 items and is annotated. There are also the bibliographies in the *Literary history of the United States* (New York: Macmillan, 1948, 3 volumes); and its *Bibliography supplementary* (1960), whose index covers references in the main work as well.

For current material there are serials:

*The year's work in English studies:* edited for the English Association, *1919–1920* to date | Oxford University Press 1921 to date

which excludes American literature. It is classified, mainly on a chronological basis, with entries—including evaluative annotations—given in narrative style. There are indexes of authors and titles, and subjects.

*Annual bibliography of English language and literature:* edited for the Modern Humanities Research Association, 1920 to date | Cambridge: Bowes 1921 to date

This is classified with literature divided chronologically. It includes both books (including reviews) and periodicals, and covers American literature. There is an author index.

*Abstracts of English studies, January 1958 to date* | Champagne, Ill.: National Council of Teachers in English 1958 to date

is a monthly publication covering both English and American language and literature, with monthly and annual subject indexes. References to older material are covered in R. S. Crane's *English literature, 1660–1800 : a bibliography of modern studies* (Princeton University Press, 1950–62, 4 volumes), which is continued once a year in the *Philological quarterly*, the original work being a reprint of the references given in the 1926–50 issues of that journal.

For pseudonymous literature there is one outstanding work:

HALKETT, SAMUEL and LAING, JOHN | *Dictionary of anonymous and pseudonymous English literature* | new and enlarged edition by James Kennedy and W. A. Smith and A. F. Johnson | 9 volumes | Edinburgh: Oliver & Boyd 1926–62

which is described in detail on page 161.

## ENGLISH POETRY

This subject is remarkably well documented. In the first place there is the famous:

GRANGER, EDITH | *Index to poetry and recitations* | 5th edition | Chicago: McClurg 1967

This index is supported by:

BRUNCKEN, H. | compiler | *Subject index to poetry* | Chicago: American Library Association 1940

which thoroughly indexes the contents of well over 200 anthologies. There are also three indexes of children's poetry:

BREWTON, JOHN EDMUND and BREWTON, SARA WESTBROOK | *Index to children's poetry: a title, subject, author and first-line index to poetry in collections for children and youth* | New York: H. W. Wilson 1942 (reprint, 1946) (Supplements, 1954 and 1965)

MACPHERSON, M. R. | compiler | *Children's poetry index* | Boston, Mass.: Faxon 1938

SELL, VIOLET and others | compilers | *Subject index to poetry for children and young people* | Chicago: American Library Association 1957

There is also a number of indexes of poetry of specific periods:

BROWN, CARLETON FAIRCHILD | *Register of Middle English religious and didactic verse* | 2 volumes | Bibliographical Society 1916–20

of which part I is devoted to a list of well over 1,000 manuscripts arranged by country, sub-arranged by libraries, and part II to indexes of first lines, and of titles and subjects. Chronicle histories, political pieces, romances, secular lyrics, charms, alchemical poems, and dramatic texts are omitted.

BROWN, CARLETON FAIRCHILD and ROBBINS, ROSSELL HOPE | *Index of Middle English verse* | 2 parts | New York: Index Society 1943

seems designed to supersede the earlier work. It is arranged by title, with references to manuscripts and to critical material in periodicals, &c., in many languages. A list of acephalous poems and a subject and title index are included in the second part. A supplement (University of Kentucky Press, 1966) extends the scope up to at least 1533, revises more than half of the original 4,500 entries, and adds another 1,500 published since 1943. For the next period there is:

> CASE, A. E. | *A bibliography of English poetical miscellanies, 1521–1750* | Bibliographical Society 1935
>
> ROLLINS, HYDER E. | compiler | *An analytical index to the ballad-entries (1557–1709) in the registers of the Company of Stationers of London* ... | Chapel Hill, N.C.: University of North Carolina Press 1924

It must also be remembered that Sears's *Song index* (described in the previous chapter) includes poems which have been set to music, especially foreign titles either in the original or in translation, many of which are not included in Granger.

## PLAYS

Readers are reminded of the supporting material on this subject described in the previous chapter under the heading THEATRE. There is a number of general indexes, of which one of the most notable is:

> *The player's library: the catalogue of the British Drama League* | 2nd edition | Faber 1950 (3 supplements, 1951–56 | new edition in preparation)

which includes about 70,000 volumes, excluding the famous Archer Collection. The main part of the work consists of an author catalogue (807 pages) which gives the general character of each play, changes of scene, and the number and kind of actors. There is a subject catalogue of books on the theatre, and title index of plays. Previous editions of this catalogue contain additional material, especially the first edition which includes brief summaries of plots. Another very useful index is:

> GREGOR, JOSEPH | *Schauspielführer* | 7 volumes | Stuttgart: Hiersemann 1953–64

which is an annotated world bibliography of plays, with special emphasis on German drama. Another, older work is still of great use:

> CLARENCE, REGINALD | *The 'Stage' cyclopaedia: a bibliography of plays* | *An alphabetical list of plays and other stage pieces of which any record can be found since the commencement of the English stage, together with descriptions, authors' names, dates and places of production, and other useful information, comprising in all nearly 50,000 plays and extending over a period of upwards of 500 years* | 'The Stage' 1909

Entries are arranged alphabetically by title, but include some subject entries (e.g. Greek plays, French plays, &c.), the index aiming to be complete for English drama and selective for foreign plays. Important revivals are included.

OTTEMILLER, JOHN H. | *Index to plays in collections: an author and title index to plays appearing in collections published between 1900 and 1962* | 4th edition | New York: Scarecrow Press 1964

is limited to full-length plays published in anthologies and general collections in Britain and the United States. Original as well as translated titles are given for foreign plays, and there is a title index.

For one-act plays there is a series of indexes:

LOGASA, HANNAH and VER NOOY, WINIFRED | compilers | *An index to one-act plays* | Boston, Mass.: Faxon 1924

to which four Supplements have been issued covering the period 1924-57. Both books and periodicals are indexed. Entries are arranged alphabetically by title, giving the number of actors, scene, and sometimes subject. Translations are included. There are indexes of authors and subjects.

Attention is also drawn to the many play catalogues issued by public libraries, such as the excellent and substantial lists published by the cities of Bristol and Sheffield and by the counties of Essex and Nottingham; and to Mathew O'Mahony's *Progress guide to Anglo-Irish plays* (Dublin, Progress House, 1960), which, like the invaluable:

*The guide to selecting plays, 1960-1961* | 2 parts | Samuel French 1960

includes summaries. Samuel French's guide devotes part I to full-length, and part II to one-act plays. Each part is arranged alphabetically by titles, with author, subject and number-of-characters indexes.

For the early period there is:

HARBAGE, ALFRED | *Annals of English drama, 975-1700: an analytical record of all plays, extant or lost, chronologically arranged and indexed by authors, titles, dramatic companies, &c.* Revised by S. Schoenbaum | Philadelphia: University of Pennsylvania Press; London, Methuen 1964

which contains entries for English, French, and Latin plays and masques devised in England, or by Englishmen abroad: these are chronologically arranged in tabular form, giving details of date, author(s), title, limits, type, auspices, and first and latest editions. There are indexes of foreign playwrights, of foreign plays translated or adapted for the English stage, of dramatic companies, and of titles. There are also very useful lists of theatres, of non-extant plays, and of extant play manuscripts of this period with their locations and catalogue numbers. There is another list of early plays:

## Plays

GREG, SIR WALTER WILSON | *A bibliography of the English printed drama to the Restoration* | 4 volumes | Bibliographical Society 1939–59

which consists of the Stationers' Company's records of plays. Entries are arranged according to the supposed date of the earliest surviving edition. Volume 3 comprises Collections, appendix and reference lists, while Volume 4 gives Introductions, additions, corrections, and an index of titles. For the latter part of the period there is:

WOODWARD, GERTRUDE LOOP and McMANAWAY, JAMES GILMER | compilers | *A check list of English plays, 1641–1700* | Chicago: Newberry Library 1945 (Supplement published 1950)

This records plays and masques, with variant editions and issues, printed in the English language in the British Isles or in other countries during this period, with locations in American libraries. It excludes reprints of classical Greek and Latin in the original, and political and critical dialogues never intended for stage presentation. Entries are arranged alphabetically by author. Note should be taken of the Supplement of additions and corrections (pp. 148–55).

The extensive bibliographies in Dr Leslie Hotson's *The Commonwealth and Restoration stage* (Oxford University Press, 1928), and Allardyce Nicoll's famous series *A history of English drama, 1660–1900* (6 volumes Cambridge University Press, 1952–9), as well as Carl J. Stratman's *Bibliography of English printed tragedy, 1565–1900* (Southern Illinois University Press, 1966), will be found of the greatest use in tracing rare and unusual material and plays. Dougald Macmillan's *Catalogue of the Larpent plays in the Huntingdon Library* (1939) covers the listing of plays submitted to the Lord Chamberlain for licensing 1737–1824, is continued by the British Museum's *Plays submitted to the Lord Chamberlain, 1824–51*. Further volumes are planned.

For later material there are:

FIRKINS, INA TEN EYCK | compiler | *Index of plays, 1900–1926* | New York: H. W. Wilson 1927

to which a Supplement, covering the years 1927–34, was published in 1935. It lists only plays in English, but includes translations of plays in foreign languages. The main part of the work consists of an author index: under each author the entries are arranged as follows: (*a*) separate publication of each play, (*b*) collected works, (*c*) composite collections, (*d*) periodicals. The second part consists of a title and subject index. There are two appendixes: A. An alphabetical list (arranged by authors) of those works which contain more than one play by the author; B. An alphabetical list (arranged by authors) of composite works. Overlapping with and continuing this period is:

> THOMSON, RUTH GIBBONS | *Index to full-length plays, 1926–1944* | Boston, Mass.: Faxon 1946

This is a title list, in alphabetical order, of English-language (including translations) plays only. Details given include the number of acts, characters, sets, and subject-matter—with period where useful. There are indexes of subjects and authors. A supplement, covering the period 1895–1925, was published in 1956.

As in poetry, there is an index of children's material:

> AMERICAN LIBRARY ASSOCIATION | *Subject index to children's plays* | Chicago 1940

which is graded for age-groups.

# FICTION

Gerald B. Cotton and Hilda McGill describe in narrative form *Fiction guides: British and American* (Bingley, 1967). Chief among the many comprehensive bibliographies of this subject is:

> BAKER, ERNEST ALBERT and PACKMAN, JAMES | *A guide to the best fiction, English and American, including translations from foreign languages* | New edition | Routledge 1932 (reprinted 1967)

This is arranged alphabetically by author. It is heavily annotated with critical notes, indications of place, plot and chief characters, and notes of alternative titles and editions. There is an index of authors, titles, subjects, historical names and allusions, places, characters, pseudonyms, and national groups of authors. Another important index which has been continued up to the present day is:

> *Fiction catalog:* 1961–65: a list of 1,524 works of fiction in the English language, with annotations | Edited by ESTELLE A. FIDELL and ESTHER V. FLORY | New York: H. W. Wilson 1966 (annual supplements)

It includes translations from foreign languages and collections of short stories. The annotations are detailed and helpful. The majority of books are entered under three or more subjects. Items particularly recommended are starred, and those highly recommended double-starred. Books suitable for young people aged fourteen to twenty are marked 'y'. Sequels are indicated. Entries are arranged in one alphabetical sequence of

Fiction | 111

authors, with an index of titles and subjects. Earlier editions should of course be retained. Another very good subject index which is arranged on a different plan is:

LENROW, ELBERT | *Reader's guide to prose fiction* | Appleton-Century 1940

in which the entries are classified according to the author's own scheme, and fully annotated. There are indexes of authors and titles.

A companion to Gregor's *Schauspielführer* provides one of the most detailed guides in existence:

OLBRICH, WILHELM | *Der Romanführer* | 12 volumes | Stuttgart; Hiersemann 1950-61

of which the first five volumes are devoted to German novels, and the remainder to fiction of other countries. Arrangement is alphabetical by authors under each country, with plot summaries and author and title indexes. Additional help can be gained from G. B. Cotton and Alan Glencross's *Cumulated fiction index, 1945-1960* (Association of Assistant Librarians, 1961) which is a subject index to some 25,000 novels and short stories, new and old published or republished in the post-war period; and from Frank M. Gardner's *Sequels* (5th edition, Association of Assistant Librarians, 1967); as well as from E. M. Kerr's *Bibliography of the sequence novel* (Minneapolis, University of Minnesota Press, 1950).

There are also indexes to various types of fiction, notably to historical tales:

BAKER, ERNEST ALBERT | *A guide to historical fiction* | Routledge 1914

This covers life of the past in the widest possible fashion, including sagas, romances, and novels of customs and manners (such as Jane Austen and George Eliot). Books suitable for children are indicated. Most parts of the world are covered, but more than half the work is devoted to Great Britain and the United States. Entries are arranged by country and sub-arranged by period, and are well annotated with notes of plots and main characters. There is an alphabetical index of authors, titles, historical names, places, events, allusions, &c. A similar work which includes later material is:

NIELD, JONATHAN | *A guide to the best historical novels and tales* | 5th edition | Elkin Mathews and Marrot 1929

which includes some translations of foreign works. The main work is arranged chronologically by centuries and is fully annotated with critical notes, indications of plots, main characters, places, &c. Books of special worth are marked with asterisks, and books suitable for children are also indicated. There are additional lists of books describing the pre-Christian era and of semi-historical fiction, as well as a bibliography of books and articles on the subject of historical fiction. Indexes of authors (including dates), titles, and subjects are included.

Short stories also have their own index:

COOK, DOROTHY E. and MONRO, I. S. | compilers | *Short story index* | New York: H. W. Wilson 1953

to which supplements, covering the periods 1950–4, 1955–8 and 1959–63, were added in 1956, 1960 and 1965 respectively. The basic volume is an alphabetical index of authors, subjects and titles of stories in well over 4,000 collections. Foreign items are included if they have been translated into English, and bibliographical details of the collections are included as an appendix. The supplements have a similar arrangement.

Two bibliographies are devoted to romances:

BRITISH MUSEUM | DEPARTMENT OF MANUSCRIPTS | *Catalogue of romances in the Department* ... 3 volumes | 1883–1910

This includes related material, and covers classical, allegorical, didactic, and miscellaneous manuscripts, legends and tales of northern and eastern origin, Aesopic fables, the Miracles of the Virgin, the Collections of Exempla, the Gesta Romanorum, miscellaneous anecdotes, &c. There are full bibliographical descriptions, and historical and critical notes.

ESDAILE, ARUNDELL | *A list of English tales and prose romances printed before 1740* | Bibliographical Society 1912

Part I of this work covers the period 1475–1642, and part II 1643–1739. Each part is arranged alphabetically by author, and full bibliographical descriptions are given, together with some annotations, including locations of copies, notes of editions, and references to other bibliographies. Translations and fables are listed, but early-printed medieval verse-romances and many jest-books have been omitted. It will be realized that Wells's *Manual of the writings in Middle English, 1050–1400*, described earlier, is also an essential work for research in this subject for the earlier period. Attention is also drawn to C. C. Misch's *English prose fiction, 1660–1700* (Charlottesville, University of Virginia Bibliographical Society, 1952. 3 volumes), and to S. Odell's *A chronological list of prose fiction in English printed in England and other countries, 1475–1640* (Massachusetts Institute of Technology 1954).

Later fiction is covered in part by:

BLOCK, ANDREW | *The English novel, 1740–1850: a catalogue including prose romances, short stories, and translations of foreign fiction* | revised edition | Dawson 1961

# Fiction | 113

McBURNEY, WILLIAM H. and TAYLOR, CHARLENE M. | *English prose fiction, 1700–1800, in the University of Illinois Library* | Urbana, Illinois University Press 1965

STEVENSON, LIONEL | *Victorian fiction: a guide to research* | Harvard University Press 1964

and by Lucien Leclaire's *A general analytical bibliography of the regional novelists of the British Isles, 1800–1950* (Paris, Belles-Lettres, 1954) and his *Le roman régionaliste dans les îles Britanniques, 1800–1950* (Clermont-Ferrand, G. de Bussac, 1954); as well as by Michael Sadleir's *XIX century fiction: a bibliographical record, based on the author's own collection* (Constable, 1951, 2 volumes).

There are two bibliographies devoted to American fiction:

GERSTENBERGER, DONNA LORINE and HENDRICK, GEORGE | *The American novel, 1789–1959; a check-list of twentieth-century criticism* | Denver, Col.: Swallow 1961

WRIGHT, L. H. | *American fiction, 1774–1850* | revised edition | San Marino, Calif.: Huntington Library 1948

of which, the first includes studies of individual works of American novelists and of their works in general, while a further section is devoted to general studies of the American novel as a genre. The second is arranged alphabetically by author, with chronological and title indexes.

There is one excellent index to fairy-tales:

EASTMAN, MARY HUSE | *Index to fairy tales, myths and legends* | 2nd edition | Boston, Mass.: Faxon 1926 (Supplements, 1937 and 1952)

This bibliography includes fables, Greek and Norse mythology, hero stories, and some modern stories such as the 'Leak in the dyke'. It is international in scope. Entries are arranged alphabetically under the last-known title with references from earlier and alternative titles. There are cross-references for subjects. Items suitable for small children are starred. There are also subject and geographical lists of books analysed.

Early children's books are dealt with in masterly fashion in:

DARTON, F. J. HARVEY | *Children's books in England* | 2nd edition | Cambridge University Press 1958

ST JOHN, JUDITH | *The Osborne Collection of early children's books, 1566–1910* | Toronto Public Library 1958

A catalogue of the Osborne Collection was published by the National Book League in 1966. Current books for children are covered in:

*Books for young people* | Library Association

LINES, KATHLEEN M. | *Four to fourteen: a library of books for children* | 2nd edition | Cambridge University Press, for the National Book League 1956

*Subject and title index to short stories for children* | Chicago: American Library Association 1955

THOMSON, JEAN | editor | *Books for boys and girls* | 3rd edition | Toronto: Ryerson Press, for Toronto Public Library 1954 (*Supplement 1953-1958*, 1960)

The Library Association pamphlets are published in three age groups and are frequently revised and supplemented.

## ESSAYS AND SPEECHES

For current material in this subject there is a comprehensive index:

*Essay and general literature index, 1900 to date* | New York: H. W. Wilson 1934 to date

This is issued every six months and cumulates into annual three-year and seven-year volumes. There is also a 'foundation volume' covering the years 1900–33 which indexes some 40,000 essays in over 2,000 volumes, with nearly 90,000 analytical entries. Entries in each volume are arranged alphabetically and include authors, subjects, and some titles for essays and articles. Variant titles are included. This index is useful also for tracing literary biography, and criticism both general and specific.

Speeches are covered by:

SUTTON, R. B. | compiler | *Speech index* | New York: H. W. Wilson 1935

to which a supplement for the period 1935–55 was issued in 1956. These two volumes index by author, type and subject, the speeches printed in some 134 collections of outstanding orations of all times.

## INDIVIDUAL AUTHORS

For most authors of any importance there is usually at least a check-list and often a comprehensive bibliography. For some modern authors so-called bibliographies of first editions have been issued which are poorly constructed and have little value for the research worker: their only use is for the first-edition collector. These are rapidly giving place to individual bibliographies of a high standard, many of which are listed below. Attention must also be drawn to the excellent *British Book News* Bibliographical series of supplements, 1950 to date (issued by Longmans, on behalf of the British Council) comprising about 100 pamphlets, each containing a reading list on an outstanding British author and a critical appreciation by a well-known author of today.

*Arnold, Matthew*

    SMART, THOMAS BURNETT | *The bibliography of Matthew Arnold* | Davy 1892

*Auden, W. H.*

    BLOOMFIELD, B. C. | *W. H. Auden: a bibliography* | University Press of Virginia 1964 (new edition in preparation)

*Austen, Jane*

    KEYNES, SIR GEOFFREY | *Jane Austen: a bibliography* | Nonesuch Press 1929

    CHAPMAN, R. W. | *Jane Austen: a critical bibliography* | 2nd edition | Oxford: Clarendon Press 1955

*Bacon, Francis*

    GIBSON, R. W. | *A Bacon bibliography* | Oxford: Scrivener Press 1950 (Supplement, 1960)

*Baring, Maurice*

    CHAUNDY, LESLIE | *A bibliography of the first editions of the works of Maurice Baring* | Dulau 1925

*Barrie, Sir James*

    CUTLER, BRADLEY DWYANE | *Sir James M. Barrie: a bibliography* | New York: Greenberg 1931

    GARLAND, HERBERT | *A bibliography of the writings of Sir James Matthew Barrie* | Bookman's Journal 1928

*Beaumont and Fletcher*

    TANNENBAUM, SAMUEL AARON | *Beaumont and Fletcher: a concise bibliography* | New York: Tannenbaum 1938

    POTTER, ALFRED CLAGHORN | *A bibliography of Beaumont and Fletcher* | Cambridge, Mass.: Harvard University Library 1890

*Beckford, William*

    CHAPMAN, GUY and HODGKIN, JOHN | *A bibliography of William Beckford of Fonthill* | Constable 1930

*Beerbohm, Sir Max*

    GALLATIN, ALBERT EUGENE and OLIVER, L. M. | *A bibliography of the works of Max Beerbohm* | Hart-Davis 1952

## 116 | Individual Authors

*Belloc, Hilaire*

CAHILL, P. | *The English first editions of Hilaire Belloc* | Cahill 1953

*Bentley, Richard*

BARTHOLOMEW, A. T. | *Richard Bentley: a bibliography* | Cambridge: Bowes & Bowes 1908

*Berkeley, George*

JESSOP, THOMAS EDMUND | *A bibliography of George Berkeley . . .* | Oxford University Press 1934

*Bierce, Ambrose*

STARRETT, VINCENT | *Ambrose Bierce: a bibliography* | Philadelphia: Centaur Book Shop 1929

*Blake, William*

BENTLEY, G. E. and NURMI, MARTIN K. | *A Blake bibliography: annotated lists of works, studies, and Blakeana* | University of Minnesota Press 1964

KEYNES, SIR GEOFFREY | *A bibliography of William Blake* | New York: Grolier Club 1921

*Borrow, George*

WISE, THOMAS JAMES | *A bibliography of the writings in prose and verse of George Henry Borrow* | 1914

*Boswell, James*

POTTLE, FREDERICK ALBERT | *The literary career of James Boswell, Esq.: being the bibliographical materials for a life of Boswell* | Oxford: Clarendon Press 1929

*Bridges, Robert*

McKAY, GEORGE L. | *A bibliography of Robert Bridges* | Oxford University Press 1933 (reprinted New York, AMS Press 1966)

*Brontës, The*

WISE, THOMAS JAMES | *A Brontë library* | 1929

WOOD, B. | *A bibliography of the Works of the Brontë family* | Bradford: Brontë Society 1895

*Browne, Sir Thomas*

KEYNES, SIR GEOFFREY | *A bibliography of Sir Thomas Browne* | Cambridge University Press 1924

*Browning, Robert*

BROUGHTON, L. N. and others | *Robert Browning: a bibliography, 1830-1950* | Ithaca, N.Y.: Cornell University Press 1953

WISE, THOMAS JAMES | *A complete bibliography of the writings in prose and verse of Robert Browning* | 1897

*Bunyan, John*

HARRISON, FRANK MOTT | *A bibliography of the works of John Bunyan* | Bibliographical Society 1932

*Burke, Edmund*

TODD, WILLIAM B. | *A bibliography of Edmund Burke* | Hart-Davies 1965

*Burns, Robert*

*Catalogue of the Robert Burns Collection in the Mitchell Library, Glasgow* | Glasgow Public Libraries 1959

EGERER, J. W. | *A bibliography of Robert Burns* | Edinburgh: Oliver and Boyd 1964

GIBSON, JAMES | *The bibliography of Robert Burns* | Kilmarnock: M'Kie 1881

*The Murison Burns Collection* | Dunfermline Public Libraries 1953

*Burton, Sir Richard*

PENZER, NORMAN M. | *An annotated bibliography of Sir Richard Francis Burton* | Philpot 1923

*Butler, Samuel*

HARKNESS, STANLEY BATES | *The career of Samuel Butler, 1835-1902: a bibliography* | Bodley Head 1955

HOPPÉ, A. J. | *A bibliography of the writings of Samuel Butler* | Bookman's Journal 1925

*Byron, Lord*

WISE, THOMAS JAMES | *A bibliography of the writings in verse and prose of George Gordon Noel, Baron Byron* | 2 volumes | 1932-3 (reprinted 1964)

NOTTINGHAM CORPORATION | *The Roe-Byron Collection, Newstead Abbey* | Nottingham 1937

FIRST EDITION CLUB | *Bibliographical catalogue of first editions, proof copies and manuscripts of books by Lord Byron exhibited at the Fourth Exhibition* | 1925

## Individual Authors

*Cabell, James Branch*

BRUSSEL, ISIDORE ROSENBAUM | *A bibliography of the writings of James Branch Cabell: a revised bibliography* | Philadelphia: Centaur Book Shop 1932

*Carlyle, Thomas*

DYER, ISAAC WATSON | *A bibliography of Thomas Carlyle's writings and ana* | Portland, Maine: Southworth Press 1928

SHEPHERD, RICHARD HERNE | *The bibliography of Carlyle* | Elliot Stock 1881

*Carpenter, Edward*

SHEFFIELD PUBLIC LIBRARIES | *A bibliography of Edward Carpenter* | Sheffield 1949

*Carroll, Lewis*

WILLIAMS, SIDNEY HERBERT and MADAN, FALCONER | *The Lewis Carroll handbook. Revised by R. L. Green* | Oxford University Press 1962

*Chaucer, Geoffrey*

HAMMOND, ELEANOR PRESCOTT | *Chaucer: a bibliographical manual* | New York: Macmillan, 1908 | (Reprint, New York: Peter Smith 1933)

*Churchill, Winston*

WOODS, FREDERICK | *A bibliography of the works of Sir Winston Churchill* | Vane 1963

*Cleveland, John*

MORRIS, BRIAN | *John Cleveland (1613-1658): a bibliography of his poems* | Bibliographical Society 1967

*Coleridge, Samuel Taylor*

WISE, THOMAS JAMES | *A bibliography of the writings in prose and verse of Samuel Taylor Coleridge* | Bibliographical Society 1913 | (Supplement, 1919)

*Conrad, Joseph*

LOHF, K. A. and SHEENY, E. P. | *Joseph Conrad at mid-century: editions and studies, 1895-1955* | Minneapolis: University of Minnesota Press 1957

WISE, THOMAS JAMES | *A Conrad library* | 1928 (reprinted 1964)

*Coppard, A. E.*

SCHWARTZ, JACOB | *The writings of Alfred Edgar Coppard: a bibliography* | Ulysses Bookshop 1931

*Cowper, William*

RUSSELL, NORMAN H. | *A bibliography of Cowper to 1837* | Oxford University Press 1963

*Crane, Stephen*

WILLIAMS, AMES W. and STARRETT, VINCENT | *Stephen Crane: a bibliography* | Glendale, Calif.: Valentine 1948

*Crane, Walter*

MASSÉ, GERTRUDE C. E. | *A bibliography of first editions of books illustrated by Walter Crane* | Chelsea Publishing Co. 1923

*Cummings, E. E.*

FIRMAGE, GEORGE J. | *E. E. Cummings: a bibliography* | Middletown, Conn.: Wesleyan University Press 1960

*Darwin, Charles*

FREEMAN, R. B. | *Charles Darwin: an annotated bibliographical handlist* | Dawsons 1965

*Defoe, Daniel*

*Catalogue of the Defoe Collection in the Boston Public Library* | Boston, Mass.: G. K. Hall 1966

MOORE, JOHN ROBERT | *A checklist of the writings of Daniel Defoe* | Indiana University Press 1960

*Dickens, Charles*

HATTON, THOMAS and CLEAVER, ARTHUR H. | *A bibliography of the periodical works of Charles Dickens* | Chapman & Hall 1933

ECKEL, JOHN C. | *The first editions of the writings of Charles Dickens, their points and values: a bibliography* | Revised edition | Maggs 1932

MILLER, WILLIAM | *The Dickens student and collector: a list of writings relating to Charles Dickens and his works, 1836-1945* | Chapman & Hall 1946

*Dobson, Austin*

DOBSON, ALBAN | *A bibliography of the first editions of published and privately printed books and pamphlets by Austin Dobson* | First Editions Club 1925

*Donne, John*

KEYNES, SIR GEOFFREY | *A bibliography of Dr. John Donne* | 3rd edition | Cambridge University Press 1958

*Douglas, Norman*

WOOLF, CECIL | *A bibliography of Norman Douglas* | Hart-Davis 1954 | (Supplement issued Christmas 1954)

*Doyle, Sir Arthur Conan*

LOCKE, HAROLD | *A bibliographical catalogue of the writings of Sir Arthur Conan Doyle, 1879-1928* | Tunbridge Wells: D. Webster 1929

*Dryden, John*

MACDONALD, HUGH | *John Dryden: a bibliography of early editions, and of Drydeniana* | Oxford: Clarendon Press 1939

*Edgeworth, Maria*

SLADE, BERTHA COOLIDGE | *Maria Edgeworth, 1767-1840: a bibliographical tribute* | Constable 1937

*Eliot, T. S.*

GALLUP, DONALD CLIFFORD | *T. S. Eliot: a bibliography* | Faber 1952

*Emerson, Ralph Waldo*

COOKE, GEORGE WILLIS | *Bibliography of Ralph Waldo Emerson* | Boston, Mass.: Houghton 1908

*Firbank, Ronald*

BENKOVITZ, MIRIAM J. | *A bibliography of Ronald Firbank* | Hart-Davis 1964

*FitzGerald, Edward*

PRIDEAUX, W. F. | *Notes for a bibliography of Edward FitzGerald* | Frank Hollings 1901

*Forster, E. M.*

KIRKPATRICK, B. J. | *E. M. Forster* | Hart-Davis 1965

*Frazer, Sir James*

BESTERMAN, THEODORE | *A bibliography of Sir James George Frazer, O.M.* | Macmillan 1934

*Frost, Robert*

CLYMER, WILLIAM BRANFORD SHUBRICK and GREEN, CHARLES ROBERT | *Robert Frost: a bibliography* | Amherst, Mass.: Jones Library 1937

*Galsworthy, John*

MARROT, H. V. | *A bibliography of the works of John Galsworthy* | Elkin Mathews & Marrot 1928

*Gibbon, Edward*

NORTON, J. E. | *A bibliography of the works of Edward Gibbon* | Oxford University Press 1940

*Gilbert, W. S.*

ALLEN, REGINALD | *W. S. Gilbert: an anniversary survey and exhibition checklist* | University Press of Virginia 1964

*Goldsmith, Oliver*

SCOTT, TEMPLE | *Oliver Goldsmith bibliographically and biographically considered ...* | New York: Bowling Green Press 1928

*Graves, Robert*

HIGGINSON, FRED H. | *A bibliography of the works of Robert Graves* | New York: Archon 1966

*Gray, Thomas*

NORTHUP, CLARK SUTHERLAND | *A bibliography of Thomas Gray* | New Haven: Yale University Press 1917

STARR, H. W. | *A bibliography of Thomas Gray* | Philadelphia: University of Pennsylvania Press for Temple University Publications 1953

*Haggard, Rider*

SCOTT, J. E. | *A bibliography of the works of Sir Henry Rider Haggard, 1856–1925* | Takeley: Elkin Mathews 1947

*Hardy, Thomas*

PURDY, R. L. | *Thomas Hardy: a bibliographical study* | Oxford University Press 1954

## Individual Authors

*Hawthorne, Nathaniel*

BROWNE, NINA ELIZA | *A bibliography of Nathaniel Hawthorne* | Boston, Mass.: Houghton 1905

*Hazlitt, William*

KEYNES, SIR GEOFFREY | *Bibliography of William Hazlitt* | Nonesuch Press 1931

*Housman, A. E.*

CARTER, JOHN and SPARROW, J. | *A. E. Housman: an annotated hand-list* | Hart-Davis 1952

*Hudson, W. H.*

WILSON, G. F. | *A bibliography of the writings of W. H. Hudson* | Bookman's Journal 1922

*Huxley, Aldous*

DUVAL, HANSON RAWLINGS | *Aldous Huxley: a bibliography* | New York: Arrow 1938

ESCHELBACH, CLAIRE JOHN and SHOBER, JOYCE LEE | *Aldous Huxley: a bibliography, 1916–1959* | Berkeley, University of California Press 1961

*Irving, Washington*

WILLIAMS, STANLEY THOMAS and EDGE, MARY ALLEN | *Bibliography of the writings of Washington Irving: a check list* | New York: Oxford University Press 1936

*James, Henry*

EDEL, LEON and LAURENCE, DAN H. | *A bibliography of Henry James* | 2nd edition | Hart-Davis 1964

PHILLIPS, LEROY | *A bibliography of the writings of Henry James* | New York: Coward, McCann 1930

*Johnson, Samuel*

ADAM, ROBERT B. | *The R. B. Adam Library relating to Dr. Samuel Johnson and his era* | 3 volumes | Oxford University Press 1929

CLIFFORD, J. L. | *Johnsonian studies, 1887–1950: a survey and bibliography* | Minneapolis: University of Minnesota Press 1951

COURTNEY, WILLIAM PRIDEAUX and SMITH, DAVID NICHOL | *A bibliography of Samuel Johnson: a reissue of the edition of 1915, illustrated with facsimiles* | Oxford: Clarendon Press 1925 | (Supplement by R. W. Chapman, 1939)

## Jonson, Ben

TANNENBAUM, SAMUEL AARON | *Ben Jonson: a concise bibliography* | New York: Scholars' Facsimiles and Reprints 1938 | (Supplement, New York: Tannenbaum 1947)

## Joyce, James

DEMING, ROBERT H. | *A bibliography of James Joyce studies* | University of Kansas Libraries 1963

O'HEGARTY, P. S. | *A bibliography of James Joyce* | Dublin: Thom 1946

PARKER, ALLAN | *James Joyce: a bibliography of his writings, critical material and miscellanea* | Boston, Mass.: Faxon 1948

SLOCUM, J. J. and CAHOON, H. | *A bibliography of James Joyce, 1882–1941* | Hart-Davis 1953

## Keats, John

MACGILLIVRAY, J. R. | *Keats: a bibliography and reference guide* ... | Toronto: University of Toronto Press 1949

## Kipling, Rudyard

LIVINGSTON, FLORA V. | *Bibliography of the works of Rudyard Kipling* | New York: Edgar H. Wells, 1927 | (Supplement, Cambridge, Mass.: Harvard University Press 1938)

MARTINDELL, E. W. | *A bibliography of the works of Rudyard Kipling (1881–1923)* | New edition | Lane 1923

## Lamb, Charles and Mary

THOMSON, J. C. | *Bibliography of the writings of Charles and Mary Lamb: a literary history* | Hull: J. R. Tutin 1908

## Landor, Walter Savage

WISE, THOMAS JAMES and WHEELER, STEPHEN | *A bibliography of the writings in prose and verse of Walter Savage Landor* | Bibliographical Society 1919

## Lawrence, D. H.

McDONALD, EDWARD D. | *A bibliography of the writings of D. H. Lawrence* | Philadelphia: Centaur Book Shop 1925 | (Supplement, 1931)

ROBERTS, F. W. | *D. H. Lawrence* | Hart-Davis 1963

## Lawrence, T. E.

DUVAL, ELIZABETH W. | *T. E. Lawrence: a bibliography* | New York: Arrow 1938

## Individual Authors

*London, Jack*

WOODBRIDGE, HENSLEY C. | *Jack London: a bibliography* | Georgetown, Calif.: The Talisman Press 1966

*Longfellow, Henry Wadsworth*

LIVINGSTON, LUTHER S. | *A bibliography of the first editions in book form of the writings of Henry Wadsworth Longfellow* ... | New York 1908

*Lowell, James Russell*

LIVINGSTON, LUTHER S. | *A bibliography of the first editions in book form of the writings of James Russell Lowell* ... | New York 1914

*Machen, Arthur*

GOLDSTONE, ADRIAN and SWEETSER, WESLEY | *A bibliography of Arthur Machen* | University of Texas Press 1965

*Mansfield, Katherine*

MANTZ, RUTH ELVISH | *The critical bibliography of Katherine Mansfield* | Constable 1931

*Marlowe, Christopher*

TANNENBAUM, SAMUEL AARON | *Christopher Marlowe: a concise bibliography* | New York: Scholars' Facsimiles and Reprints 1937 | (Supplement | New York: Tannenbaum 1947)

*Masefield, John*

HANDLEY-TAYLOR, GEOFFREY | *John Masefield, o.m., The Queen's Poet Laureate: a bibliography* | Cranbrook Tower Press 1966

SIMMONS, CHARLES H. | *A bibliography of John Masefield* | Oxford University Press 1930

*Maugham, Somerset*

STOTT, RAYMOND TOOLE | *Maughamiana: the writings of W. Somerset Maugham* | Heinemann 1950

STOTT, RAYMOND TOOLE | *The writings of William Somerset Maugham: a bibliography* | 2nd issue | Rota 1963

BASON, FREDERICK T. | *A bibliography of the writings of William Somerset Maugham* | Unicorn Press 1931

*Meredith, George*

FORMAN, MAURICE BUXTON | *A bibliography of the writings in prose and verse of Meredith* | Bibliographical Society 1922 | (Supplement 1924)

*Mill, John Stuart*

MACMINN, NEY and others | *Bibliography of the published writings of John Stuart Mill...* | Evanston, Ill.: Northwestern University 1945

*Miller, Henry*

*Henry Miller bibliography*. Minneapolis, Henry Miller Literary Society, 1961 (Supplement 1964)

*Milton, John*

THOMPSON, ELBERT N. S. | *John Milton: topical bibliography* | New Haven: Yale University Press 1916

STEVENS, DAVID HARRISON | *Reference guide to Milton from 1800 to the present day* | Chicago: University of Chicago Press 1930

HUCKABAY, CALVIN | *John Milton: a bibliographical supplement, 1929-1957* | Pittsburg, Duquesne University Press 1960

*Morris, William*

FORMAN, HARRY BUXTON | *The books of William Morris described, with some account of his doings in literature and in the allied crafts* | Frank Hollings 1897

SCOTT, TEMPLE | *A bibliography of the works of William Morris* | Bell 1897

*Newton, Sir Isaac*

GRAY, G. J. | *A bibliography of the works of Sir Isaac Newton, together with a list of books illustrating his works* | 2nd edition | Cambridge: Bowes & Bowes 1907

*O'Neill, Eugene*

SANBORN, RALPH and CLARK, BARRETT H. | *A bibliography of the works of Eugene O'Neill* | Bronx, N.Y.: Blom 1965

*Phillpotts, Eden*

HINTON, PERCIVAL | *Eden Philpotts: a bibliography of first editions* | Birmingham: Greville Worthington 1931

*Poe, Edgar Allan*

HEARTMAN, CHARLES FREDERICK and CANNY, JAMES R. | *A bibliography of first printings of the writings of Edgar Allan Poe...* | Hattiesburg, Mo.: The Book Farm 1940

*Pope, Alexander*

WISE, THOMAS JAMES | *A Pope library: a catalogue of plays, poems and prose writings...* | 1931

## Individual Authors

GRIFFITH, REGINALD HARVEY | *Alexander Pope: a bibliography* | Volume 1—Pope's own writings | Austin, Texas: University of Texas 1922-7

*Pound, Ezra*

GALLUP, DONALD | *A bibliography of Ezra Pound* | Hart-Davis 1964

*Powys, John Cowper*

LANGRIDGE, DEREK | *John Cowper Powys: a record of achievement* | Library Association 1966

SIBERELL, LLOYD EMERSON | *A bibliography of the first editions of John Cowper Powys* | Cincinatti: Ailanthus Press 1934

*Powys, T. F.*

RILEY, PETER | *T. F. Powys: a bibliography* | Hastings: R. A. Brimmell 1966

*Richardson, Samuel*

SALE, WILLIAM MERRITT | *Samuel Richardson: a bibliographical record of his literary career, with historical notes* | New Haven: Yale University Press 1936

*Robinson, Edwin Arlington*

LIPPINCOTT, LILLIAN | *Bibliography of the writings and criticisms of Edwin Arlington Robinson* | Boston, Mass.: Faxon 1937

*Ruskin, John*

WISE, THOMAS JAMES and SMART, JAMES P. | *A complete bibliography of the writings in prose and verse of John Ruskin...* | 2 volumes | 1889-93

*Sassoon, Siegfried*

KEYNES, SIR GEOFFREY | *A bibliography of Siegfried Sassoon* | Hart-Davis 1962

*Scott, Sir Walter*

CORSON, JAMES CLARKSON | *A bibliography of Sir Walter Scott: a classified and annotated list of books and articles relating to his life and works, 1797-1940* | Edinburgh: Oliver & Boyd 1943

RUFF, WILLIAM | *A bibliography of the poetical works of Sir Walter Scott, 1796-1832* | (Edinburgh Bibliographical Society | *Transactions* 1937: pp. 99-239, 279-81)

WORTHINGTON, GREVILLE | *A bibliography of the Waverley novels* | Constable 1931

## Shakespeare, William

EBISCH, WALTHER and SCHÜCKING, LEVIN L. | *A Shakespeare bibliography* | Oxford: Clarendon Press 1931 | (Supplement 1937)

JAGGARD, WILLIAM | *Shakespeare bibliography* ... | Stratford-upon-Avon: Shakespeare Press 1911 (Reprint 1913)

*Shakespeare survey*, volume 1- | Cambridge University Press, 1948 to date

SMITH, GORDON ROSS | *A classified Shakespeare bibliography, 1936–1958* | Pennsylvania State University Press 1963 (continuing Ebisch)

## Shaw, Bernard

WELLS, GEOFFREY H. | *A bibliography of the books and pamphlets of George Bernard Shaw* | Bookman's Journal 1928

BROAD, C. LEWIS and BROAD, VIOLET M. | *Dictionary to the plays and novels of Bernard Shaw, with bibliography of his works and of the literature concerning him, with a record of the principal Shavian play productions* | Black 1929

## Shelley, Percy Bysshe

WISE, THOMAS JAMES | *A Shelley library: a catalogue of printed books, manuscripts and autograph letters of Percy Bysshe Shelley, Harriet Shelley and Mary Wollstonecraft Shelley* | 1924

FORMAN, HARRY BUXTON | *The Shelley library: an essay in bibliography* | Reeves & Turner 1886

## Sitwell family

FIFOOT, E. R. S. | *Edith, Osbert and Sacheverell Sitwell* | Hart-Davis 1963

## Spenser, Edmund

JOHNSON, FRANCIS R. | *A critical bibliography of the works of Edmund Spenser printed before 1700* | Baltimore: Johns Hopkins Press 1933

ATKINSON, DOROTHY F. | *Edmund Spenser: a bibliographical supplement* | Baltimore: Johns Hopkins Press 1937

CARPENTER, FREDERICK IVES | *A reference guide to Edmund Spenser* | Chicago: University of Chicago Press 1923 (Reprinted 1950)

## Sterne, Laurence

HARTLEY, LODWICK | *Laurence Sterne in the twentieth century: an essay and a bibliography of Sternean studies* | University of North Carolina Press 1966

## Individual Authors

*Stevenson, Robert Louis*

McKAY, G. L. | *A Stevenson library* | 2 volumes | New Haven: Yale University Press 1951-2

PRIDEAUX, W. F. | *A bibliography of the works of Robert Louis Stevenson* | New edition | Frank Hollings 1917

*Summers, Montague*

SMITH, TIMOTHY D'ARCH | *A bibliography of the works of Montague Summers* | Kaye 1966

*Swift, Jonathan*

STATHIS, JAMES L. | *A bibliography of Swift studies. 1945-65* | Vanderbilt University Press 1967

TEERINK, H. | *A bibliography of the writings of Jonathan Swift* | 2nd edition | Pennsylvania University Press 1967

*Swinburne, Algernon*

WISE, THOMAS JAMES | *Bibliography of the writings in prose and verse of Algernon Charles Swinburne* | 2 volumes | 1919-20

*Symonds, John Addington*

BABINGTON, PERCY L. | *Bibliography of the writings of John Addington Symonds* | John Castle 1925

*Tennyson, Lord*

THOMSON, J. C. | *Bibliography of the writings of Alfred, Lord Tennyson* | 1905

WISE, THOMAS JAMES | *A bibliography of the writings of Alfred, Lord Tennyson* | 2 volumes | 1908

*Thackeray, William Makepeace*

VAN DUZER, HENRY SAYRE | *A Thackeray library ...* | New York 1919

*Thomas, Dylan*

ROLPH, J. A. | *Dylan Thomas: a bibliography* | Dent 1956

*Thoreau, Henry*

ALLEN, FRANCIS HENRY | *A bibliography of Henry David Thoreau* | Boston, Mass.: Houghton Mifflin 1908

*Trollope, Anthony*

SADLEIR, MICHAEL | *Trollope: a bibliography* | Constable 1928 (*Addenda and corrigenda, 1934*) (reprinted 1964)

*Twain, Mark*

JOHNSON, MERLE | *A bibliography of the works of Mark Twain* . . . | New York: Harper 1935

*Vaughan, Henry*

MARILLA, E. L. | *A comprehensive bibliography of Henry Vaughan* | University, Ala.: University of Alabama Press 1948

*Walpole, Horace*

HAZEN, A. T. | *A bibliography of Horace Walpole* | New Haven: Yale University Press 1948

*Walton, Izaak*

OLIVER, PETER | *A new chronicle of the* Compleat Angler, *1653-1936* | New York: Paisley Press 1936

*Wells, H. G.*

*H. G. Wells: a comprehensive bibliography* | The H. G. Wells Society 1966

WELLS, GEOFFREY H. | *The works of H. G. Wells, 1887-1925: a bibliography, dictionary and subject-index* | Routledge 1926

*White, Gilbert*

MARTIN, EDWARD A. | *A bibliography of Gilbert White, the naturalist and antiquarian of Selborne* | Revised edition | Halton 1934

*Whitman, Walt*

*Walt Whitman: a catalog* | Washington: Library of Congress, Reference Department 1955

WELLS, CAROLYN and GOLDSMITH, ALFRED H. | *A concise bibliography of the works of Walt Whitman* . . . | Boston: Houghton Mifflin 1922

*Whittier, John Greenleaf*

CURRIER, THOMAS FRANKLIN | *A bibliography of John Greenleaf Whittier* | Cambridge, Mass.: Harvard University Press 1937

*Wilde, Oscar*

FINZI, JOHN CHARLES | *Oscar Wilde and his literary circle: a catalog of manuscripts and letters* | Berkeley: University of California Press for the William Andrews Clark Memorial Library 1957

MASON, STUART | *Bibliography of Oscar Wilde* | Reprint, with addenda and a new introduction by Timothy d'Arch Smith | Rota 1967 ('Stuart Mason' was the pseudonym of Christopher Millar. His bibliography was originally published in 1914)

## Individual Authors

*Williamson, Henry*

GIRVAN, I. WAVENEY | *A bibliography and a critical survey of the works of Henry Williamson* | Alcuin Press 1932

*Wordsworth, William*

HEALEY, GEORGE HARRIS | *The Cornell Wordsworth Collection* | Ithaca, N.Y.: Cornell University Press 1957

WISE, THOMAS JAMES | *A bibliography of the writings in prose and verse of William Wordsworth* | 1916

*Yeats, W. B.*

SYMONS, A. J. A. | *A bibliography of the first editions of books by William Butler Yeats* | First Editions Club 1924

WADE, A. | *A bibliography of the writings of W. B. Yeats* | Hart-Davis 1951

Further material on these and other authors can be found in the works listed in the section on Bibliographies of Bibliographies in the second part of this book. The bibliographies issued by Thomas James Wise were privately printed and very few copies—sometimes no more than twenty—were published; nevertheless, many of them are to be found in the larger reference libraries.

## GERMAN LITERATURE

The great bibliography on this subject is one which has only just reached the beginning of the nineteenth century in some sixty years of research:

GOEDEKE, KARL | *Grundriss zur Geschichte der deutschen Dichtung aus den Quellen* | 14 volumes | 2nd edition | Dresden: Ehlermann 1884 to date (Supplement, 1955 to date)

which gives some biographical and critical comment on the authors, critical and other notes on individual works, sources, &c., and exhaustive bibliographies of editions, treatises, histories, biographical and critical articles, &c. There is a detailed index in each volume. The main work covers the period up to 1830, while the supplement, *Neue Folge*, lists items issued during the next fifty years. Additional material for this bibliography is announced in the first volume of the new series *Bibliotheca Bibliographica* under the general editorship of Dr Moriz Grolig:

*Nicht bei Goedeke: viertausend in Goedekes 'Grundriss der deutschen Dichtung' fehlende Schriftsteller und Werke* | Vienna: Walter Krieg 195-

German Literature | 131

Another useful and comprehensive work is:

KÖRNER, JOSEF | *Bibliographisches Handbuch des deutschen Schrifttums* | 3rd edition | Bern: Francke 1949

This is divided into four parts: I. General, covering bibliographies of bibliography, literary history, serials, &c.; II. Writings before Goethe; III. Writings of Goethe's times; IV. Writings since Goethe up to the present time. It is international in scope, and includes criticism in books and periodicals. There are indexes of names and subjects.

For more recent material there is:

ARNOLD, ROBERT FRANZ | *Allgemeine Bücherkunde zur neueren deutschen Literaturgeschichte* | 3rd edition | Berlin: de Gruyter 1931

KUNISCH, HERMANN and HENNECKE, HANS | *Handbuch der deutschen Gegenswartliteratur* | Munich: Nymphenburger Verlagshandlung 1965

In Arnold entries are classified and include some for histories and criticism. There are also entries for general encyclopaedias, biographical dictionaries, special encyclopaedias, with notes assessing their use for students of German literature. Kunisch and Hennecke is a comprehensive work providing bibliographies of authors who have done their most significant work since 1910. Short historical essays are included. In this connexion it should be remembered that the Meyer and Brockhaus encyclopaedias may often supply in their bibliographical notes at the end of articles material which cannot easily be traced elsewhere. A special index from America is of great assistance to students of modern German plays:

JOHNS HOPKINS UNIVERSITY | LIBRARY | *Fifty years of German drama: a bibliography of modern German drama, 1880–1930, based on the Loewenberg collection* | Baltimore 1941

while the first two volumes of Gregor's *Schauspielführer* (see p. 107) cover the whole period of German drama. Similarly, the first five volumes of Olbrich's *Romanführer* (see p. 111) partly supply the need for a bibliography of German fiction.

Current material is covered by three serials:

*Bibliographie der deutschen Literaturwissenschaft, volume 1, 1945 to date* | Frankfurt-am-Main: Klostermann 1957 to date

*Jahresbericht für deutsche Sprache und Literatur, volume 1, 1960 to date* | Berlin: Akademie-Verlag 1960 to date

*Jahresbericht über die wissenschaftlichen Erscheinungen auf dem Gebiete der neueren deutschen Literatur ... 1921 to date* | Berlin: de Gruyter 1924 to date

132 | French Literature

of which the last is published under the auspices of the Literaturarchivgesellschaft in Berlin, and was itself preceded by:

*Jahresberichte für neuere deutsche Literaturgeschichte, 1890–1915* | (Berlin: Behr 1892–1919)

For translations into English there is:

MORGAN, BAYARD QUINCY | *A critical bibliography of German literature in English translation, 1481–1927, with supplement . . . 1928–35* | 2nd edition | Stanford, Calif.: Stanford University Press 1938

which is arranged alphabetically by author. Entries are evaluated by the use of symbols and occasional comments. Anonymous writings are listed separately, and there is an appendix of collections, and an index of translators. A Supplement, covering the period 1928–55 was published by the Scarecrow Press in 1965.

## FRENCH LITERATURE

The outstanding bibliography of French literature is:

LANSON, GUSTAVE | *Manuel bibliographique de la littérature française moderne, 1500–1900* | New edition | Paris: Hachette 1921

This is selective but has over 23,000 entries, including many analyticals for periodical material. There is an appendix of literature of the Great War, 1914–18. A great new bibliography bids fair to replace Lanson:

CABEEN, D. C. | editor | *A critical bibliography of French literature* | 7 volumes | Syracuse, N.Y.: Syracuse University Press 1947 to date

Coverage is very wide, and material is evaluated. Each volume is devoted to a period, and contributions from experts are included. There is also a special bibliography of mediaeval literature, R. Bossuat's *Manuel bibliographique de la littérature française du moyen âge* (Melun, Argences, 1951), to which a Supplement was published in 1955. Alexandre Cioranescu's *Bibliographie de la littérature francaise de dix-septième siècle* (Paris, 1966 to date) attempts to list all publications concerning French literature 1601 to 1715, and critical reviews up to 1960. Part I gives a classified list of 6,500 items relating to general studies. Part II is a bibliography of about 6,000 authors, listing original and subsequent editions, and critical reviews.

For modern literature there is an important bibliography:

TALVART, HECTOR and PLACE, JOSEPH | *Bibliographie des auteurs modernes de langue française (1801–1936)* | volumes | Paris: Chronique des Lettres Françaises 1928 to date

French Literature | 133

Which is arranged alphabetically by author, giving very brief biographical details, a chronological list of publications and editions with short bibliographical descriptions, followed by selections, works written in collaboration with other authors, prefaces, and criticism and reviews about the author and his work, including much analytical material from books and periodicals. Later volumes cover material up to the date of their publication. There is another bibliography covering the same period:

THIEME, HUGO PAUL | *Bibliographie de la littérature française de 1800 à 1930* | 3 volumes | Paris: Droz 1933

The first two volumes are arranged alphabetically by author, giving dates of birth and death, a chronological list of (1) books, (2) prefaces, (3) articles, (4) references to the author, (5) references in periodicals from many countries. Volume III is devoted to 'La civilisation'—a classified list of books and articles on questions of the day: e.g. dowries, the education of women, &c. This, too, is international in scope. Thieme includes more authors than Talvart and Place but does not give so much information about each. His bibliography is continued by:

DREHER, S. and ROLLI, M. | *Bibliographie de la littérature française, 1930–1939* | Lille: Giard 1948 to date

DREVET, M. L. | *Bibliographie de la littérature française, 1940–1949* | (Geneva, Droz 1955)

which are also arranged alphabetically by authors and gives dates and places of birth and death. Under each author they list his works in chronological order, followed by periodical articles, and give references to outstanding criticism in books and periodicals in a number of languages.

These bibliographies can be supplemented by the bibliographical notes at the end of the articles in the Larousse encyclopaedia which are very good for the older material.

Current research and criticism are recorded in two bibliographies:

*Bibliography of critical and biographical references for the study of contemporary French literature, 1940 to date* | New York and London: Stechert Hafner 1949 to date

*Bibliographie der französischen Literaturwissenschaft, 1956 to date* | Frankfurt-am-Main: Klostermann 1960 to date

of which the first is prepared by the French Group of the Modern Language Association of America; while the second gives all headings and explanatory text in French.

## ITALIAN LITERATURE

The bibliography of Italian literature is not at all well covered, but the bibliographies (international in scope) at the end of the articles in the great *Enciclopedia Italiana* will assist the reader when other sources fail. There is a useful small manual:

MAZZONI, G. | *Avviamento allo studio critico delle lettere italiane* | 4th edition | Florence: Sansoni 1951

This covers general reference works, texts, literary criticism, literary history, and language. For recent literary criticism there is:

PREZZOLINI, GIUSEPPE | *Repertorio bibliografica della storia e della critica della letteratura italiana dal 1902 al 1932* | 2 volumes | Rome: Edizioni Roma 1937

to which a Supplement in two volumes, covering the years 1932–42 (New York: S. F. Vanni), was added in 1946. In both the main work and the supplement entries are arranged in one alphabetical sequence of persons and subjects concerned. It is international in scope, covering books and periodicals. There is an analytical subject index. An additional index in this field is:

FUCILLA, JOSEPH G. | *Universal author repertoire of Italian essay literature* | New York: Vanni 1941

in which entries are arranged alphabetically by subjects, covering biographical and critical articles on authors—mostly Italian, but including outstanding writers of other countries—in nearly 1,700 collections of Italian essays.

Additional assistance can be gained from the bibliographies contained in the following two reference works:

GARDNER, EDMUND GARRATT | editor | *Italy: a companion to Italian studies . . .* | Methuen 1934

*Storia letteraria d'Italia . . .*| 3rd edition | 10 volumes | Milan: Vallardi, 1942 to date (the standard large history of the subject)

## PORTUGUESE LITERATURE

On this subject there is a useful small guide:

BELL, AUBREY FITZGERALD | *Portuguese bibliography* | Oxford University Press 1922 which contains chapters on general works, texts, anthologies, folk-lore, popular poetry, &c., the Portuguese language, dictionaries, and individual authors.

## SPANISH LITERATURE

A similar handbook to that for Portuguese bibliography is available:

FITZMAURICE-KELLY, JAMES | *Spanish bibliography* | Oxford University Press 1925

In this there are chapters of bibliographies, works of reference, the history of the theatre, collections, of texts, anthologies, works of reference on each period of Spanish literature, and editions of individual authors and commentaries on their work. An important recent work is:

SIMON DIAZ, JOSE | *Manual de la literatura española* | Barcelona: Gil: 1963

This includes some 20,000 entries for Spanish and Spanish colonial publications from the Middle Ages to 1961 and for critical works (from other countries) relating to them. Items are arranged by period and locations are given for those which are rare. There are detailed indexes of authors and subjects. Three-year supplements are promised.

The great bibliography of Spanish literature is now well under way:

GRISMER, RAYMOND L. | *A new bibliography of the literatures of Spain and Spanish America...* | volumes | Minneapolis, Minn.: Perine Book Company 1941 to date

Entries for authors and subjects are arranged in one alphabetical sequence, and include both books and periodical articles.

There are two other major works in course of publication:

SERIS, H. | *Manual de bibliografía de la literatura española* | 7 parts | Syracuse, N.Y.: Centro de Estudios Hispánicos, Hall of Languages 1948 to date

SIMON DIAZ, JOSE | *Bibliografía de la literatura hispánica* | volume 1– | Madrid: Consejo Superior de Investigaciones Científicas, Instituto 'Miguel de Cervantes' de Filología Hispánica 1950 to date

of which the second includes Latin American literature.

Students of Spanish drama will find the 1927 special volume of the *Berliner Titeldrucke* of particular use:

*Spanisches Theater* | Berlin 1928

which records a comprehensive collection alphabetically by author. Another and smaller collection is:

ROGERS, PAUL PATRICK | *Spanish drama collection in the Oberlin College Library: a descriptive catalogue* | Oberlin, Ohio: Oberlin College 1940

which covers the period from the last quarter of the seventeenth century to 1924. Some 7,530 entries are arranged alphabetically by author.

For Spanish-American literature there are two reference sources:

GRISMER, RAYMOND L. | *A reference index to 12,000 Spanish-American authors* ... | New York: H. W. Wilson 1939

TOPETE, J. M. | *A working bibliography of Latin American literature* | St. Augustine, Fla. 1952

the first of which is a simple alphabetical list of authors with references to standard works in which they are mentioned. Dates of birth and death are given where possible, and pseudonyms are included. Topete's bibliography was compiled for the Inter-American Bibliographical and Library Association, and includes translations into English.

There is also a bibliography of translations into English:

PANE, REMIGIO UGO | *English translations from the Spanish, 1484-1943: a bibliography* | New Brunswick, N.J.: Rutgers University Press 1944

This includes work in periodicals. Entries are arranged alphabetically by original author, with dates of birth and death. Titles are sub-arranged chronologically. The original and the translated titles and publication details are given, but no annotations. There is an index of translators.

For additional bibliographical material the bibliographies at the end of relevant articles in the great Spanish encyclopaedia usually known as the *Espasa* will be found of considerable assistance.

## LATIN AND GREEK LITERATURE

A useful introductory guide to this subject is:

NAIRN, J. A. | *Classical hand-list* | 4th edition | Oxford: Blackwell 1960

which is a classified list giving author, brief title, publisher, and date only. It covers general reference works, collections and individual texts, histories of Greek and Latin literature, philology, palaeography, papyrology, epigraphy, history, religion and mythology, philosophy, music, science, mathematics and medicine, geography, archaeology, art, numismatics, and periodicals. Unfortunately there are no indexes. There is also a similar but more scholarly work:

OOTEGHEM, J. VAN | *Bibliotheca graeca et latina: à l'usage des professeurs des Humanités gréco-latines* | 2nd edition | Brussels: Editions de la Revue les Etudes Classiques 1946

Latin and Greek Literature | 137

in which the first part is devoted to general matters—bibliography, geography, history, grammar, metre, and dictionaries—while the second and third parts deal with Greek and Latin literature respectively, each part being sub-arranged alphabetically by authors. Periodical articles are included, important works are marked with an asterisk, but here again there are no indexes. The great guides, especially for the older material, are:

ENGELMANN, WILHELM | *Bibliotheca scriptorum classicorum: 8. Auflage, umfassend die Literatur von 1700 bis 1878... neu bearb. von E. Preuss*| 2 volumes | Leipzig: Engelmann 1880-2 (reprinted 1959)

Volume I is devoted to Greek and volume II to Latin literature. The first part of each volume lists collections, and the second is arranged alphabetically by author. Under each author is given first his original works (beginning with collected editions), followed by critical works, alphabetically arranged by editor. The bibliography was continued by:

KLUSSMANN, RUDOLF | *Bibliotheca scriptorum classicorum et graecorum et latinorum: die Literatur von 1878 bis 1896, einschliesslich umfassend* | 2 volumes in 4 | Leipzig: Reisland 1909-12 (reprinted in 2 volumes in 1961)

which is arranged similarly to Engelmann. There is also an important library catalogue:

SOCIETIES FOR THE PROMOTION OF HELLENIC AND ROMAN STUDIES | *A classified catalogue of the books, pamphlets and maps* | Macmillan 1924

This has only short entries with brief bibliographical particulars, and there are no indexes. The catalogue is kept up to date by means of annual supplements published in the *Journal of Hellenic Studies*.

Current material is recorded in:

*L'Année philologique: bibliographie critique et analytique de l'antiquité gréco-latine, 1924-26 to date* | Paris: Société d'Edition 'Les Belles Lettres', 1928 to date

This was preceded by two volumes entitled *Dix années de bibliographie classique...*, *1914-1924*, compiled by J. Marouzeau (who still edits the *Année philologique*) in 1927-8. The annual bibliography covers more than 700 periodicals in many languages and includes literature, philology, history and transmission of texts, archaeology, epigraphy, numismatics, political history, institutions, religions and mythology, philosophy, law, science, history, and methods of study from pre-history to the end of the Byzantine and Gallo-Roman epochs. Entries are classified under these headings, and there are indexes of Latin and Greek names and of authors in each volume.

Another bibliography in serial form is:

*Bibliotheca philologica classica, 1874 to date* | Leipzig: Reisland 1875 to date

which was published annually and had a very wide range. There was also an English bibliography which has unfortunately ceased publication:

*The year's work in classical studies, 1906-1947* | The Classical Association 1907-50

which consists of bibliographies, in narrative form, of Greek and Latin literature, Greek and Roman history, Greek and Roman religion, ancient philosophy, Greek archaeology and excavation, and Italian archaeology and excavation. There is an index of subjects, but unfortunately none of authors.[1]

Translations are listed in three well-known bibliographies:

PALMER, HENRIETTA R. | *List of English editions and translations of Greek and Latin classics printed before 1641* | Bibliographical Society 1911

This records the translations in the British Museum, the Bodleian and the Cambridge University Libraries, with references to their descriptions in standard bibliographies. Entries are arranged alphabetically by original author.

SMITH, F. SEYMOUR | *The classics in translation: an annotated guide to the best translations of the Greek and Latin classics into English* | Scribner 1930

evaluates individual translations to a certain extent by means of asterisks. Entries are arranged alphabetically by authors and translators in two sequences—one for each language. Original titles are not usually given. There is an appendix of writings by the Apostolic Fathers.

For Greek literature alone there is:

FOSTER, FINLEY MELVILLE KENDALL | *English translations from the Greek: a bibliographical survey* | New York: Columbia University Press 1918

This covers literature up to A.D. 200, but does not include Josephus or the Early Christian Fathers. Original titles are not given. Entries are arranged alphabetically by original authors, and some reprints are included. There is an index of translators.

[1] An appendix of Addenda and Corrigenda to volumes I-IV is printed in Volume V (1936-45), 1950.

## Latin and Greek Literature | 139

N. I. Herescu's *Bibliographie de la littérature latine* (Paris, Belles Lettres, 1943) and P. Masquéray's *Bibliographie pratique de la littérature grecque, des origines à la fin de la période romaine* (Paris, Klincksieck, 1914) are extensive guides to the literature of the classical period. There is considerable additional bibliographical material at the end of the articles in the monumental encyclopaedia of classical studies known familiarly as Pauly-Wissowa.

*Blackwell's Byzantine handlist* (Oxford, Blackwell, 1938) lists the principal texts, translations and commentaries (arranged alphabetically by the authors of the texts); as well as the chief works on the literature, literary history, history, geography, culture, economics, religion, law, art, archaeology, numismatics, monasticism, etc., of the period, and the main reference works and periodicals.

## ORIENTAL CLASSICS

The staff of Columbia University's Oriental Studies Program prepared, under the editorship of Theodore de Bary and Ainslee T. Embree, *A guide to oriental classics* (Columbia University Press 1964). This annotated list of translations into Western languages of the classic religious, philosophical and literary works of Islam, India, China and Japan, is supplemented by a selection of historical, critical, and biographical works.

# 10 | Geography | History | and Biography

'*For the use of scientists*,' wrote John Kirtland Wright and Elizabeth T. Platt, '*bibliographies that include the titles of books only are normally of much less value than those that also contain references to periodical articles, since many of the most significant results of scientific research never find their way into books. Other things being equal, a bibliographical aid that furnishes information about separate maps and maps in books and periodicals is of more use to the geographer than one that fails to do so.*'

This quotation occurs in an invaluable introduction to the literature of geography:

WRIGHT, JOHN KIRTLAND and PLATT, ELIZABETH T. | *Aids to geographical research: bibliographies, periodicals, atlases, gazetteers and other reference books* | 2nd edition | New York: Columbia University Press 1947

This bibliography was published for the American Geographical Society. It is in three parts: I. General aids—bibliographies, periodicals and series, manuals, gazetteers, guidebooks, maps, and atlases; II. Topical aids—historico-geographical studies, geographical education and methodology, physical and mathematical geography, geography of plants and animals, and human geography; III. Regional aids and general geographical periodicals, sub-arranged by regions. Many analyticals for periodical articles are included, and the entries are fully annotated and criticized where necessary. There is an index of authors, titles, and subjects.

The Commission on College Geography of The Association of American Geographers published in 1966 *A basic geographical library*. This lists, with brief annotations some 1,400 books and serials (mostly in English) on (1) geography in general (2) geographical methods (3) thematic geography (4) regional geography. There is an author index. Another excellent bibliography is:

COX, EDWARD GODFREY | *A reference guide to the literature of travel, including voyages, geographical descriptions, adventures, shipwrecks and expeditions* | 3 volumes | Seattle: University of Washington 1935-49

A fourth volume is projected. The first volume is devoted to the Old World, the second to the New World, and the third to Great Britain. Each volume is arranged geographically and covers works in the English language including translations from foreign tongues and foreign translations of English books. There are full annotations, and indexes of personal names. Two older bibliographies are of use in tracing historical material:

STEIN, HENRI | *Manuel de bibliographie générale* | Paris: Picard 1897 (section on geography, pp. 325-400)

JACKSON, JAMES | *Liste provisoire de bibliographies géographiques spéciales* | Paris: Delgrave 1881

The principal library catalogue is:

AMERICAN GEOGRAPHICAL SOCIETY | *Research catalogue* | 15 volumes | Boston, Mass. G. K. Hall 1962–

which comprises a General Section, followed by regional sections—North America; South America; Europe; Africa; Asia; Australasia; the Polar Regions; Oceans; and, the Tropics.

Of atlases, there are several important bibliographies and catalogues:

*The Harold Whitaker Collection of county atlases, road books and maps* ... | Leeds: Brotherton Library 1937

*A description of Ordnance Survey small-/medium-/[and] large-scale maps* | Chessington, Surrey, Ordnance Survey (frequently reissued)

CHUBB, THOMAS | *The printed maps in the atlases of Great Britain and Ireland: a bibliography, 1579-1870* ..., with an introduction by F. P. SPRENT, and biographical notes on the map makers, engravers and publishers by THOMAS CHUBB ... | Homeland Association 1927

The last is divided into three parts—England and Wales, Scotland, and Ireland. Under each entries are arranged chronologically with full details of scale, size, &c. This bibliography is based on the British Museum's atlas collection:

BRITISH MUSEUM | *Catalogue of printed maps, charts and plans...* | 5 volumes | 1967

This is a photolithographic reproduction of the Museum's guard-books incorporating the 2-volume catalogue of 1885 and the annual accessions to 1964.

LIBRARY OF CONGRESS | *List of geographical atlases in the Library of Congress* | compiled by PHILIP LEE PHILLIPS | 5 volumes | Washington 1909-58

The main work (the first two volumes) describes 3,470 atlases, including the 'atlases of cities, those printed to accompany voyages, historical works, and scientific expeditions, and reproductions in atlases to accompany reports on boundary disputes between nations. The maps relating to America, and material of special interest not usually found in atlases, are brought to the attention of the student in bibliographical notes and contents.' Volume I is devoted to full descriptive titles, and volume II contains a complete author list of abridged titles giving full name of author, and dates where known. The supplements, listing a further 3,000 titles, are arranged in similar fashion.

THIELE, WALTER | *Official map publications: a historical sketch, and a bibliographical handbook of current maps and mapping services in the United States, Canada, Latin America, France, Great Britain, Germany, and certain other countries* | Chicago: American Library Association 1938

includes Austria, Hungary, the Netherlands, and Norway, as the 'certain other countries' mentioned in the title. For British Ordnance Survey, Hydrographic Survey, and Land Utilization maps, the catalogues and guides issues by the official publishing bodies should be studied, see also The National Council of Social Service's *The historian's guide to Ordnance Survey maps* (1965) which covers the whole period from 1801 to date, and in this connexion another useful official guide to maps issued before and during the war is the catalogue of G.S.G.S. maps. Note also the *Index to maps in books and periodicals* of the Map Department of the American Geographical Society (Boston, Mass., G. K. Hall 1967), which is arranged alphabetically by subjects and geopolitical divisions, entries being sub-arranged chronologically.

For recent and current material there are five important guides:

*Current geographical publications, 1938 to date* | New York: American Geographical Society of New York (monthly list of books, periodical articles and maps International coverage)

*New geographical literature and maps, 1951 to date* | Royal Geographical Society (a monthly list which now indexes the contents of 20 outstanding British and foreign journals)

*Geographisches Jahrbuch, 1866–* | Gotha: Justus Perthes 1866– (an annual which is a kind of documented 'year's work in geography' with emphasis given to different subjects in different years | A full analysis of the earlier volumes is given on pp. 52–57 of Wright and Platt's *Aids to geographical research*, 1947)

*Bibliotheca geographica: Jahresbibliographie der geographischen Literatur, 1891/92–1911/19* | Berlin: Gesellschaft für Erdkunde 1895–1917 (included books and periodical articles in classified sequence—mainly geographical—with an author index | No annotations)

*Bibliographie géographique internationale, 1891 to date* | Paris: Colin 1894 to date (once known as *Annales de géographie*)

Geography | 143

This last is issued in two parts: I. General, including history, mathematical geography and cartography, physical and human geography. The second part is arranged by regions, subdivided by continents and countries. It includes books, periodical articles, and maps, and gives signed critical annotations. There is an author index.

In January 1966 the publishers, Geo Abstracts, of *Geomorphological abstracts* extended their coverage of geography by adding three further abstracting services covering literature from 1965 onwards. The present pattern is therefore:

A. *Geomorphological abstracts*—including structured geomorphology, ocean floors, weathering and slopes, rivers, glacial morphology, periglacial, karst, arid areas, coasts and regional physiography

B. *Climatology, biogeography and cartography*—including aspects of climatology, synoptic meteorology and oceanography relevant to geographers, soils, plant ecology, plant distributions, evolution of crop plants, and cartography

C. *Economic geography*—including agriculture, forestry and fishing, land utilisation, conservation, mining, energy, manufacturing, trade, transport, tourism, regional planning and urban economic studies

D. *Social geography*—including the geography of man in society, the geography of population composition and growth, population movements, man in relation to environment, medical geography, urban and rural settlement patterns, the geography of political units and boundaries, military geography, and geographical nomenclature

Each volume is issued in six parts: the last part each year including author and regional indexes.

For maps there is a serial bibliography:

*Bibliographie cartographique internationale 1936 to date* | Paris: Colin 1938 to date

This is published under the auspices of the Comité National Français de Géographie and the Union Géographique Internationale, with the powerful and welcome support of Unesco. Entries are arranged by continent, sub-arranged by country, with size and publication details. A comprehensive list of periodicals is given in Chauncey D. Harris and Jerome D. Fellmann's *International list of geographical serials* (University of Chicago, Department of Geography, 1960) which is arranged alphabetically by country, with a title index. The first author has also compiled an *Annotated world list of selected current geographical serials in English* (Department of Geography. Research Paper no. 96, 1964).

# HISTORY

The most important bibliography of this subject in general is:

*A guide to historical literature* | new edition | New York: Macmillan 1961

This remarkable work, which is sponsored by the American Historical Association and which supersedes the 1931 edition (known as 'Dutcher', after its editor), is a model of what an adequate bibliography should be. Entries are arranged in classified order, each section being under the general editorship of an expert, and each entry having a signed annotation, usually very brief, but sometimes detailed. Subjects included are the Near East in ancient times, Ancient Greece and the Hellenistic world, Rome, the history of Christianity, the history of Mohammedanism and Moslem peoples, medieval times, modern Europe, contemporary times, exploration and colonial expansion, Great Britain and Ireland, France, Spain and Portugal, Italy, Germany, Austria and Switzerland, the Netherlands and Belgium, the Scandinavian countries, Russia, Poland, Czechoslovakia and the borderlands, South-eastern Europe and South-western Asia, Asia—including India, China and Japan, Oceania, Africa, the United States, Hispanic America, and British North America. There is an index of authors and subjects. A very useful guide to bibliographies of history is:

COULTER, EDITH M. and GERSTENFELD, MELANIE | *Historical bibliographies: a systematic and annotated guide* | Berkeley, Calif.: University of California Press 1935 (reprinted 1965)

Entries are arranged by period, country, and episode, and have good evaluative annotations, including references to reviews. Both books and periodical articles are covered, and there is an index of authors, titles, and subjects.

A very helpful series is of considerable value:

*Helps for students of history:* edited by CHARLES JOHNSON, J. P. WHITNEY and HAROLD W. V. TEMPERLEY | Society for the Promotion of Christian Knowledge, 1918-24; Historical Association, 1950 to date

Each volume is a small paper-bound pamphlet and in many libraries the series will be found bound up in a number of large volumes each containing several of these pamphlets. In each volume the subject is outlined and bibliographies are given. A complete list of the volumes is to be found in *Guide to historical literature*, 1961.

An old but still important bibliography must be mentioned:

LANGLOIS, CHARLES VICTOR | *Manuel de bibliographie historique* | 2 volumes | Paris: Hachette 1901-4 of which part I is devoted to general works, bibliographies, &c., and part II to the bibliography of European history from the Renaissance to the end of the nineteenth century, with special emphasis on France and books in French. There are very full evaluative annotations.

On medieval history a comprehensive bibliography has been published:

PAETOW, LOUIS JOHN | *A guide to the study of medieval history* | Revised edition | New York: Crofts 1931 (reprinted 1960)

This is international in scope, and covers both books and periodical articles. There are many full critical annotations. Part I is devoted to general works, part II to the general history of the Middle Ages, and part III to medieval culture. Under each specific section the arrangement of material is: A. Outline of main events; B. Special recommendations for reading; C. Bibliography, ending with references to other bibliographies. There is a detailed index of authors, editors, subjects, and titles of large collections. A new edition is in preparation. For older material there is Ulysse Chevalier's *Répertoire des sources historiques du moyen âge* (2 volumes in 4. Paris, Picard, 1894-1907. Reprinted 1960), of which the first part deals with 'Bibliographie', and the second 'Topo-bibliographie'). Current material is listed in the *International guide to medieval studies*, 1961/62 to date (Darien, Conn., American Bibliographical Service).

The valuable bibliographies in the Cambridge histories of ancient, medieval, and modern history, and of the British Empire, should not be overlooked, and it will be found that most substantial historical works are well documented and can act as supporting bibliographies from time to time.

Serials in the field of history are recorded in:

CARON, P. and JARYC, M. | editors | *World list of historical periodicals and bibliographies* | Oxford: International Committee of Historical Sciences 1939

BOEHM, ERIC H. and LALIT, ADOLPHUS | editors | *Historical periodicals* | Santa Barbara, Calif.: and Munich, Clio Press 1961

KRAMM, HEINRICH | *Bibliographie historischer Zeitschriften, 1939-1951* | Marburg, Rausch, 1952-54

Kramm continues Caron and Jaryc with a list of over 3,000 titles, but excludes the publications of the western hemisphere. Boehm and Lalit is an annotated world list of some 5,000 serials, with title index. Local history, diplomatics, genealogy, heraldry, iconography, numismatics, palaeography, and toponymy are included, and many entries are annotated.

For current material the most important sources are:

*International bibliography of historical sciences, 1926 to date* | Paris: Colin 1930 to date

*Historical abstracts, 1955 to date* | Santa Barbara, Calif.: 1955 to date

*Historical abstracts*, issued quarterly with annual and 5-year indexes, covers articles on political, diplomatic, economic, social, cultural and intellectual history for the period 1775 to 1945. The *International bibliography*, which is issued by the International Committee of Historical Science, under the auspices of Unesco, takes all history as its field. Entries are classified, mainly chronologically, and include many analyticals for periodical articles from about 3,000 periodicals. There are indexes of authors and subjects, and places. Additional material can be found in the bibliographies included in the *American historical review* and the *English historical review*, and in:

*Annual bulletin of historical literature:* published for the Historical Association | 1911 to date

This contains chapters in narrative form briefly reviewing the year's publications in the various fields of history, more especially those in the English language. Both books and periodical articles are included, and there is an author index.

For the period of the war when the *International bibliography* was in abeyance, a British bibliography took its place to a certain extent:

FREWER, LOUIS B. | *Bibliography of historical writings published in Great Britain and the British Empire, 1940–1945* | Oxford: Blackwell 1947

This was compiled on the same lines, and is a selective bibliography of historical writings covering all aspects of history down to the beginning of the war published in Great Britain and the Commonwealth, including articles and reviews in 120 periodicals. American books marketed in Great Britain by the Oxford and Cambridge University Presses are included. Entries are arranged in classified sequence, but there are no annotations. There is an index of persons and places. A kind of sequel exists in Joan C. Lancaster's *Bibliography of historical works issued in the United Kingdom 1946–1956* (University of London, Institute of Historical Research, 1957, reprinted 1964).

## GREAT BRITAIN AND THE COMMONWEALTH

There is one major library catalogue which is especially useful for tracing material on the Commonwealth, and, in particular, on the less-known parts of it:

ROYAL COMMONWEALTH SOCIETY | *Subject catalogue of the Library* . . . , by EVANS LEWIN | 5 volumes | 1930–61

which is fully described on page 28, on which will also be found details of A. R. Hewitt's valuable reference work.

For purely British history the resources of the Public Record Office must not be overlooked:

PUBLIC RECORD OFFICE | *Guide to the contents of the Public Record Office* | 2 volumes | H.M.S.O. 1963

Based on M. S. Giuseppi's great *Guide* of 1923–24, this brings the information up-to-date to 1960. The first volume describes the legal records, and the second the state papers and the records of public departments.

The following two bibliographies will also be found of use:

MULLINS, E. L. C. | *Texts and calendars: an analytical guide to serial publications* | Royal Historical Society 1958

GROSS, CHARLES | *Bibliography of British municipal history, including gilds and parliamentary representation* | New York: Longmans 1897 (reprint 1915)

The latter covers the governmental or constitutional history of Great Britain. Purely topographical works and parish histories are omitted, but standard county histories are included. Some of the entries have critical annotations. Part I is devoted to general authorities, central and county; part II to individual towns arranged alphabetically by name. A new reprint (Leicester University Press, 1966) with an introductory essay by Dr. G. H. Martin, promises a continuation to assimilate the literature published since 1897.

Special bibliographies are available for many periods in British history:

BONSER, WILFRID | *A Romano-British bibliography* [55 B.C.–A.D. 449] | 2 volumes | Oxford: Blackwell 1964

BONSER, WILFRID | *An Anglo-Saxon and Celtic bibliography (450–1087)* | Oxford: Blackwell 1957

148 | History

GROSS, CHARLES | *The sources and literature of English history from earliest times to about 1485* | 2nd edition | Longmans 1915

The last is a model of its kind. More than 3,000 items—books, periodical articles, and transactions of learned societies—are minutely classified under the following main headings: (*a*) General authorities, (*b*) origins, (*c*) Anglo-Saxon period, (*d*) period between 1066 and 1485. There are short but good critical annotations, and a detailed index. There are also four appendixes: reports of the Deputy Keeper of the Public Records; the Historical Manuscripts Commission, the Rolls Series; and chronological tables of the principal sources. Following on this is:

READ, CONYERS | *Bibliography of British history: Tudor period, 1485–1603* | 2nd edition | Oxford: Clarendon Press 1959

This, and the next item, were issued under the auspices of the Royal Historical Society and the American Historical Association. It is intended to continue Gross, subsequent volumes having been planned to cover the remaining period up to the present day. International in scope, it includes books, periodical articles, documents, and society transactions, but is selective. Entries are arranged in classified order. A list of English county 'notes and queries' is included. Immediately following this in the same series is:

DAVIES, GODFREY | *Bibliography of British history: Stuart period, 1603–1714* | Oxford: Clarendon Press 1928

This is on the same lines and is arranged as follows: political and constitutional history, military history, naval history, religious history, economic history, social history, literature, ballads and journalism, fine arts, science, political science, local history, Scotland, Ireland, Wales, voyages and travels, and colonial history. Items are further sub-arranged chronologically. For part of this period there is an important comprehensive bibliography:

MORGAN, WILLIAM THOMAS and MORGAN, CHLOE SINER | *A bibliography of British history (1700–1715) with special reference to the reign of Queen Anne* | 5 volumes | Bloomington, Ind.: University of Indiana 1934–42

This monumental work is of special value to all students of the period for it is in effect a complete record of the publications of these years, and a storehouse of sources on all the historical, political, economic, and cultural aspects of the times. Another bibliography which continues Davies is:

PARGELLIS, STANLEY and MEDLEY, D. J. | *The eighteenth century, 1714–1789* | Oxford: Clarendon Press 1951

# History | 149

which is in the same series as Read and Davies. A volume in this series to cover the nineteenth century is in preparation. Overlapping with Pargellis is the very interesting:

GROSE, CLYDE LECLARE | *A select bibliography of British history 1660–1760* | Chicago: University of Chicago Press 1940

in which over 8,000 entries for books and periodical articles are arranged by subject with many annotations. Diplomatic, political, social, economic, cultural, and literary aspects are all covered. There is a detailed index of authors and subjects. And for the next ninety years some help can be obtained from:

WILLIAMS, JUDITH BLOW | *A guide to the printed materials for English social and economic history, 1750–1850* | 2 volumes | New York: Columbia University Press 1926

The use of this is somewhat limited owing to its exclusion of periodical articles, but it is nevertheless an important work in its field owing to its scholarship and critical annotations. International in scope, in part I it covers research material: bibliographies and general reference works, and in part II a number of special subjects: industry, transport, political, social and economic conditions and movements.

*Writings on British history: a bibliography of books and articles on the history of Great Britain from about 450 A.D. to 1914, published during the year . . . , with an Appendix containing a select list of publications . . . on British history since 1914*, compiled by ALEXANDER TAYLOR MILNE 1934 to date | Royal Historical Society 1937 to date

This includes art material when definitely historical, but the domestic history of colonies and dominions is only noted when it directly concerns the mother country. The local and national history of both Wales and Scotland is included. Part I consists of general material—auxiliary sciences, bibliography, historiography, and British history in general. Part II is arranged by periods, sub-divided by classes corresponding to those in part I. Some brief annotations are included, and references are made to authoritative reviews of important items. A retrospective series (5 volumes. 1967–68) covers the period 1901–33.

There are two major bibliographies of British topography:

ANDERSON, JOHN PARKER | *The book of British topography: a classified catalogue of the topographical books in the Library of the British Museum relating to Great Britain and Ireland . . .* | Satchell 1881

This has a classified arrangement: entries are arranged by country—England, Wales, &c.—then alphabetically by county, sub-divided alphabetically by town. There is an index of authors and subjects.

HUMPHREYS, ARTHUR LEE | *A handbook to county bibliography: being a bibliography of bibliographies relating to the counties and towns of Great Britain and Ireland* | Strangeways 1917

includes systematic bibliographies, and calls attention to source books, indexes, &c., of local historical and topographical material, and also to local manuscript and printed collections. It is arranged alphabetically by county, sub-arranged alphabetically by town. Note the Addenda, pp. 315-45. There is an appendix of general works on England, Scotland, Ireland, and Wales, and a detailed index of authors and subjects. In addition, there are a number of great regional bibliographies—notably those of the Birmingham and Gloucester Public Libraries—which reflect the history of Britain in miniature, and which should not be overlooked by any student or research worker who wishes to make a thorough survey of his subject. Note also the Historical Association's *English local history handlist: a short bibliography for the study of local history and antiquities*(1965).

## ARCHAEOLOGY

General works on archaeology are listed in the Preedy Memorial Library's *Catalogue* described on page 76. Current material is recorded in:

*Archäologische Bibliographie: Beilage zum Jahrbuch des Deutschen Archäologischen Instituts, 1913 to date* | Berlin: de Gruyter

which is systematically arranged and has an index of authors in each annual issue.

Material on Britain is covered by:

*Index of archaeological papers, 1665-1910* | Constable 1892-1914 | 21 volumes

which was prepared under the auspices of the Congress of Archaeological Societies and of the Society of Antiquaries. Current items are listed in the annual:

*Archaeological bibliography for Great Britain and Ireland, 1940 to date* | Council for British Archaeology

which includes material up to 1600 with a selection of items for the next century. Attention is also called to the recent:

*Current publications on Old World archaeology 1958 to date* | Cambridge, Mass.: Council for Old World Archaeology 1958 to date

comprising 22 area reports, on the archaeology of the entire Old World from Palaeolithic to recent historical times, including annotated bibliographies.

## BIOGRAPHY AND GENEALOGY

The one indispensable bibliography for biography is:

RICHES, PHYLLIS M. | *Analytical bibliography of universal collected biography: comprising books published in the English tongue in Great Britain and Ireland, America and the British dominions* ... | Library Association 1934

which is limited to works written in, or translated into, English. It consists of: (*a*) an alphabetical index of 55,000 names of subjects of biographies; (*b*) an annotated list of books analysed; (*c*) a bibliography of biographical dictionaries; (*d*) a subject index classifying persons whose lives are recorded; (*e*) a chronological index. There is a similar but more comprehensive work:

ARNIM, MAX | *Internationale Personalbibliographie, 1800–1959* | 2nd edition | 3 volumes | 1963

This is arranged in alphabetical order and gives references to books, bibliographies, and periodical articles in a large number of languages. Robert Bigney Slocum's *Biographical dictionaries: a bibliography* (Gale Research 1966) lists, with some annotations, about 4,500 items issued since 1700, entries being arranged geographically. The importance of the bibliographies at the end of the articles in the *Dictionary of national biography* and the *Dictionary of American biography* for prominent figures of all times in the English-speaking world should never be overlooked, more especially for those people who have never warranted full-length biographies, material for their lives being contained in a few periodical articles, manuscripts, or private collections. Similarly the great national encyclopaedias will be found to be especially strong in biographical material. For general purposes there are the *Britannica* and *Chambers's*, while for France there is *Larousse*, for Italy the great *Italiana*, for Spain and Latin-America, the *Espasa*, for Switzerland the *Schweizer-Lexicon*, for Germany *Brockhaus* and *Meyer*, and there are corresponding reference works for the smaller countries. A good source for earlier publications is Eduard Marie Oettinger's *Bibliographie biographique universelle* (2 volumes Brussels, Stienon, 1854).

A recent index has already proved its worth in providing easy reference to the mass of biographical material contained in periodicals and in books of collective biography:

*Biography index: a cumulative index to biographical material in books and magazines, 1946 to date* | New York: H. W. Wilson 1946 to date

This is issued quarterly and cumulates annually and three-yearly. It

## 152 | Biography and Genealogy

includes biographical material appearing in all the periodicals now covered by the Wilson indexes and in selected professional journals; current books of individual and collected biography in the English language (wherever published) including biographical fiction, drama, poetry, and children's books; incidental but frequently valuable biographical material (such as prefaces) as currently indexed and analysed in the *Standard Catalog*, the *Essay and general literature index*, and the *Vertical file index*; obituaries found in all the periodical sources and some published in the *New York Times*; portraits whenever they appear in connexion with indexed material; and material about individuals both living and dead. The index consists of a main alphabetical index by name, and an index of occupations and professions. In the main index wherever possible dates of birth and death, nationality, and occupation or profession are included in the headings.

Additional useful information of this kind, including—in the case of writers—the titles of outstanding works, can be found in:

*Current biography, 1940 to date* | New York: H. W. Wilson 1940 to date

Each entry includes source material and, if possible, a portrait. This publication is issued monthly, cumulating into annual volumes, with a cumulated index which includes the names in all previous annual volumes.

Further useful sources include Donald H. Simpson's *Biography catalogue*, which is volume V of the Royal Commonwealth Society's *Subject catalogue* described on page 28; and:

MATTHEWS, WILLIAM | compiler | *British autobiographies: an annotated bibliography of British autobiographies published or written before 1951* | Berkeley: University of California Press 1955

MATTHEWS, WILLIAM | *British diaries: an annotated bibliography of British diaries written between 1442 and 1942* | Berkeley: University of California Press 1950

MATTHEWS, WILLIAM | *Canadian diaries and autobiographies* | Berkeley: University of California Press 1950

MATTHEWS, WILLIAM | *American diaries: an annotated bibliography of American diaries written prior to the year 1861* | Berkeley: University of California Press 1945

KAPLAN, LOUIS | *A bibliography of American autobiographies* | Madison: University of Wisconsin Press 1961

which between them record many thousands of published and unpublished works. Kaplan comprises well over 6,000 items published in book form before 1945, and is thus supplemented to some extent by Jane Kline's *Biographical sources for the United States* (Washington, D.C., Library of Congress, 1961) which lists principally biographies published between 1945 and 1960.

For the student of family histories, genealogies, and heraldry there are a number of useful guides:

THOMSON, T. R. | compiler | *A catalogue of British family histories* | 2nd edition | Beck 1935

FERGUSON, J. P. S. | *Scottish family histories held in Scottish libraries* | Edinburgh: Scottish Central Library 1960 (reprinted 1964)

Thomson is arranged alphabetically by family surname. It does not include biographies, printed pedigree sheets, reprints from genealogical magazines, peerage claims, or American publications even if they deal with British families. Ferguson comprises some 2,000 works. There are also the following guides:

MARSHALL, GEORGE WILLIAM | *The genealogist's guide: being a general search through genealogical, topographical, and biographical works, family histories, peerage claims, &c.* | 4th edition | Guildford 1903 (arranged alphabetically by family name)

BRIDGER, CHARLES | *An index to printed pedigrees contained in county and local histories, the Herald's visitations, and in the more important genealogical collections* | John Russell Smith 1867

WHITMORE, J. B. | *A genealogical guide* | Walford 1953

Whitmore is a sequel to Marshall. Bridger contains some 16,000 entries. It is arranged alphabetically by counties, followed by a section of general works. There is an index of family names. But the most comprehensive guide to the subject is:

LIBRARY OF CONGRESS | *American and English genealogies . . .* | 2nd edition | Washington 1919

This is mainly limited to genealogies separately published, periodical articles, &c., being for the most part omitted. There are over 7,000 entries and some are briefly annotated. There is an index of authors.

A very helpful introduction to the whole subject is:

HARRISON, H. G. | *A select bibliography of English genealogy, with brief lists for Wales, Scotland and Ireland: a manual for students* | Phillimore 1937

of which part I is a general classified list of standard reference works on the subject. Part II is a geographical list of sources arranged by counties. There are brief annotations, and a subject index to part I. D. E. Gardner and F. Smith's *Genealogical research in England and Wales* (2 volumes, Salt Lake City, Utah, Bookcraft Publications, 1956-59) and Manchester Public Libraries' *Reference Library subject catalogue, Section 929: Genealogy* (3 volumes, 1956-58) are two further invaluable guides in this field. Note also Donald Lines Jacobus's *Index to genealogical periodicals* (3 volumes. The author 1932-53. Reprinted: Baltimore, Genealogical Publishing Co., 1963-64).

For heraldry a convenient bibliography of current material has been published recently:

COPE, S. TREHEARNE | *Heraldry, flags, and seals: a select bibliography, with annotations, covering the period 1920 to 1945* | Aslib 1948

This was reprinted from the *Journal of Documentation*. It is arranged alphabetically by authors and is heavily annotated. Both books and periodical articles are included, and details of illustrations—which are of especial importance in this particular case—are given. There is a detailed index of subjects. Special note should be taken of the supplement of additional material on pp. 144-6.

# PART TWO
Universal and National Bibliographies

# 11 Universal Bibliographies and Bibliographies of Bibliographies

It is not intended to treat the second part of this book in as detailed a fashion as the first. International and national bibliographies have been well described in many other standard works (to which attention will be drawn in the final chapter on Further Reading), so that here it is only necessary to indicate the outstanding items and to give rather fuller information concerning those publications which have appeared during the last years and are not yet familiar to the majority of readers.

For the most part users of recorded information are interested in books from the *subject* point of view, wanting very much more frequently to know what books have been published on a certain subject, rather than what books have been written by a certain author. But when the latter inquiry arises, or when it is necessary to identify a work of which the particulars given are incomplete or suspect and the subject uncertain, it is of great use to have some acquaintance with the main universal bibliographies and also with the great national bibliographies of individual countries. If this knowledge includes some idea of the scope of each bibliography much time may be saved in deciding which is the most likely to help in tracing the item required.

The most generally useful of all general bibliographies are those which are not limited to any particular time, country, or language, and foremost among these are the catalogues of the great national libraries. In these it is possible to search with some hope of success for an item without regard to its origin or subject. In addition, as some of these catalogues—notably that of the British Museum—have subject indexes, they can also be used for tracing the main background material on individual subjects. There is also the advantage that these catalogues are the result of much careful and scholarly research and may yield valuable information on such points as full names, the identity of anonymous and pseudonymous writers, the origin of others, and so on.

## 158 | Universal Bibliographies

From the point of view of the British reader the most valuable catalogue is:

BRITISH MUSEUM | *Catalogue of printed books* | 95 volumes | 1881–1900

to which a Supplement of thirteen volumes was published in 1900–5. A new edition is in progress at the present time, the first 124 volumes (1931 to date) covering the letters A to Kno. It is hoped to complete the catalogue in some three hundred volumes by 1967. Both editions are arranged in alphabetical order of author, but the first edition contains a number of form headings of which the most important are 'Academies' for the publications of associations, learned societies, &c., and 'Periodical publications'. There is also a subject index for works added to the Library since 1881, and for works issued before this period there is a series of selective indexes by R. A. Peddie.

Another catalogue which is especially valuable for works in the English language and for the more prominent foreign items is:

LIBRARY OF CONGRESS | *Catalog of the books represented by Library of Congress printed cards issued to July 31, 1942* | 167 volumes | *1942–6*

To this author catalogue two supplements, comprising 66 volumes in all, were added, covering the period 1942–52. Subsequent accessions are incorporated in:

*The national union catalog: a cumulative author list representing Library of Congress printed cards and titles reported by other American libraries, 1952 to date* | Washington, D.C.: Library of Congress 1956 to date

which represents the holdings of over 800 large American libraries. Subject catalogues of the Library of Congress's own stock are also available for the period 1950 onwards.

Other valuable catalogues are those of the London Library (author catalogues covering the period up to 1950, and subject index up to 1953), Edinburgh University Library (published 1918–23), the National Library of Scotland (formerly known as the Advocates' Library, published 1857–79), and John Rylands Library (for early printed books in English).

For foreign material there are two great national catalogues:

*Catalogue général des livres imprimés de la Bibliothèque Nationale* | volumes | Paris 1897 to date

*Berliner Titeldrucke: Verzeichnis der von der Staatsbibliothek, den preussischen Universitätsbibliotheken und den Bibliotheken der preussischen Technischen Hochschulen erworbenen neueren Druckschriften* | volumes | Berlin 1892 to date

## Universal Bibliographies | 159

and in addition there are a number of smaller catalogues issued by the national libraries of other countries.

At all times there have existed individual bibliophiles who have devoted their lives to building up vast bibliographies of what they regarded as the more important works, and later bookmen owe much to their researches, more especially for the earlier period of the printed book. The most famous of these is probably:

BRUNET, JACQUES CHARLES | *Manuel du libraire et de l'amateur de livres* | 5th edition | 6 volumes | Paris: Didot 1860–5

to which a Supplement in two volumes was issued in 1878–80. This lists more than 40,000 important works and is especially strong in French and Latin items. A similar work, which Schneider calls 'der Englische Brunet' is:

LOWNDES, WILLIAM THOMAS | *The bibliographer's manual of English literature* | New edition | 6 volumes | Bell 1857–64

which includes English literature printed abroad. There is also:

WATT, ROBERT | *Bibliotheca Britannica: or, a general index to British and foreign literature* | 4 volumes | Edinburgh 1824 (reprinted 1965)

which is specially useful for eighteenth-century items and for its subject index. A more modern compilation which is still of great use is:

SONNENSCHEIN, WILLIAM SWAN | *The best books: a reader's guide* | 3rd edition | 6 volumes | 1910–35

This is a classified bibliography of over 100,000 items, with occasional brief annotations, and a comprehensive index of authors, titles, and subjects. Sonnenschein was a genius in recording the important books on a subject, no matter how rare, and his guide contains entries for many obscure but valuable items.

For the special subject of incunabula, there are fortunately several detailed reference works:

HAIN, LUDWIG | *Repertorium bibliographicum* | 2 volumes in 4 | Stuttgart: Cotta 1826–38 (reprinted 1920, 1925 and 1948)

to which Supplements and corrections were published by W. A. Copinger (1895–1902), Dietrich Reichling (1905–14), and Konrad Burger (1891–1908). Hain is important for he lists most of the important works published before 1500 and many works of reference and booksellers' catalogues refer to individual books by Hain's reference numbers, but his bibliography is difficult to use and—as the supplements show—not always reliable. It is

## 160 | Universal Bibliographies

therefore encouraging that two more comprehensive and authoritative catalogues are now in course of issue, notably the famous "GKW":

*Gesamtkatalog der Wiegendrucke: herausgegeben von der Kommission für den Gesamtkatalog der Wiegendrucke* | volumes | Leipzig 1925 to date

This monumental work has reached volume VIII, and although its progress has been held up by the war it has not altogether been checked. It is estimated that ultimately it will record well over 30,000 items. Arranged in alphabetical order of author, it gives full bibliographical particulars, and includes locations in libraries throughout the world. A work of less but still considerable importance comes from Britain:

BRITISH MUSEUM | *Catalogue of books printed in the fifteenth century, now in the British Museum* | volumes | 1908 to date (corrected reprint 1962)

This reached its ninth volume in 1962, but a further volume (for Spain and Portugal) is in the press. Entries are arranged in the now famous 'Proctor-order' established in Robert Proctor's *An index to the early printed books in the British Museum from the invention of printing to the year 1500, with notes of those in the Bodleian Library* (2 volumes, Kegan Paul, 1898–9; reprinted, with the four supplements and Konrad Burger's index, London 1960), by which incunabula are arranged first by countries and then by presses, sub-arranged chronologically. Theodore Besterman's *Early printed books to the end of the sixteenth century: a bibliography of bibliographies* (2nd edition. Geneva, Societas Bibliographica, 1961) lists well over 2,000 bibliographies.

There are three other bibliographies which are of some use in tracing early publications:

PANZER, GEORG WOLFGANG | *Annales typographici ab artis inventae origine ad annum 1536* | 11 volumes | Nuremberg 1793–1803

MAITTAIRE, MICHAEL | *Annales typographici ab artis inventae origine ad annum 1664* | 5 volumes | The Hague 1719–89

GEORGI, GOTTLIEB | *Allgemeines europäisches Bücherlexikon: vor dem Anfange des XVI | Seculi bis 1739* | 4 parts | Leipzig 1742 (Supplements, 1750–8)

but these, which are particularly valuable for the post-incunabula period, are only to be found in the larger libraries.

## ANONYMOUS AND PSEUDONYMOUS WORKS

The most difficult class of works to discover are those which have been published anonymously or pseudonymously. Fortunately there are several tools devoted to tracing such items:

## Anonymous and Pseudonymous Works | 161

HALKETT, SAMUEL and LAING, JOHN | *Dictionary of anonymous and pseudonymous literature:* new and enlarged edition by JAMES KENNEDY and W. A. SMITH and A. F. JOHNSON | 9 volumes | Edinburgh: Oliver & Boyd 1926-62

The main work is arranged alphabetically by titles, with notes of author and publication details. There are many annotations, including the authority for the ascriptions. The first supplement is contained in volume VI: asterisks are placed against entries which correct or add to entries in the main sequence. Volume VII contains a second supplement, and a detailed index of authors (with inclusive dates of books indexed), as well as an index of initials and pseudonyms. Volume VIII covers items published in the first half of the twentieth-century.

QUÉRARD, JOSEPH MARIE | *Les supercheries littéraires dévoilées* | 2nd edition | 7 volumes | Paris: Daffis, 1869-79 (Supplement, 1889)

is mainly devoted to French works, but includes some foreign and classical items. For German literature there are two main works:

HOLZMANN, MICHAEL and BOHATTA, HANS | *Deutsches Pseudonymen-Lexikon* | Vienna 1906

HOLZMANN, MICHAEL and BOHATTA, HANS | *Deutsches Anonymen-Lexikon* | 7 volumes | Weimar, 1902-28

which between them cover about 100,000 works. For additional works of reference covering many different countries, Archer Taylor and Fredric J. Mosher's excellent *The bibliographical history of anonyma and pseudonyma* (Chicago University Press, for the Newberry Library, 1951) should be consulted.

## BIBLIOGRAPHIES OF BIBLIOGRAPHIES

Of all the many introductions to bibliographies the finest handbook is volume I of:

MALCLES, LOUISE-NOËL | *Les sources du travail bibliographique* | volumes | Geneva, Droz: Lille, Giard 1950 to date

This is a remarkable achievement since it not only lists the outstanding bibliographies and standard reference works of all the more important countries, but also describes them in considerable detail, and evaluates them with great care.

The outstanding work in the English language to treat of bibliographies and reference works is:

WINCHELL, CONSTANCE M. | *Guide to reference books* | 8th edition | Chicago: American Library Association 1967

This is a standard work throughout the English-speaking world since it is truly international in scope, although slightly more detail is naturally given to American publications and interests. Its especial value is in its subject arrangement and its informed and evaluative annotations. There is a similar work for Britain:

WALFORD, A. J. | *Guide to reference material* | 2nd edition | 3 volumes | Library Association 1966–68

which omits some of the older works listed in Winchell, but lists a large number of 'hidden' bibliographies. It is superbly annotated.

The works so far mentioned include bibliographies but are not entirely devoted to them. The most comprehensive recent index to bibliographies is:

BESTERMAN, THEODORE | *A world bibliography of bibliographies* | 4th edition | 5 volumes | Geneva: Societas Bibliographica 1965–66

which is restricted to some 117,000 bibliographies in 49 languages published separately. Entries are arranged by 16,000 subjects in alphabetical order, and there is a comprehensive index of authors and subjects in the fourth volume. There is also a current index of bibliographical material:

*Bibliographic index: a cumulative bibliography of bibliographies, 1937 to date* | New York: H. W. Wilson 1938 to date

This is issued quarterly and cumulates into annual and multi-annual volumes. It is a subject index only and includes bibliographies published separately as books and pamphlets, and those published as parts of books, pamphlets, and periodical articles. References to new editions and supplements are included. In the preliminary pages of each issue valuable information is given of new bibliographic publications, changes, &c.

Recent bibliographies are noted in *Bibliographical services throughout the world, 1950–1959, 1960–64* (2 volumes. Paris, Unesco, 1961–67), in the volumes of the *Index bibliographicus* (4th edition. The Hague, Fédération Internationale de Documentation, 1959 to date), and in Unesco's invaluable bi-monthly *Bibliography, documentation and terminology*, 1961 to date.

For the older material the most useful reference works are:

PETZHOLDT, JULIUS | *Bibliotheca bibliographica: kritisches Verzeichnis der das Gesamtgebiet der Bibliographie betreffenden Literatur des In-und Auslandes in systematischer Ordnung* | Leipzig: Engelmann 1886 (reprinted 1961)

Petzholdt has long been a standard work owing to its international scope and careful annotations. On it was modelled another but less important work:

### Bibliographies of Bibliographies | 163

STEIN, HENRI | *Manuel de bibliographie génèrale: bibliotheca bibliographica nova* | Paris: Picard 1897 (reprinted 1961)

which is best on the subject rather than the national bibliography aspect. Thus the next work:

LANGLOIS, CHARLES VICTOR | *Manuel de bibliographie historique* | 2nd edition | Paris: Hachette 1901-4

is of use since it is valuable for its critical annotations of general and national bibliographies. Its treatment of subject bibliographies is not, however, of the same standard.

The last work to be mentioned in this field is:

COURTNEY, WILLIAM PRIDEAUX | *A register of national bibliography: with a selection of the chief bibliographical books and articles printed in other countries* | 3 volumes | Constable 1905-12

which Schneider calls an excellent work. It is international in scope but especially strong in English material. Entries are arranged alphabetically by subjects and cover bibliographies published separately and also those contained in books and periodicals.

# 12 | National Bibliographies

The records of the publications of the different nations are for the most part incomplete and indifferent: only for British, German-language and American works is there anything approaching a comprehensive range of bibliographies covering the whole period from the beginning of printing, and even now additional titles hitherto unknown are constantly being discovered. The records of the publications of most other nations are very much less satisfactory, and in all cases the period for which bibliographies are weakest is the eighteenth century when an immense amount of important material appeared. In this chapter are noted the most important of the reference tools to which the reader should turn for assistance: there is a large amount of supporting material which although sometimes unreliable may still be of service from time to time, and these will be found in the more detailed reference works obtainable in most large reference libraries. The best guides to the subject are Helen F. Conover's *Current national bibliographies* (Washington, D.C., Library of Congress, 1955) and Olga Pinto's *Le bibliografie nazionali* (2nd edition. Florence, Olschki, 1951).

## GREAT BRITAIN AND THE U.S.A.

The main work of reference in this field is clearly the *General catalogue* of the British Museum which has already been described in the previous chapter. In addition, the catalogue of the Library of Edinburgh University and that of the National Library of Scotland (formerly the Advocates' Library) will be found of use, especially in tracing Scottish publications.

For the earliest period, up to 1500, the main work of reference is the British Museum's *Catalogue of books printed in the 15th century*, 1912 to date, supported by Proctor's *Index to the early printed books in the British Museum from the invention of printing to the year 1500* . . . , 1898–9, both of which have already been described. In addition, there is:

DUFF, EDWARD G. | *Fifteenth-century English books: a bibliography of books and documents printed in England and of books for the English market printed abroad* | Bibliographical Society 1917

# NATIONAL BIBLIOGRAPHY

## GREAT BRITAIN

| General | To 1640 | 1641–1700 | 1700–99 | 1801–99 | 20th century |
|---|---|---|---|---|---|
| British Museum Catalogues and Subject-indexes<br>Cambridge bibliography of English literature<br>Lowndes's Bibliographer's manual<br>Peddie's Subject indexes<br>Dictionary of national biography | British Museum Catalogue ... to 1640<br>Pollard and Redgrave's S.T.C.<br>Proctor's Index<br>Sayle's Early English printed books | Wing's S.T.C.<br>Transcripts of Registers of Stationers' Company<br>Thomason tracts | London Catalogue<br>Watt's Bibliotheca Britannica | English Catalogue | English Catalogue<br>Whitaker's Cumulative Book List (since 1926)<br>Cumulative Book Index (since 1930)<br>British national bibliography (since 1950) |

## FRANCE

| General | 1470–1600 | 1601–99 | 1700–1899 | | Current |
|---|---|---|---|---|---|
| Bibliothèque Nationale Catalogue<br>Brunet's Manuel<br>Cabeen's Critical bibliography<br>Lanson's Manuel<br>Répertoire de bibliographie française | Brunet's La France littéraire<br>British Museum Short-title catalogue | Georgi's Allgemeines europäisches Bücherlexikon | Quérard's La France littéraire<br>Lorenz<br>Bibliographie de la France<br>Thieme's Bibliographie<br>Vicaire's Manuel | | Biblio<br>Bibliographie de la France<br>Bibliographie française<br>Librairie française<br>Lorenz<br>Talvart's Bibliographie<br>Thieme's Bibliographie |

## GERMANY

| General | To 18th Century | 1700–99 | 1800–99 | | 20th Century |
|---|---|---|---|---|---|
| Berliner Titeldrucke | Hain's Repertorium<br>Gesamtkatalog der Wiegendrucke<br>Panzer's Annales<br>Maittaire's Annales<br>Georgi's Allgemeines europäisches Bücherlexikon | Heinsius<br>Kayser (from 1750)<br>Halbjahrs-Verzeichnis (from 1798) | Halb-Jahrs-Verzeichnis<br>Heinsius (to 1892)<br>Kayser<br>Börsenblatt (from 1834)<br>Wöchentliches Verzeichnis (from 1842)<br>Allgemeine Bibliographie (from 1856)<br>Fünfjahrs-Katalog (from 1851) | | Kayser (to 1910)<br>Fünfjahrs-Katalog (to 1912)<br>Wöchentliches Verzeichnis (to 1931)<br>Deutsche Bibliographie (from 1947)<br>Deutsche National-bibliographie (from 1931) |

## 166 | National Bibliographies

This is an exhaustive series of standard descriptions arranged alphabetically by authors and titles, followed by facsimiles and a short-title list in 'Proctor-order', listing in all 431 books. The same author also compiled a list of publications for the next period:

DUFF, EDWARD G. and others | *Hand-lists of books printed by London printers, 1501–1556* | Bibliographical Society 1913

which covers the interim period up to the published entries in the Registers of the Company of Stationers of London:

STATIONERS' COMPANY | *Transcript of the registers . . . 1554–1640*, edited by EDWARD ARBER | 5 volumes | 1875–94

which unfortunately contains no index. There are also several bibliographies which cover the entire period up to 1640, notably:

CAMBRIDGE UNIVERSITY | *Early English printed books in the University Library . . . 1475–1640* | 4 volumes | 1900–7

which is usually known as 'Sayle' after the name of its compiler, C. E. Sayle. Entries are arranged in 'Proctor-order' and include works published on the Continent. There are full indexes of authors and titles, printers and stationers, &c. There is also:

BRITISH MUSEUM | *Catalogue of books . . . printed in England, Scotland and Ireland, and of English books printed abroad to the year 1640* | 3 volumes 1884

which was hastily prepared and does not include all that the British Museum possesses for this period. Another important source (since it includes the treasures of the Bibliotheca Lindesiana) records a collection in Manchester:

JOHN RYLANDS LIBRARY | *Catalogue of books . . . printed in England, Scotland and Ireland, and of books in the English language printed abroad to the end of the year 1640* | Manchester: Cornish 1895

which was edited by Edward G. Duff, and maintains a high standard of accuracy. There is also the famous:

POLLARD, ALFRED W. and REDGRAVE, G. R. | compilers | *A short-title catalogue of books printed in England, Scotland and Ireland, and of English books printed abroad, 1475–1640* | Bibliographical Society 1926 (reprinted 1950; new edition in preparation)

POLLARD, ALFRED W. and REDGRAVE, G. R. | *Index of printers, publishers and booksellers . . .* by P. G. MORRISON (Charlottesville: Bibliographical Society of Virginia 1950)

This has already become a standard work owing to its accuracy, but as it gives only brief details, reference to the other works already described is

## National Bibliographies | 167

necessary for additional information. A new edition is in preparation. Since its publication additional titles have been discovered, some of which are recorded in:

NEWBERRY LIBRARY | *English books and books printed in England before 1641 in the Newberry Library: a supplement to the record in the S.T.C.*, compiled by GERTRUDE L. WOODWARD | Chicago 1939

RAMAGE, DAVID | *A finding list of early English books to 1640 in libraries in the British Isles* (Durham University Library, 1958) and others are now being found during the compilation of a union catalogue of early printed books in the cathedral libraries by Miss Hands.

Other sources of information include:

AMES, JOSEPH | *Typographical antiquities: or an historical account of the origin and progress of printing in Great Britain and Ireland ... considerably augmented ... by William Herbert ...* | 3 volumes | 1785-90

COLLIER, JOHN PAYNE | *Bibliographical and critical account of the rarest books in the English language* | 4 volumes | New York: Scribner 1866

For the next twenty years, there is one very important catalogue:

BRITISH MUSEUM | THOMASON COLLECTION | *Catalogue of the pamphlets, books, newspapers and manuscripts relating to the Civil War, the Commonwealth, and Restoration, collected by George Thomason, 1640-1661* | 2 volumes | 1908

Over 20,000 entries are arranged chronologically, newspapers being catalogued separately at the end. This is a remarkably complete collection, since Thomason collected everything he could discover except folio volumes. Two sets of transcripts are also helpful:

STATIONERS' COMPANY | *Transcript of the registers ... from 1640-1708:* edited by G. E. B. EYRE | 3 volumes | Roxburghe Club 1913-15

The entries were transcribed by H. R. Plomer by whose name it is sometimes known. There is no index.

ARBER, EDWARD | editor | *The term catalogues, 1668-1709 A.D., with a number for Easter term 1711 A.D.: a contemporary bibliography of English literature in the reigns of Charles II, James II, William and Mary, and Anne* edited from the very rare quarterly lists of new books issued by the booksellers of London | 3 volumes | Arber 1903-6

The arrangement of entries is naturally rather inconvenient, and use is further impeded by very poor indexes. These bibliographies are, however, superseded for the most part by:

WING, DONALD | *A short title catalogue of books printed in England and in Scotland, Ireland, Wales and British America, and of English books printed in other countries, 1641-1700* | 3 volumes | New York: Index Society 1945-51

## 168 | National Bibliographies

WING, DONALD | *Index to printers, publishers and booksellers . . .* by P. G. MORRISON | Charlottesville: Bibliographical Society of the University of Virginia 1955

which continues Pollard and Redgrave. Various supplementary lists of additional titles and further locations have already appeared for both British and American holdings.

Bibliographies and catalogues specifically related to the eighteenth century and of any considerable reliability are non-existent. The most useful work is Watt's *Bibliotheca Britannica*, 1824, which is described in the previous chapter. Apart from this, the only other source is the *London catalogue of books since 1700*, 1773, but this is practically useless since dates and publishers are omitted and sometimes even authors.

Two other sources of information are the *Gentleman's Magazine*, 1731 to 1907, and Tobin's *Eighteenth-century English literature and its cultural background*, 1939 (reprinted 1967), in addition to the material which has been described in the section on English literature.

For British publications since the beginning of the nineteenth century the records are much more satisfactory. The main source of reference is:

*The English catalogue of books, giving in one alphabet, under author and title, the size, price, month of publication, and publisher of books issued in the United Kingdom, 1801 to date* | London 1864 to date

This annual has a very useful supplement of the publications of learned societies, associations, clubs, &c., and a directory of publishers. It is based on the weekly lists of publications included in the *Publishers' circular* which are themselves cumulated into monthly lists. Six volumes cover the whole of the nineteenth century, and since that date five-yearly cumulative volumes have been issued which facilitate speedy reference.

For the last forty-two years another trade list is also available:

*Whitaker's cumulative booklist, 1926 to date* | Whitaker 1926 to date

This is based on the weekly lists in the *Bookseller* and is issued quarterly, cumulating throughout the year into annual volumes and later into five-yearly volumes. It has the advantage of being arranged in classified form, with an index of authors and titles. Neither of these lists is completely comprehensive, so that the issue of the:

*British national bibliography, 1950 to date* | Council of the British National Bibliography 1950 to date

based on the accessions to the British Museum, is very welcome for its careful cataloguing and for its inclusion of much rare material. Entries are fully catalogued in accordance with the Anglo-American Code and are classified according to the Dewey Decimal Classification. They are

## National Bibliographies | 169

arranged in classified order in each weekly issue, and there are weekly and monthly indexes of authors, titles, subjects, significant references, &c. These are cumulated into annual volumes and permanent cumulations (1951–54, 1955–59, etc.), also in classified order, with cumulated indexes. Useful notes of such items as dates of previous editions, &c., are included. A printed card service is also available, covering publications from 1956 to date.

In 1874 Joseph Whitaker, founder of *Whitaker's Almanack*, issued *The reference catalogue of current literature*, representing all books in print at that time. It was subsequently issued at three- and four-yearly intervals (apart from the 1940's), and the latest edition comprises the publications of some 1,800 British publishers (2 volumes. Whitaker, 1961), an invaluable source of reference. The first volume is an author index and the second a title index with some subject groupings.

Readers are also reminded of the resources of the *Cumulative book index* which is described later in this chapter, since this is the most direct form of reference for publications throughout the English-speaking world issued since 1928.

### THE UNITED STATES OF AMERICA

American publications issued prior to 1928 can be traced in a series of bibliographies which cover almost the whole period since the beginning of printing. Two bibliographies deal with the first period:

EVANS, CHARLES | editor | *American bibliography: a chronological dictionary of all books, pamphlets and periodical publications printed in the United States of America from the genesis of printing in 1639 down to and including the year 1800: with bibliographical and biographical notes* | 14 volumes | Worcester, Mass.: American Antiquarian Society 1903–59

It includes books, pamphlets, and periodicals, and there are indexes of authors, subjects, publishers, and printers. Overlapping with this but containing additional items is:

SABIN, JOSEPH | *Dictionary of books relating to America, from its discovery to the present time* | 29 volumes | Bibliographical Society of America 1868–1936 (reprinted Amsterdam 1961)

which is generally referred to either by its author's name or by the title *Bibliotheca Americana*. Whereas Evans is arranged chronologically, Sabin is alphabetically arranged by authors. The gap, 1801–19, is gradually being covered by Ralph R. Shaw and Richard H. Shoemaker's *American bibliography: a preliminary check list for 1801–[1819]* (New York, Scarecrow Press, 1958 to date).

Another *Bibliotheca Americana* is available for the next period:

ROORBACH, ORVILLE AUGUSTUS | editor | *Bibliotheca americana: catalogue of American publications including reprints and original works from 1820 to 1860 inclusive, together with a list of periodicals published in the United States* | 4 volumes | New York: Roorbach 1852-61

in which entries are arranged alphabetically by author. Richard H. Shoemaker's *A checklist of American imprints for 1820-1825* (Scarecrow Press, 1964 to date) is intended to bring Roorbach up-to-date with selected locations. Periodicals and newspapers are not included. Roorbach is continued by:

KELLY, JAMES | editor | *American catalogue of books, original and reprints, published in the United States from January 1861 to January 1871* | 2 volumes | New York: Wiley 1866-71

and then by a series of issues of the *American catalogue* each of which recorded the volumes then in print (an equivalent of the British *Reference catalogue of current literature*). These were published annually from 1881 to 1911 and cover the period 1876 to 1910. At the turn of the century a new and far superior index came into being and is now the standard reference work for current material:

*Cumulative book index, 1898 to date* | New York: H. W. Wilson, 1898 to date

This is issued monthly, cumulating throughout the year into annual volumes, and later into multi-annual volumes. It is an index long famed for its high standards of bibliographical accuracy, and its arrangement of entries for authors, titles, and subjects in one alphabetical sequence has ensured its popularity and continued use. Since 1928 it has included the publications of the remainder of the English-speaking world.

In addition to this remarkably complete record of American publications, it should also be remembered that the catalogue of the Library of Congress, which has now been issued in book form and is being kept up to date by the regular issue of Supplements (see page 158) provides an unrivalled reference work for many of those publications which cannot be traced elsewhere.

In 1960 publication began of the *American book publishing record* (known as the *BPR*), a monthly cumulation from the trade listings in the *Publishers' weekly*. This aims to be a complete and accurate record of American current book production. Entries are arranged in classified order, with—in many cases—brief annotations and there is an author and title index to each issue. The American current equivalent of the British *Reference catalogue* is the annual *The publishers' trade list annual* which has appeared each year since its first issue in 1873. Since 1948 an index of authors and titles, *Books in print*, has been added to each issue, and in 1957 a further volume comprising an alphabetical *Subject guide* has been issued. *Books in print* is supplemented by the bi-monthly *Forthcoming books* (January 1966 to date). All these publications are issued by the R. R. Bowker Company of Philadelphia and New York.

Pamphlet material, which is only partly covered by the publications given above, is more fully treated in the monthly alphabetical subject list *Vertical file index* (New York, H. W. Wilson Company), which has been issued since 1932. It has a title index. Annual cumulations are published.

## FRANCE

The earlier publications of France are not fully recorded in its trade and bibliophile catalogues, and readers should keep in mind the *Catalogue général* of the Bibliothèque Nationale which records much rare material and which is described in the previous chapter. Other useful works for the early period are Brunet's *Manuel du libraire et de l'amateur de livres* (already described) and his:

BRUNET, GUSTAVE | *La France littéraire au $15^e$ siècle: ou, Catalogue raisonné des ouvrages en tout genre imprimés en langue française jusqu'à l'an 1500* | Paris: Franck 1865

and another useful handlist for the period up to 1600 is:

BRITISH MUSEUM | *Short-title catalogue of books printed in France, and of French books printed in other countries from 1470 to 1600* | 1924

There is no special bibliography of French books for the seventeenth century, and reference must be made to the general bibliographies mentioned in the previous chapter, and especially to Brunet's *Manuel* and to Georgi's *Allgemeines europäisches Bücherlexikon*, of which part V is devoted to French publications.

For the eighteenth century there is:

QUÉRARD, JOSEPH MARIE | *La France littéraire: ou, dictionnaire bibliographique des savants, historiens et gens de lettres de la France, ainsi que des littérateurs étrangers qui ont écrit en français, plus particulièrement pendant les $xviii^e$ et $xix^e$ siecles* | 12 volumes | Paris: Didot 1827-64 (reprinted, 12 volumes in 10, by Stechert-Hafner 1964)

which is arranged alphabetically by authors and includes brief biographical notes. This is also of use for the nineteenth century and so is the author's:

QUÉRARD, JOSEPH MARIE and others | *La Littérature française contemporaine, 1827-49* | 6 volumes | Paris: Daguin 1842-57

Another bibliography which covers almost the whole of the nineteenth century but is rather selective is:

VICAIRE, GEORGES | *Manuel de l'amateur de livres du 19ᵉ siècle, 1801–1893* | 8 volumes | Paris: Rouquette 1894–1920

which is well annotated, and gives full bibliographical details. For most of the century a trade list is available:

*Bibliographie de la France: ou, Journal général de l'imprimerie et de la librairie, 1811 to date* | Paris: Cercle de la Librairie 1811 to date

which is equipped with annual author and title indexes and an alphabetical list of periodicals. A list which has become the standard trade bibliography commenced rather later:

*Catalogue général de la librairie française, 1840 to date* | Paris: Champion 1867 to date

This is the equivalent of the British *English catalogue* and, in volumes covering periods of three years (many more in the older volumes), gives an alphabetical list of authors and titles, with a subject list at the end. This is far more comprehensive than Vicaire but lacks its annotations. It is very often referred to by the name of its first author, Lorenz.

The French equivalent of the *Reference catalogue* is the:

*Librairie française: catalogue général des ouvrages en vente . . . , 1930 to date* | Paris 1930 to date

which gives separate author and title lists of books in print. Another useful trade list is:

*Biblio: bibliographie; littérature* | *1933 to date* | Paris: Hachette 1933 to date

which includes authors, titles, and subjects in one alphabetical sequence. It is published monthly, cumulating into annual volumes.

## GERMANY

The early publications of the German-speaking areas are to be found recorded mainly in the purely general bibliographies such as Georgi, and in the national libraries of Germany and other countries. For the eighteenth-century onwards, there are:

HEINSIUS, WILHELM | *Allgemeines Bücherlexikon, 1700–1892* | 19 volumes | Leipzig: Brockhaus 1812–94

KAYSER, CHRISTIAN GOTTLOB | *Vollständiges Bücher-Lexikon, 1750–1910* | 36 volumes | Leipzig: 1834–1910

Subject indexes to the latter were published for the period 1750–1832 (1838) and 1891–1910 (5 volumes, 1896–1912).

In 1834 a daily trade list of the German publishing output began publication under the title *Börsenblatt für den deutschen Buchhandel*, and this was followed in 1842 by a weekly list as well, the *Wöchentliches Verzeichnis*, and in 1856 by a monthly list, the *Allgemeine Bibliographie*. But the main bibliographical record for the whole of the nineteenth century was the German book-trade's:

*Halbjahrs-Verzeichnis der im deutschen Buchhandel erschienenen Bücher, Zeitschriften, Landkarten* ... , *1798–* | Leipzig: Verlag des Börsensvereins der Deutscher Buchhändler 1798–

a comprehensive series, complemented since the middle of the century by the:

*Fünfjahrs-Katalog der im deutschen Buchhandel erschienenen Bücher, Zeitschriften, Landkarten, etc.; Titel Verzeichnis und Sachregister, 1851– 1912* | Leipzig: Hinrichs 1857-1913

usually referred to simply as 'Hinrichs'. Gustav Thelert published a *Supplement* (Grossenheim, Baumert, 1893) to these works to cover items published since 1850 which they had overlooked, and Karl Georg added a *Schlagwort-Katalog*, published at intervals of five years (Hannover, Lemmermann, 1889-1913) to enable books published during the years 1883-1912 to be traced by means of their 'catchword' titles.

The *Wöchentliches Verzeichnis* was superseded in 1931 by the:

*Deutsche Nationalbibliographie: Gesamtverzeichnis des in Deutschland erschienenen Schrifttums und der deutschsprachigen Schriften des Auslands, 1931 to date* | Leipzig: Deutsche Bücherei und Börsenverein der deutschen Buchhändler 1931 to date

of which the weekly Section A covers commercially-published books and maps, and the half-monthly Section B covers official and other non-commercial publications. From 1945 annual cumulations of Section A have been published under the title *Jahresverzeichnis des deutschen Schrifttums*, and a ten-year cumulation *Deutsches Bücherverzeichnis, 1941– 1950* (which includes the more important non-commercial items) is being followed by five-yearly cumulations. *Nova*, a monthly annotated classified selective trade list of new books has been issued regularly since 1957.

A rival West German weekly publication:

*Deutsche Bibliographie: wöchentliches Verzeichnis, 1947 to date* | Frankfurt-am-Main: Buchhändler-Vereinigung 1947 to date

whose title from 1947 to 1952 was *Bibliographie der deutschen Bibliothek* (monthly), has cumulated under the same main title as the *Halbjahres Verzeichnis* since 1951, and five yearly cumulations cover the period from 1945. Since 1954 there has also been an annual author and subject index.

## National Bibliographies

From the first issue of 1965 the *Deutsche Bibliographie* appeared in three series:

**Reihe A** listing, weekly, publications available in the book trade, including atlases but *not* maps, with weekly indexes cumulating monthly. Separate quarterly indexes include Austrian and Swiss German-language publications, and will be cumulated in half-yearly and 5-year lists

**Reihe B** listing, monthly, non-book-trade publications. Monthly indexes are cumulated annually. Selected titles from Reihe B will be included in the half-yearly and 5-year cumulated lists of Reihe A

**Reihe C** listing, bi-monthly, maps. Indexes cumulated annually

Printed catalogue cards for entries in these series are available from the Deutsche Bibliothek, which is responsible for the preparation of all bibliographical details, and for the preparation of the selective annotated bi-monthly *Das deutsche Buch* (1950 to date).

Both the *Deutsche Nationalbibliographie* and the *Deutsche Bibliographie* attempt to cover all German publications and all publications in the German language.

# 13 | Serial Publications

The increasingly important part played by serial publications in modern learning and research obliges the serious reader to have some acquaintance with the reference works which will enable him to identify a periodical from a reference and to trace a given article without too much delay. Fortunately, there are a number of excellent aids (recorded in The Library of Congress's *Union lists of serials: a bibliography* 1964), chief of which is the remarkable scholarly and detailed:

> GREGORY, WINIFRED | editor | *Union list of serials in libraries of the United States and Canada* | 3rd edition | New York: H. W. Wilson 1965

This is the most complete of all the bibliographies of periodicals throughout the world, and lists both current and extinct items. Dates and place of publication are included, and also changes of name. Entries are arranged alphabetically, and there are also locations for sets in America. The work of this bibliography was continued in *Serial titles newly received, 1951-52*, and its successor:

> *New serial titles, 1953 to date* | Washington, D.C.: Library of Congress 1953 to date

a monthly, annual and multi-annual publication, listing alphabetically the items received by outstanding American libraries. Coverage is international. A classified list *New serial titles-classed subject arrangement* is also issued monthly. The first ten-year cumulation of *New serial titles* was issued in 1962, and was followed by the 1961-65 cumulation (3 volumes. New York: Bowker 1967).

The British equivalent is a work already affectionately known (by its initials) as BUCOP:

> *British union-catalogue of periodicals: a record of the periodicals of the world, from the seventeenth century to the present day, in British libraries* | Edited by J. D. STEWART | 4 volumes | Butterworth 1955-8 (Supplement, 1962)

which lists alphabetically nearly 150,000 serials in some 400 British libraries and is continued by the quarterly *British union-catalogue of periodicals, incorporating World list of scientific periodicals: new periodical titles* (1964 to date), which has annual and 5-year cumulations.

Another very important list is:

*Union catalogue of the periodical publications in the university libraries of the British Isles* | Joint Standing Committee on Library Co-operation 1937

which is also arranged alphabetically by title, and gives details of publication. There is a Supplement of international congresses. A third list, equally important, is the *World list of scientific periodicals published in the years 1900–1960*, 1966: this, and the *Handlist* of the Science Library, are described in the chapter on Science.

There are two other very useful lists:

TIMES, THE | *Tercentenary handlist of English and Welsh newspapers, magazines, and reviews* | 1920

which is divided into two sections: London, and the provinces. Under each section entries are arranged chronologically, with indexes of titles.

GREGORY, WINIFRED | editor | *List of the serial publications of foreign governments, 1815–1931* | New York: H. W. Wilson 1932

For older material there are five outstanding bibliographies:

BRITISH MUSEUM | *Catalogue of printed books ... periodical publications* | 2nd edition | 2 volumes | 1899–1900

BRITISH MUSEUM | *Catalogue of printed books ... newspapers published in Great Britain and Ireland, 1801–1900* | 1905

MILFORD, R. T. and SUTHERLAND, D. M. | *A catalogue of English newspapers and periodicals in the Bodleian Library, 1622–1800* | 1936

WARD, WILLIAM S. | compiler | *Index and finding list of serials published in the British Isles, 1789–1832* | Lexington: University of Kentucky Press 1953

CRANE, R. S. and KAYE, F. B. | 'A census of British newspapers and periodicals, 1620–1800.' | *Studies in philology*, January 1927 (published by the University of North Carolina Press)

The last includes newspapers, magazines, reviews, essay sheets in the *Spectator* tradition, annuals, &c.—Scottish, Irish, and Welsh, as well as English. Entries are arranged in alphabetical order of title, and there is a geographical index of periodicals published outside London, and a chronological index of the whole. Ward's locations supplement those in Gregory's *Union list of serials*. An essay and bibliography by Katherine Kirtley Weed and Richmond Pugh Bond on 'Studies of British newspapers and periodicals from their beginning to 1800: a bibliography' (*Studies in philology*, December 1946) is designed to complement primary lists such as Crane and Kaye by gathering together the titles of numerous

## Serial Publications | 177

secondary works—some of them obscure and hard to come upon—which deal with British newspapers and periodicals issued before 1800. Additional items are listed in the *Cambridge bibliography of English literature* (see p. 103). There is also a very good German index:

*Gesamtverzeichnis der ausländische Zeitschriften, 1914–1924* | Berlin: Staatsbibliothek 1927–9

which is arranged alphabetically by the 'Schlagwort' or significant word of the title, with cross-references from other forms. This is often referred to by the abbreviation G.A.Z.

For current material one of the most helpful though selective lists is:

*Ulrich's international Periodicals directory: a classified guide to a selected list of current periodicals* | 12th edition | New York: Bower 1967 and annual supplements from 1966 onwards)

which is international in scope. Entries are arranged in classified order in 2 volumes: 1—scientific, technical, and medical periodicals (about 20,000 titles); 2—the arts, humanities, social sciences, and business (about 35,000 titles). Each entry indicates the presence of abstracts, book reviews, bibliographies, illustrations, statistics, &c., and states in what cumulative services the journal is abstracted or indexed. Ulrich is kept up-to-date in the *Library journal*. Another useful list is:

CAMBRIDGE UNIVERSITY LIBRARY | *current periodicals* ..., *1960* | Cambridge University Press 1960

which includes the proceedings of learned societies, shows entries for college and departmental libraries, and is thus also useful for tracing the whereabouts of serials. Other such lists include those of the Bodleian and the University of London library, and various regional lists such as the *London union list of periodicals* (LULOP).

A special list of abstracts is available:

ROYAL SOCIETY | *A list of periodicals and bulletins containing abstracts published in Great Britain: with an appendix giving partial list of journals containing abstracts published in the British Commonwealth* | June 1949

This is selective, choosing only those which fulfil the Society's high standards. Entries are arranged in classified order, and scope, method, and publication details are given. There is an index of titles and organizations.

It is often of importance to be able to ascertain whether cumulative indexes are available for a given serial. The answer can frequently be obtained from:

HASKELL, DANIEL C. | *Check list of cumulative indexes to individual periodicals in the New York Public Library* | New York: Public Library 1942

In addition to the entries in *New serial titles* new periodicals are recorded (first number only) in the *British national bibliography*, 1950 to date, and many government and special libraries record the issue of new serials in their accessions lists (for example, the library of the Victoria and Albert Museum). In addition, notes of new periodicals are given regularly—together with notes of changes of title, cessation of publication, &c.—in the preliminary pages of the various H. W. Wilson periodical indexes. The national trade indexes of current periodicals are also useful in tracing specific items: the chief lists are mentioned at the end of this chapter.

For tracing specific articles there is an immense range of periodical indexes, some general, and many more devoted to a special subject or group of subjects. Of the latter, notable examples are the *Public affairs information service*, the *Engineering index*, the *Applied science and technology index*, the *Art index*, and many others, each of which is described in the appropriate chapter. In addition there are four general indexes:

*British humanities index, 1915–22, 1926 to date* | Library Association 1915 to date

*Readers' guide to periodical literature, 1900 to date* | New York: H. W. Wilson 1901 to date

*Social sciences and humanities index, 1907 to date* | New York: H. W. Wilson 1916 to date

UNITED NATIONS | LIBRARY | *Monthly list of selected articles* | 1947 to date

The first, known until 1961 as the *Subject index to periodicals*, is issued monthly, cumulating annually; supplementary regional lists are also issued. The *Social sciences and humanities index*, formerly the *International index*, is of more interest to British readers than the *Readers' guide* since it covers more British periodicals, but both are monuments of careful indexing. The *Readers' guide* indexes about 130 periodicals, of general interest. Author and subject entries are given for each article, and title entries are included for stories. Poems, films, and plays are also listed by title under 'Poems', 'Moving picture plays', and 'Dramas' respectively. It is issued fortnightly, cumulates throughout the year into annual and three-yearly volumes. The *Social sciences and humanities index* is an author and subject index to about 200 periodicals devoted to pure science and the humanities. Subjects include: astronomy, general science, geography, geology, anthropology, philology and literature, nursing, palaeontology, religion, ethics and philosophy, psychology, law, mathematics, archaeology, sociology, history, economics, political science, physics, and zoology. Many periodicals of general interest are also indexed. Some foreign material is included. It cumulates throughout the year into annual and three-yearly volumes. The United Nations *Monthly* list is a classified list of outstanding periodical articles from important periodicals, mainly in the field of the social sciences.

For the nineteenth century there is:

*Poole's index to periodical literature, 1802-1906* | 7 volumes | Boston, Mass.: Houghton 1888-1908 (reprinted 1938)

which is very useful but not always easy to use since articles are arranged in alphabetical order by the significant word of the title, which makes tracing rather haphazard. This is gradually being superseded by Walter Edwards Houghton's *The Wellesley index to Victorian periodicals, 1824-1900* (University of Toronto Press 1966 to date) which identifies many of the contributors and provides bibliographies of their articles and stories; and by the:

*Nineteenth century readers' guide to periodical literature . . .* | New York: H. W. Wilson 1944 to date

of which the first two volumes, covering the years 1890-9, have already been issued. They include some supplementary indexing for the twentieth century of important periodicals.

Attention must be drawn to the great German work *Internationale Bibliographie der Zeitschriftenliteratur*, the most comprehensive index to periodical literature ever published. With its supplementary volumes it covers German periodicals for over 100 years, while non-German periodicals are indexed from 1911. In its later years it has indexed more than 6,000 journals, compared with the few hundred covered by British and American indexes. Details are:

*Internationale Bibliographie der Zeitschriftenliteratur*

Abteilung A: *Bibliographie der deutschen Zeitschriftenliteratur, 1896 to date* | (Supplement, in 20 volumes, covers the years 1861-95)

Abteilung B: *Bibliographie der fremdsprachigen Zeitschriftenliteratur, 1911 to date*

Abteilung C: *Bibliographie der Rezensionen und Referate, 1900-1943* | 77 volumes | Osnabrück: Dietrich 1897 to date

In its later years Abteilung A indexes well over 4,000 German serials, and the Supplement devotes six of its volumes to additions to the main work. Abteilung B covers about 3,000 foreign (i.e. non-German) serials, and is particularly strong in English-language, French and Italian items. From 1912 onwards, Abteilung C added book reviews in non-German periodicals, listing them in a separate section. The basic volumes of the *Internationale Bibliographie*, to approximately 1944, have recently been reprinted (238 volumes. New York, Kraus Reprint Corporation, 1960-2).

Book reviews are also covered in the following:

*Book review digest, 1905 to date* | New York, H. W. Wilson, 1905 to date

*An index to book reviews in the humanities, 1960 to date* | Detroit, Phillip Thomson 1960 to date

The first is issued monthly, cumulating into annual volumes. It is arranged alphabetically by author. There is a subject and title index which cumulates annually and 5-yearly. Digests of reviews of some 4,000 current books in 70 journals are provided each year. The second indexes reviews in nearly 700 journals. It is issued quarterly.

The following directories of periodicals and newspapers will be found of use in identifying incomplete or abbreviated references:

*Annuaire de la presse française et étrangère, et du monde politique, 1878 to date* | Paris: Roux-Bluysen

*N. W. Ayer and Son's Directory [of] newspapers and periodicals, 1880 to date* | Philadelphia, Ayer (covers United States and its possessions, Canada, Bermuda, Cuba, and the Philippines)

*Newspaper press directory and advertisers' guide, 1846 to date* | Benn (covers Great Britain, Northern Ireland, Eire, the Commonwealth and foreign newspapers, magazines, reviews and periodicals | Often known as Mitchell's, after its former publisher)

*La presse francaise* | 3rd edition | Paris: Hachette 1967 (lists both alphabetically and by subject French and French-language periodicals published throughout the world)

*Sperling's Zeitschriften- und Zeitungs-Adressbuch: Handbuch der deutschen Presse, 1858 to date* | Leipzig

TOASE, M. | *Guide to current British periodicals* | Library Association 1962

*Willing's press guide, 1874 to date* | Willing's Press Service (comprehensive for Great Britain; selective for the Commonwealth and foreign countries | Includes lists of changed titles | Supplements issued quarterly)

## Serial Publications | 181

*Willing's European press guide*, 1966/67 to date | Willing's (a classified list of journals published on the Continent)

*The writers' and artists' year book*, *1902 to date* | Black (describes subject coverage of British and American periodicals)

*Handbuch der Auslandspresse* | Bonn: Athenäum-Verlag, 1960 | (A companion volume to the Berlin Free University's Institut für Publizistik's *Die deutsche Presse* | Covers the press of nearly 200 countries and territories)

MERRILL, JOHN C. | *A handbook of the foreign press* | revised edition | Baton Rouge: Louisiana State University Press 1959

RAUX, H. F. | *Répertoire de la presse et des publications périodiques françaises, 1960* | Paris: Editions de la Documentation française 1961

# 14 | Further Reading

At best this book can but be an introduction to a vast subject. Those who have visited the University Library at Senate House in London will no doubt have seen and admired the astonishing collection of bibliographies in what is known as the Middlesex North Library, yet even this excellent aid to bibliographical research is but a selection of what is available. And to what has already been published is daily added more and more so that the research worker finds a wealth of material from which it is difficult to distinguish the most useful.

For those who wish to pursue this subject in more detail there are no better guides than those described on pp. 161–62. To keep up to date with current material it is necessary to consult the issues of the *Bibliographic index* (also described in the section named above) as they appear, and to read the chapters on bibliographies in the issues of the *Five year's work in librarianship* (Library Association). The *Times Literary Supplement* usually reviews the more general bibliographies, and there are some reviews of this nature in the *Library Association Record*, which is published monthly. New English bibliographies are recorded in the *British national bibliography* (January 1950 to date) at the beginning of each weekly issue. In addition, Unesco's *Bibliography, documentation, terminology* provides excellent information on national bibliographical developments and on individual new bibliographies and bibliographical services from all parts of the world.

Finally there can be no better ending to this book than the words written by Lord Passfield in his Introduction to the *London bibliography of the social sciences*:

'I stoutly maintain that every orderly arranged bibliography, however incomplete, will be of use to somebody. For many years I have made it a practice to begin my counsel to would-be researchers—indeed to everyone wishing to make any genuine investigation—by urging them to start by compiling a list of books, pamphlets, and reports bearing on the chosen subject. The mere survey of their titles, publication dates, and tables of contents is a necessary preliminary to every voyage of discovery after new truth. The second step is—not reading through these innumerable volumes, all of them more or less obsolescent or at any rate of exhausted fertility—but skipping lightly over their pages, pencil in hand to note down all the hints and hypotheses, cavilling objections and, irresponsible interrogations that will arise in the investigator's mind as he turns irreverently, or even mockingly, over the pages in which the craziest cranks have printed their fancies and venerable 'authorities' enshrined their 'standard' doctrines. Then and not till then, is the researcher in a position effectively to begin his serious business of investigation for the discovery of new truth. Without a whole assortment of hypotheses, any pregnant observation of facts is difficult, if not impossible.'

# Index of Subjects and Personal Names

Abstracts   177
Accountancy   39
Adam, R. B.   122
Adventures   140
Advertising   4
Aeronautics   66, 71–2
Aesthetics   8, 9, 10, 78, 87
Agriculture   47, 66, 73–5, 143
Air mail   72
Airships   72
Alchemy   54
Allen, F. H.   128
Altmann, W.   92
Alston, R. C.   102
Altick, R. D.   102
Altsheler, B.   58
Ames, J.   167
Anatomy   46, 58
Anderson, J. P.   149
Anderson, R. B.   32
Angling   98
Anglo-Saxon language   103
Animals   45, 55, 61–4, 73, 74
  behaviour   11
  distribution   140
  flight   72
  industrial aspects   74
Anonymous literature   100, 105, 160–1
Anthony, L. J.   46, 53
Anthropology   13, 21, 22, 23, 59, 179
  philosophical aspects   9
  physical   46
Apel, W.   87
Apocrypha of the Bible   17
Apostolic Fathers   13, 138
Appleton, Sir E.   45
Applied entomology   62
Arber, E.   166, 167
Arbitration   33

Arboriculture   60
Archaeology   16, 76, 78, 80, 136, 137, 138, 139, 150, 179
Architecture   77, 78, 79–80, 85
Archives   xvii, 4, 5, 30
Arias   91
Arnim, M.   151
Arnold, M.   115
Arnold, R. F.   131
Arnott, J. F.   95
Art   76–86, 136
Art exhibitions   78, 85, 86
Artists   77, 78, 79, 85, 86
Astrology   51
Astronautics   72
Astronomy   46, 47, 48, 49, 178
Astrophysics   47, 52
Atkinson, D. F.   127
Atlases   140–43
Atomic energy   53
Atwood, A. C.   60
Auden, W. H.   115
Aufricht, H.   27
Austen, J.   111, 115
Authors   6, 85, 100, 104, 114–30
Authorship   4, 5
Autobiographies   152
Autogiros   72
Autographs   77
Automation   70
Automobiles   71
Aviation   71–72
Ayer, N. W.   180

Babington, P. L.   128
Backus, E. N.   90
Bacon, F.   115
Bacteriology   46, 47, 59

185

# Index of Subjects and Personal Names

Baillie, G. H.   80
Baker, B. M.   96
Baker, E. A.   110, 111
Baker, E. Alan   75
Baldwin, J. M.   8
Ballads   91, 107, 148
Ballen, D.   43
Ballet   97, 98
Balloons   72
Bank notes   82
Banks and banking   21, 31, 39
Banned Books   101
Baptist faith   18-19
Baring, M.   115
Baron, G.   41
Barrie, Sir J.   115
Barrow, J. G.   16
Bartholomew, A. T.   116
Bary, T. de   139
Bason, F. T.   124
Bates, W.   14
Bateson, F. W.   103
Batson, H. E.   29
Beale, J. H.   31
Beardsley, A. S.   34
Beaumont, C. W.   97
Beaumont, Sir F.   115
Becker, F.   76, 85
Beckford, W.   115
Beerbohm, Sir M.   115
Beethoven, L. van   88
Beliefs   43
Belknap, S. Y.   98
Bell, A. F.   134
Belloc, H.   116
Benkovitz, M. J.   120
Bentley, G. E.   116
Bentley, R.   116
Berkeley, G.   116
Bernal, J. D.   65
Berolzheimer, D. D.   54
Besterman, T.   xv, 121, 160, 162
Beverages   75
Bewick, T.   77
Bible, The   14, 16, 17-18, 20
 criticism   13
 translation   17, 104

Bibliographical references   xvi
Bibliographies   6
 form   xv-xvi
 qualities   xvi-xvii, 167-8
 varieties   xiv-xv
Bibliographies, National   149, 150-60
Bibliographies, Universal   182-3
Bibliographies of bibliographies   161-3
Bibliography   4, 5, 6
Bibliotheca Osleriana   163
Bibliotheca Patrum   13
Bicycles   72
Bierce, A.   116
Bigmore, E. C.   3
Biochemistry   47, 58
Biogeography   57
Biography   137-9, 151-54
Biology   13, 46, 47, 48, 58-9, 68, 74
Biophysics   47, 52, 58
Birds   63-4
Bitner, H.   34
Black, G. F.   44
Blacker Library of Zoology   63
Blades, W.   4
Blake, S. F.   60
Blake, W.   116
Blanchard, J. R.   73
Blanck, J.   104
Blaustein, A. P.   35
Blindness   39
Block, A.   112
Bloomfield, B. C.   115
Bochenski, I. M.   10
Boehm, E. H.   27, 145
Bohatta, H.   161
Bollandine Acta Sanctorum   13
Bolton, H. C.   54
Bond, D. F.   101
Bond, R. P.   176
Boni, A.   87
Bonser, W.   44, 147
Book plots   99
Book production   3
Book reviews and reviewing   5, 180
Book trade   4

## Index of Subjects and Personal Names | 187

Bookbinding   3, 4, 5, 77
Books   5, 6
Bookselling   4
Borrow, G.   116
Bossuat, R.   132
Boswell, J.   116
Botany   46, 58, 59, 61, 74
Bottle, R. T.   53, 58
Boxing   98
Brandreth, H. R. T.   18
Breed, P. F.   92
Brewton, J. E.   106
Brewton, S. W.   106
Bridger, C.   153
Bridges, R.   116
Brie, G. A. de   9
Broad, C. L.   127
Broad, V. M.   127
Broadcasting   93–4
Brockett, P.   71, 72
Brontë family   116
Broughton, L. N.   117
Brown, A. A.   90, 95
Brown, C. F.   106
Brown, C. R.   35
Brown, H. M.   90
Browne, N. E.   84, 122
Browne, Sir T.   116
Browning, R.   117
Bruncken, H.   106
Brunet, G.   171
Brunet, J. C.   159, 171
Brussel, I. R.   118
Buccaros   81
Buddhism   20
Buffalo Bill   97
Bunyan, J.   117
Burger, K.   159, 160
Burke, E.   117
Burkett, J.   70
Burns, R.   117
Burton, M.   5
Burton, Sir R.   117
Business   22, 28
Butler, S.   117
Byron, Lord   117
Byzantine culture   139

Cabeen, D. C.   132
Cabell, J. B.   118
Cabinet making   80
Cabot, P. S. de Q.   38
Cahill, P.   116
Cahoon, H.   123
Cannons, H. G. T.   6
Canny, J.   125
Canon law   16
Carlyle, T.   118
Carnivals   96
Caron, P.   145
Carpenter, E.   118
Carpenter, F. I.   127
Carpentry   80
Carrick, N.   78
'Carroll, L.'   118
Carter, J.   122
Carter, P. G.   25
Cartography   56, 57, 142, 143
Carving   77
Case, A. E.   107
Case, S. J.   18
Catalan language and literature   92
Cataloguing   6
Cathedral libraries   17
Catholic literature   15, 16, 19
Celtic culture   79, 102
Censuses   25–6
Ceramics   66, 78, 81–2
Chamber music   88, 89, 92–3
Chamberlin, M. W.   77, 84
Chamberlin, W. J.   62
Champneys, M. C.   41
Chapbooks   43
Chapman, G.   115
Chapman, R. W.   115
Charms, D. de   92
Charophytes   60
Chaucer, G.   104, 118
Chaundy, L.   115
Chemical compounds   53
Chemical engineering   47, 48, 54, 66
Chemical physics   52
Chemistry   46, 47, 48, 49, 51, 53–5, 56
Chevalier, U.   145

Children
  books  7, 42
  courts  37
  libraries  5, 6
  plays  110
  poetry  106
  songs  92
  stories  103, 105–6, 113–14
China  66, 78, 81–2
Chivalry, Orders of  16
Choral Music  89
Choreography  98
Christ  18
Christian unity  18
Christianity  13–19, 144
Chronicles, Mediaeval  104
Chronometry  52
Chubb, T.  141
Church, The  16
Church furnishings  80
Church re-union  18
Church vestments  83
Churchill, Sir W.  118
Cinema  87, 94–5, 96
Cioranescu, A.  132
Circus  96, 97
Civics  38
Civil engineering  70
Clarence, R.  107
Clark, B. H.  125
Clark Powell, L.  ix
Classical literature  136–9
Classification  6
Cleaver, A. H.  119
Clemens, S. L. ('Mark Twain')  129
Cleveland, J.  118
Clifford, J. L.  122
Clifford-Vaughan, F. M. McA.  34
Climatology  57
Clocks  80
Clough, F. F.  93
Clymer, W. B. S.  121
Coal  56
Coins  77, 82, 136, 137, 139, 145
Colas, R.  83
Coleman, A.  41
Coleridge, S. T.  118

Colin, P.  86
Collier, J. P.  167
Collison, R. L.  7, 94, 100
Colonies  21, 27–8
Commerce  21, 22, 29, 30, 143
Communication  24
Communications  42–3, 143
Company law  34
Compound interest  39
Conan Doyle, Sir A.  120
Conflict of laws  33
Congregationalism  19
Conjuring  96, 97
Conover, H. F.  27, 164
Conrad, J.  118–9
Constitutional law  34
Control  70
Cook, D. E.  83, 112
Cooke, G. W.  120
Co-operation  18
Cope, S. T.  154
Copinger, W. A.  159
Coppard, A. E.  119
Copyright  6
Corson, J. C.  126
Costume  80, 83–4, 97
Cotton, G. B.  110, 111
Coulter, E. M.  144
Counties  141, 147, 148, 150
Courtney, W. P.  122, 163
Courts of justice  37
Cowley, A. E.  20
Cowper, W.  119
Cox, E. G.  140
Crafts  78
Crane, E. J.  53
Crane, R. S.  105, 176
Crane, S.  119
Crane, W.  119
Crerar, J.  45, 65
Cricket  98
Criminology  36–8
Cross, T. P.  vi, 101
Cruikshank, G.  77
Crustacea  62
Cryptogams  61
Crystallography  49, 52

Index of Subjects and Personal Names | 189

Culture 23
 philosophy 9, 10
Culver, D. C. 37
Cuming, G. J. 93
Cumming, Sir J. 36
Cummings, E. E. 119
Currier, T. F. 129
Cushing, H. G. 92
Customs and habits 23, 43
Cutler, B. D. 115

Dairying 74
Dalton, B. H. 69
Dances and dancing 97-8
Daniel, R. S. 12
Darling, J. 13
Darlow, T. H. 17
Darmstädter, L. 46
Darrell, R. D. 87
Darton, F. J. H. 105
Darwin, C. 119
Davies, A. M. 56
Davies, G. 148
Davies, J. H. 88
Day, C. L. 91
De Bary, T. 139
De Charms, D. 92
Deafness 39
Dean, B. 64
Dean-Smith, M. 91
Décor 97
Decoration 77, 78, 80
Defence 23
Defoe, D. 119
Deism 14
Delinquency 37-8
Deming, R. H. 123
Demography 25-6, 38, 143
Demonology 12
Dendrology 60
Dentistry 68
Dewey, M. 7
Dexter, H. M. 19
Diaries 152
Diaz, J. Simon 135
Dickens, C. 119

Dictionaries 100
 scientific & technical 50
Diehl, K. S. 16
Diepenbroick-Grüter, H. D. von 84
Dime novels 97
Diplomacy 26, 33, 34
Diplomatics 145
Discographics 87, 88, 93
Divinity 13
Dobson, A. 120
Dr Williams's Library 14
Dodgson, C. L. ('Lewis Carroll') 118
Donne, J. 120
Douglas, N. 120
Doyle, Sir A. Conan 120
Drake, K. H. ix
Drama 95-7, 107-10, 131, 135-6, 178
Drawing and drawings 77, 85
Dreher, S. 133
Dress 80, 83-4, 97
Drevet, M. L. 133
Driers (printing) 5
Drugulin, W. E. 84
Dryden, J. 120
Duckles, V. 87
Duff, E. G. 164-6
Duncan, G. S. 82
Dutcher, G. M. 144
Duval, E. W. 123
Duval, H. R. 122
Duzer, H. S. Van 128
Dyer, I. W. 118
Dyson, G. M. 53

Early Christian Fathers 13, 138
Earth sciences 47
Eastman, M. H. 43, 113
Eastwood, W. 104
Ebisch, W. 127
Ecclesiastical matters 13, 80, 83
Eckel, J. C. 119
Ecology 74
Economic geography 57
Economic geology 56

## 190 | Index of Subjects and Personal Names

Economics  13, 21-2, 23, 26, 27, 28-31, 102, 179
Ecumenical movement  16, 18
Edel, L.  122
Edge, M. A.  122
Edgeworth, M.  120
Education  9, 22, 23, 40-42, 45, 48, 50, 102
  philosophy  9, 10
Educational psychology  11
Edwardes, M.  99
Egerer, J. W.  117
Eitner, R.  88
Eldridge, H. T.  25
Electrical engineering  48, 70
Electricity  52
Electronics  52, 66, 70
Electrotyping  5
'Eliot, G.'  111
Eliot, T. S.  120
Ellis, Mrs J. C.  58, 85
Embree, A. T.  139
Emerson, R. W.  120
Encyclopaedias  7
Engelmann, W.  137
Engineering  47, 50, 69-72
English language & literature  99-130, 164-71
Engraving and engravings  77, 86
Enser, A. G. S.  95
Entomology  58, 62, 74
  applied  62, 74
Epigraphy  136, 137
Epistemology  9
Epistles  17
Eppelsheimer, H. W.  99
Equitation  97
Eschelbach, C. J.  122
Esdaile, A.  15, 112
Essays  114, 134
Etching & etchings  86
Ethics  8-10, 13-14, 16, 45, 179
Ethnology  9
Evans, A. P.  100
Evans, C.  169
Evans, M. A. ('George Eliot')  111
Ewald, K.  43

Examinations  41
Exempla  112
Expeditions  140, 142
Exploration  72, 98
Eyre, G. E. B.  167

Fables  43, 112, 113
Fairy tales  113
Family histories  153-4
Farish, M. K.  93
Farming  47, 73-5
Farquhar, J. N.  20
Farrar, C. P.  100
Fashion  83-4
Fauna  60, 63
Fellmann, J. D.  143
Ferguson, J. P. S.  153
Fertilisers  73, 74
Fiction  100, 110-14
Fidell, E. A.  110
Field Crops  74
Fifoot, E. R. S.  127
Filmed books and plays  95
Films  87, 94-5, 96, 178
Finance  21, 28-31, 39
Fine arts  76-98, 102
  philosophy  9, 10
Finzi, J. C.  129
Firbank, R.  120
Firkins, I.  109
Firmage, G. J.  119
Fish  64, 73, 143
Fishing  98
FitzGerald, E.  120
Fitzmaurice-Kelly, J.  135
Fitzmyer, J. A.  18
Flags  154
Fleischer, E. A.  90
Fleming, T. P.  47
Fletcher, J.  115
Flora  60-61, 63
Flory, E. V.  110
Folk dances  97
Folk songs and music  43, 91, 93
Folk tales  43
Folklore  13, 16, 43-4, 102, 135

Index of Subjects and Personal Names | 191

Food 74, 75
Ford, W. K. 90
Foreign affairs 16, 21, 22, 23, 26-8, 33
Foreign law 35-36
Forestry 60, 73, 74, 75, 143
Forman, H. B. 125, 127
Forman, M. B. 124
Forrester, F. S. 98
Forster, E. M. 120
Foskett, D. J. 40, 75
Foster, F. M. K. 138
Fowler, M. J. 49
Frazer, Sir J. 121
Freeman, R. B. 119
French, S. 108
French language & literature 100, 132-3
Frewer, L. B. 146
Friend, W. L. 31
Friends, Society of 19
Frost, R. 121
Fry, Sir E. 33
Fucilla, J. G. 134
Fuller, C. 22
Furniture 76, 80-81
Fussell, G. E. 73

Gallatin, A. E. 115
Gallup, D. C. 120, 126
Galsworthy, J. 121
Gamble, W. B. 72
Games 98
Gaols 37
Gardens & gardening 74, 77
  equipment 80
Gardner, D. E. 153
Gardner, E. G. 134
Gardner, F. M. 100, 111
Garland, H. 115
Garrison, F. H. 66
Gazetteers 140
Gems 56, 76, 83
Genealogy 145, 153-4
Genetics 47, 59, 74
Geoastrophysics 57

Geodesy 48, 52
Geosciences 56, 57
Geography 27, 46, 48, 136, 137, 140-3, 178
Geological Survey 57
Geology 46, 48, 55-8, 59, 66, 179
Geomorphology 57, 143
Geophysics 48, 49, 52
Georg, K. 173
Georgi, G. 160, 171, 172
German language and literature 130-2
Gerstenberger, D. L. 113
Gerstenfeld, M. 114
Gesta Romanorum 112
Gibbon, E. 121
Gibson, J. 117
Gibson, R. W. 115
Gilbert, W. S. 121
Gilder, R. 96
Gillett, C. R. 14
Girvan, I. W. 130
Giuseppi, M. S. 147
Glanzman, G. S. 18
Glass 82
Glencross, A. 111
Gliders & gliding 72
Global physics 47
Goedeke, K. 130
Goethe, J. W. von 131
Gohdes, C. 105
Goldman, S. 69
Goldsmith, A. H. 129
Goldsmith, O. 121
Goldstone, A. 124
Good, J. T. 104
Gospels 17, 18
Government publications 21, 22, 25, 40, 42
Gower, J. 104
Grammars, 100
Gramophone records 87, 88, 93
Granger, E. 106, 107
Graphic arts 3-5, 77, 78, 79
Graves, R. 121
Gray, G. J. 125
Gray, T. 121

14

## Index of Subjects and Personal Names

Greek language and literature 136–9
Green, C. R. 121
Greenfield, E. 93
Greg, Sir W. W. 109
Gregor, J. 107, 111, 131
Gregory, W. 175, 176
Grierson, P. 82
Griffith, R. H. 126
Grinstein, A. 12
Grismer, R. L. 135, 136
Grolig, M. 130
Grose, C. L. 148
Gross, C. 147, 148
Grove, Sir G. 87
Grüter, H. D. von Diepenbroick- 84
Guidebooks 140
Guitar music 93
Gurney, E. 12
Gypsies 44

Haggard, Sir R. 121
Hagiography 16, 17
Hain, L. 151, 159
Hair styles 83
Halkett, S. 105, 161
Hall, H. A. 30
Hall, M. 31
Hammond, E. P. 118
Hammond, W. A. 10, 78
Hampton, J. F. 98
Hand, M. S. G. 17, 167
Handel, G. F. 89
Handicrafts 78
Handley-Taylor, G. 124
Hanson, L. W. 28
Harbage, S. 108
Harding, J. S. 57
Hardy, T. 121
Harkness, S. B. 117
Harp music 93
Harris, C. D. 143
Harrison, F. M. 117
Harrison, H. G. 153
Hartley, L. 127
Harwood, K. 93

Harzberg, H. 83
Haskell, D. C. 178
Hastings, J. 13
Hatton, T. 119
Hawkins, R. R. 47
Hawthorne, N. 122
Haycraft, H. 100, 104
Hazen, A. T. 129
Hazlitt, W. 122
Headicar, B. M. 22, 33
Healey, G. H. 130
Health 67–8
Health insurance 39
Heartman, C. F. 125
Heinsius, W. 172
Heinzel, E. 84
Held, H. L. 20
Helicopters 72
Helminthology 74
Hemmings, E. F. 75
Hendrick, G. 113
Hennecke, H. 131
Heraldry 79, 145, 153–4
Herbage 74
Herbals 60
Herbert, W. 167
Herescu, N. T. 139
Heroes 113
Hewitt, A. R. 28, 147
Heyer, A. H. 91
Hicks, F. C. 34
Higginson, F. H. 121
Higgs, H. 28
Higson, C. W. J. 41
Hiler, H. 83
Hiler, M. 83
Hind, A. M. 86
Hinrichs, J. C. 173
Hinton, P. 125
Hirsch, P. 90
Historical Manuscripts Commission 148
History 4, 5, 136, 137, 138, 144–50
 fiction 111–12
 modern times 26, 27
 philosophy 9, 10
Hodgkin, J. 115

## Index of Subjects and Personal Names | 193

Holdsworth, Sir W. S.  31
Holzmann, M.  161
Homilies, Mediaeval  104
Hoppé, A. J.  117
Hornby, H. F.  77, 86
Horticulture  74
Hoselitz, B. F.  22
Hospitals  6, 68
Hotson, L.  109
Houghton, B.  66
Houghton, W. E.  179
Household equipment  80
Housing  80
Housman, A. E.  122
Houzeau, J. C.  51
Howard, J.  36
Huckabay, C.  125
Hudson, W. H.  122
Hughes-Hughes, A.  89
Human geography  140
Humanities  47
Humphreys, A. L.  150
Hurd, J. C.  18
Huxley, A.  122
Hygiene  67
Hypnosis  12

Iconography  78, 145
Illustration and illustrations  3, 77, 78, 83, 84-5
  clocks and watches  81
  costume  83
  nature  58
  paintings  84-5
  portraits  84-5
  prints  77
  processes  3, 77
  travel  85
Illumination  70
Income  31
Incunabula  73, 159-60, 164, 166, 167, 171
Indexing  6
Industrial arts  48, 65-75
Industrial design  78, 80
Industrial psychology  11

Industry  22, 29, 30, 65-75
Information and information services  6, 24
Ink  4, 5
Instrumental music  89, 90, 92-3
Instrumentation  50
Insurance  39
Intellectual life  23
Interior decoration  78, 80
International affairs  16, 21, 22, 23, 26-8, 33-4
International conciliation  27
International languages  101
International law  26, 27, 33-5
International meetings  27, 49
International organisations  21, 23, 27, 40
Inventions  46
Irving, W.  122
Irwin, R.  vii, 64
Islam  19, 139, 144
Italian language and literature  76, 100, 134

Jackson, B. D.  60
Jackson, J.  141
Jacobus, D. L.  154
Jaggard, W.  127
Jails  37
Jainism  20
James, H.  122
Japan  139
Jaryc, M.  145
Jessop, T. E.  116
Jesus  18
Jewellery  56, 76, 83
Jews  20
  religion  15, 19-20
Johnson, A. F.  105, 161
Johnson, C.  144
Johnson, F. R.  127
Johnson, H. T.  70
Johnson, I.  47
Johnson, M.  129
Johnson, S.  122
Jones, H. M.  105

## Index of Subjects and Personal Names

Jonson, B.  123
Josephson, A. S.  65
Joyce, J.  123
Judaism  15, 19–20
Juridical law  34
Juvenile courts  37
Juvenile delinquency  37–8, 41

Kaplan, L.  152
Kaplan, S. R.  56
Karpel, B.  78
Kaye, F. B.  176
Kayser, C. G.  172
Keats, J.  123
Keller, H. R.  99
Kelly, E. C.  69
Kelly, J.  170
Kelly, J. Fitzmaurice-  135
Kennedy, A. G.  102
Kennedy, J.  105, 161
Kent, F. L.  vii
Kerr, E.  100, 111
Keynes, Sir G.  115, 116, 120, 122, 126
Kilns  82
Kinema  87, 94–5, 96
Kipling, R.  123
Kirkpatrick, B. J.  120
Kites  72
Kline, J.  153
Klussmann, R.  137
Körner, J.  131
Kramm, H.  145
Kuhlman, A. F.  37
Kunisch, H.  131
Kunitz, S. J.  100, 104
Küp, K.  4

La Bigne, M. de  13
Labour  30, 38
Laing, J.  105, 161
Lalit, A.  145
Lamb, C.  123
Lamb, M.  123
Lancaster, J. C.  146
Land management  73

Landor, W. S.  123
Landscape architecture  78
Lane, W. C.  84
Langlois, C. V.  144, 163
Langridge, D.  126
Language  9, 99–139
  philosophy  9, 10
  teaching  41
Lanson, G.  132
Lasswell, H. D.  24
Latin American languages and literatures  135–6
Latin language and literature  108 136–9
  mediaeval period  101
Laurence, D. H.  122
Law  21, 22, 23, 31–8, 45, 137, 179
  history  31
  international  26, 27
  philosophy  9, 10
Law of aviation  72
Lawrence, D. H.  123
Lawrence, T. E.  123
League of Nations  27
Learned societies  14, 30, 46, 102
Leclaire, L.  113
Legal history  31
Legends  104, 113
Lehmann, R. P.  20
Lehmann-Haupt, H.  3
Leigh, C. W. E.  39
Leisure  38
Lende, H.  39
Lenrow, E.  111
Leslie, S.  97
Lettering  3
Levis, H. C.  86
Lewin, E.  147
Lewis, H. K.  47
Lewis, P. R.  21–2
Libraries and librarianship  4–7
Libretti and librettists  88, 91
Life assurance  39
Life sciences  55
Lighting  70
Lindley Library  61, 74
Lines, K. M.  114

## Index of Subjects and Personal Names | 195

Linguistics 48, 99, 100
Linnaeus, C. 59
Lipperheide, Freiherr von 83
Lippincott, L. 126
Literary prizes 100
Literature 85, 99–139
Lithography 5
Livingston, F. V. 123
Livingston, L. S. 124
Lloyd, R. W. 98
Local government and history 21, 30, 145, 150
Locke, H. 120
Loewenberg, A. 91, 96
Logasa, H. 108
Logic, 8, 9, 10
Lohf, K. A. 118
London, J. 124
Long-playing records 87, 88, 93
Longfellow, H. W. 124
Lorenz, O. 172
Louttit, C. M. 10–11, 12
Lowe, R. W. 95
Lowell, J. R. 124
Lowndes, W. T. 159
Lucas, E. L. 78
Ludwig, R. M. 105

McAlpine Collection 14
McBurney, W. H. 113
McColvin, E. R. 85
McCulloch, J. R. 28
McDonald, E. D. 123
Macdonald, H. 120
Macfie, R. A. S. 44
McGill, H. 110
MacGillivray, J. R. 123
Machen, A. 124
McKay, G. L. 116, 128
McManaway, J. G. 109
Macmillan, D. 109
MacMinn, N. 125
McMurtrie, D. C. 3
Macpherson, M. R. 106
Madan, F. 118
Magazines 175–81

Maggs Bros. 72
Magic 43, 96
Magriel, P. 97, 98
Maittaire, M. 160
Malclès, L. N. 161
Maller, S. ix
Maltby, A. 31
Mammals 62
Management 30
Mansfield, K. 124
Mantz, R. E. 124
Manz, H. P. 95
Maps 140–43
March, A. C. 20
Margerie, E. de 55
Marilla, E. L. 129
Marine architecture and engineering 71
Marionettes 97
Marlowe, C. 124
Marouzeau, J. 137
Marrot, H. V. 121
Marshall, G. W. 153
Martin, E. A. 129
Martin, G. H. 147
Martindell, E. W. 123
Masefield, J. 124
Mason, B. 56
Mason, S. 129
Masquéray, P. 139
Masques 97, 108, 109
Massé, G. C. E. 119
Masui, M. 31
Materials testing 70
Mathematicians 50
Mathematics 39, 46–51, 59, 69, 136, 179
  method 29
Mathews, E. B. 56
Matthews, W. 152
Maugham, W. S. 124
Maxwell, W. H. 35
Mazzoni, G. 134
Mechanical engineering 48, 70
Mechanics 46
Medals 82
Medicine 47, 55, 65, 66–9, 136

## 196 | Index of Subjects and Personal Names

Mediterranean region  28
Medley, D. J.  148
Mellon, M. G.  53
Menninger, K. A.  12
Mental disorders  11, 12, 38
Meredith, G.  124
Merrill, J. C.  181
Metallurgy  48, 66
Metalwork, Art  77
Metaphysics  9, 10, 45
Meteorology  46, 57-8, 143
Metzger, B. M.  18
Microbiology  47, 58, 74
Migel, M. C.  39
Middle English language and literature  103, 104, 106
Milford, R. T.  176
Military affairs  27
Military orders  16
Mill, J. S.  125
Millar, C.  129
Miller, G. A.  50
Miller, H.  125
Miller, W.  119
Milne, A. T.  149
Milton, J.  125
Mime  97
Mineralogy  46, 56, 58, 73
Mining  56, 73, 143
Misch, C. C.  112
Missions  16
Modern language teaching  41
Monasticism  139
Money  28-31, 82
Monro, I. S.  83, 84, 112
Monro, K. M.  84
Monroe, W. S.  40
Moore, C. K.  70
Moore, J. R.  119
Morals  13
Morgan, B. Q.  132
Morgan, C. S.  148
Morgan, W. T.  148
Morris, B.  118
Morris, R. P.  16
Morris, W.  125
Morrison, P. G.  166, 168

Morsch, L. M.  6
Morton, L. T.  66
Mosher, F. J.  161
Motion pictures  87, 94-5, 96, 178
Motor fuels and lubricants  71
Motor industry  71
Motorcycles  71
Moule, H. F.  17
Mountaineering  98
Mulhall, M. G.  24
Mullens, W. H.  63
Mullins, E. L. C.  145
Murrie, E. B.  91
Museums  30, 56, 78, 79, 81
Music  87-93, 102, 136
  ballet  98
  gypsy  44
  Islamic  19
  Jewish  20
Music Hall  95-7
Mycology  74
Myths and mythology  13, 16, 113, 136, 137


Nairn, J. A.  136
National defence  23
Natural history  58-9
Natural resources  56, 73
Naturalists  62
Ncave, S. A.  62
Needlework  83
Nervous diseases  11
New Testament  18
News films  95
Newspapers  175-81
Newton, A.  62
Newton, Sir I.  125
Nicoll, A.  109
Nield, J.  111
Night clubs  96
Niles, D.  97
Nooy, W. Ver  108
Norse mythology  113
Northup, C. S.  102, 121
Norton, J. E.  121
Novels  100, 110-14

# Index of Subjects and Personal Names | 197

Nuclear sciences  47, 53, 54
Nuffield College  28
Numismatics  77, 82, 136, 137, 139, 145
Nurmi, M. K.  116
Nursing  68, 179
Nutrition  74, 75

Observatories  80
Occult, The  12, 16
Occupational welfare  68
Oceans & oceanography  56, 141, 143
Odell, S.  112
Oettinger, E. M.  151
Official publications  21, 22, 25, 40
O'Hegarty, P. S.  123
Olbrich, W.  111, 131
Old Testament  17, 18
Olivart, Marquis de  33
Oliver, L. M.  115
Oliver, P.  129
O'Mahony  108
O'Neill, E.  125
Ooteghem, J. van  136
Opera  88, 91
Ophthalmology  69
Oppenheim, L.  33, 34
Orchestral music  89, 90, 92–3
Orders of chivalry  16
Ore deposits  56
Organ music  88
Oriental literature  139
Oriental religions  16, 19–20
Orman, O. C.  34
Ornament  78
Ornithology  61, 63–4, 73
Osborne Collection  113
Osler, Sir W.  63
Ostvold, H.  73
Ottemiller, J. H.  108
Ottley, G.  42

Packman, J.  110
Paetow, L. J.  xv, 145
Pafford, J. H. P.  ix

Painting  77, 78, 79, 80, 85–6
Paintings  84–5
Palaeography  4, 5, 102, 136, 146
Palaeontology  46, 56, 57, 58, 64, 179
Palfrey, T. R.  99
Palmer, H. R.  138
Pamphlets  171
Pane, R. U.  136
Pantomime  97
Panzer, G. W.  160
Paper  3, 4, 5, 66
Papyrology  136
Parachutes  72
Pardon  37
Paremiology  44
Pargellis, S.  148
Parke, N. G.  50, 52
Parker, A.  123
Parole  37
Passfield, Lord  182–3
Patents  54, 66
Pathology  47, 58, 59
Patten, N. Van  102
Pattison, A. S. Pringle  8
Pauly, A. F. von  139
Pazdirek, F.  88
Peace  27, 34
Pearl, R. M.  56
Pearson, J. D.  19
Peddie, R. A.  42, 158
Pedigrees  153–4
Pemberton, J. E.  50
Penology  36–8
Pentateuch  17
Penzer, N. M.  117
Performing arts  95–8
Periodicals  175–81
Perkins, W. F.  73
Pests & pest control  73
Petroleum  56
Petzholdt, J.  162
Phanerogams  60
Pharmacology  47, 55, 68
Phillips, L.  122
Phillips, P. L.  141
Phillpotts, E.  125
Philology  9, 10, 48, 99–139, 179

## Index of Subjects and Personal Names

Philosophers  8, 9, 10
Philosophy  8, 10, 13, 14, 16, 20, 45, 102, 136, 137, 138, 139, 179
Photography  52, 72, 77, 86-7
  aerial  72
  printing processes  5
Physics  46, 47, 48, 49, 51-53, 66, 69, 179
Physiology  46, 52, 58, 74
Piano music  88
Pinto, O.  164
Place, J.  132
Plants  60, 73, 74, 143
  behaviour  11
  folklore  60
  geography  140
  poisons  61
Plastics  66
Platt, E. T.  140, 142
Playbills  96
Plays  95-7, 107-10, 131, 135-6, 178
Plomer, H. R.  167
Plots, Book  99
Plumb, P.  70
Pneumatic engineering  70
Poe, E. A.  125
Poetry  106-7, 178
Poggendorf, J. C.  49
Poisons  47
  plants  61
Polar regions  26, 28, 72, 141
Police  36
Politics  21, 22, 23, 24, 26-8, 30, 45, 102, 137, 179
  philosophy  9
Pollard, A. W.  166
Poole, W. F.  179
Pope, A.  125-6
Population  25-6, 38, 143
Porcelain  66, 78, 81-2
Porter, E. C.  98
Portraits  84-5, 104
Portuguese language and literature  134-5
Potter, A. C.  115
Pottery  77, 81
Pottle, F. A.  116

Poultry  64, 74
Pound, E.  126
Powell, L. Clark  ix
Power  70
Powys, J. C.  126
Powys, T. F.  126
Preedy Memorial Library  76, 150
Prezzolini, G.  134
Price, H.  12
Price, M. O.  34
Prideaux, W. F.  120, 128
Pringle-Pattison, A. S.  8
Printing  3-6
Prints  77, 86
Prisons  37
Pritzel, G. A.  59, 60
Private presses  4
Probabilities  39
Probation  37
Proctor, R.  160, 166
Production  29
Prohibited books  101
Propaganda  24
Protestant faith  16
Provençal language and literature  101
Proverbs  43, 44, 104
Pseudonymous literature  100, 104, 105, 110, 160-1
Psychiatry,  12
Psychical research  12
Psychoanalysis  12
Psychologists  8
Psychology  8-13, 16, 22, 41, 45, 47, 59, 102, 179
Public administration  21, 22, 23
Public health  67, 68
Public opinion  24
Public records  30, 147
Publishers and publishing  4, 5, 6
Punishment  37
Purdy, R. L.  121


Quakers  19
Quérard, J. M.  161, 171

## Index of Subjects and Personal Names | 199

Radar 70
Radio 93–4, 96
Radium 52
Radzinowicz, L. 36
Railways 21, 42, 66
Ramage, D. 167
Rand, B. 8, 10, 11
Ransom, W. 4
Raux, H. F. 181
Ravage, Mme D. ix
Read, C. 148
Readers 6
Reading 5
Recitations 106
Recorded music 87, 88, 93
Redgrave, G. R. 166
Reed, T. B. 4
Reference works 7, 161, 162
Reformatories 37
Rehder, A. 60
Reichling, D. 159
Religion and religions 9, 13–20, 23, 101, 136, 137, 138, 139, 179
  history 16
  non-Christian 16, 19–20
  philosophy 8, 9, 10
Religious orders 16
Renooij, D. C. 25
Reproduction (printing, etc.) 6
Research & Development 49, 66
Reuss, J. D. 46
Richardson, E. C. 15
Richardson, S. 126
Riches, P. M. 151
Rickman, J. 12
Riddles 43
Riley, P. 126
Road books 147
Roads 43
Robbins, R. H. 106
Roberts, F. W. 123
Robin Hood 43
Robinson, E. A. 126
Robinson, J. W. 95
Rogers, P. P. 136
Rolle, R. 104
Rolli, M. 133

Rollins, H. E. 107
'Rolls Series' 148
Rolph, J. A. 128
Roman Catholic Church 15, 16, 19
Romance languages and literatures 99
Romances, medieval 43, 104
Roorbach, O. A. 170
Roumanian language and literature 99, 101
Rowland, B. 78
Rubber 66
Ruff, W. 126
Rural sociology 73, 74
Ruskin, J. 126
Russell, N. H. 119
Ryder, J. 4
Rylands, J. 158, 166

Sabin, J. 169
Sacred music 89
Sadleir, M. 113, 128
Safety 68
Sagas 113
Sage, R. 38
St John, J. 113
Sale, W. M. 126
Saltonstall, C. D. 92
Sanborn, R. 125
Sands, D. B. 103
Sarton, G. 45–6
Sassoon, S. 126
Sayle, C. E. 166
Schnapper, E. B. 90
Schneider 163
Schools 41
Schücking, L. L. 127
Schwartz, J. 119
Science 45–64, 65, 101, 136–7
  history 9, 45–6, 48
  philosophy 9
Scientific discoveries 46
Scientific instruments 50
Scientists 49
Scott, J. E. 121
Scott, T. 121, 125
Scott, Sir W. 126

## Index of Subjects and Personal Names

Sculpture  77, 78, 80, 85
Seals  82, 154
Seaplanes  72
Sears, M. E.  92, 107
Sell, V.  106
Senaud, A.  18
Sequel stories  100, 110, 111
Serial publications  175-81
Seris, H.  135
Sermons  13
Seymour Smith, F.  138
Shakespeare, W.  127
Shapiro, N.  92
Sharp, D.  80
Shaw, G. B.  127
Shaw, R. R.  169
Sheeny, E. P.  118
Shelley, P. B.  127
Shepherd, R. H.  118
Shipbuilding  71
Shipwrecks  140
Shober, J. L.  122
Shoemaker, R. H.  169, 170
Shores, L.  40
Short stories  112
Siberell, L. E.  126
Simmons, C. H.  124
Simms, R.  vii, xiii-xiv, xv
Simon Diaz, J.  135
Simpson, D. H.  152
Simpson, N. D.  61
Singer, H. W.  84
Sitwell family  127
Slade, B. C.  120
Slavonic languages and literatures  101
Slocum, J. J.  123
Slocum, R. B.  151
Smart, J.  60, 63
Smart, J. P.  126
Smart, T. B.  115
Smith, B. L.  24
Smith, D. N.  122
Smith, F.  154
Smith, F. S.  138
Smith, G. R.  127
Smith, H. C.  92
Smith, J. A.  19
Smith, J. F.  50
Smith, M. Dean-  91
Smith, R. C.  62
Smith, T. D'A.  128, 129
Smith, W. A.  105, 161
Social geography  57
Social psychology  38
Social sciences  21-44, 66
Social service  38-9
Society of Friends  19
Sociology  13, 21-45, 48
  philosophy  9
Soil science  73, 74, 143
Solon, L. M. E.  81
Somerset Maugham, W.  124
Songs  88, 89, 90, 91-2
  children  92
  gypsies  44
Sonneck, O. G. T.  91
Sonnenschein, W. S.  xv, 159
Sotheran, Henry, & Co.  51, 54
Space sciences  53, 72
Spanish language and literature  135-6
Sparrow, J.  122
Specifications  66, 69
Spector, H. K.  37
Speeches  114
Spencer, K. J.  70
Spenser, E.  127
Spherical astronomy  51
Spinoza  20
Sport  98
Sprent, F. P.  141
Squire, W. B.  89
Staffordshire  xiii-xiv
Stage  95-7
Standards  66, 69
Starr, E. C.  19
Starr, H. W.  121
Starrett, V.  116, 119
Stathis, J. L.  128
Statistics  21, 22, 24-6, 39, 45
Statutes  32
Statutory law  34
Stein, H.  141, 163
Steinschneider, M.  19

# Index of Subjects and Personal Names | 201

Stephens, T. A.  44
Stereo records  93
Stereoscopy  87
Stereotyping  3, 5
Sterne, L.  127
Steven, Sir J. F.  36
Stevens, D. H.  125
Stevenson, L.  113
Stevenson, R. L.  128
Stewart, J. D.  17
Stollreither, K.  35
Stoneware  81
Stott, R. Toole-  97, 124
Stratman, C. J.  109
Strong, R. M.  64
Structure of matter  47
Summers, M.  128
Superstition  43
Surveying, aerial  72
Sutherland, D. M.  176
Sutton, R. B.  114
Swann, H. K.  63
Sweetser, W.  124
Swift, J.  128
Swinburne, A.  128
Symonds, J. A.  128
Symons, A. J. A.  130
Szladits, C.  36

Tableware  80
Talvart, H.  132
Tannenbaum, S. A.  115, 123, 124
Taxonomic zoology  58, 62, 64
Taylor, A.  161
Taylor, C. M.  113
Taylor, G.  60
Technical dictionaries  50, 69
Technical education  41
Technical reports  66
Technology  46, 50, 65–75
  history  9
Teerink, H.  128
Teggart, F. J.  42
Telecommunications  70
Television  70, 93–4, 96, 98
Temperley, H. W. V.  144

Tennyson, Lord  128
Terra-cotta, architectural  81
Terra sigillata  81
Testing of materials  70
Textbooks
Textiles  66
Thackeray, W. M.  128
Theatre  95–7, 107–10, 131, 135–6
Thelert, G.  173
Theologians  16
Theology  13–20
Thiele, W.  142
Thieme, H. P.  133
Thieme, U.  76, 85
Thomas, D.  128
Thomason, G.  167
Thompson, E. N. S.  125
Thompson, S.  43
Thomson, J.  114
Thomson, J. C.  123, 128
Thomson, P.  180
Thomson, R. G.  110
Thomson, T. R.  153
Thoreau, H.  128
Tiles, decorative  81
Timber  80
*Times Literary Supplement*  xvii
Toase, M.  180
Tobin, J. E.  168
Todd, W. B.  117
Tokens  82
Tomkinson, Sir G.  4
Toole-Stott, R.  97, 124
Topete, J. M.  136
Town planning  77, 80, 143
Toxicology  47, 61
Toy theatres  97
Trade  21, 22, 29, 30, 143
Traditions  43
Translations  xvii, 100, 132, 136, 138, 141
Transport  21, 23, 42–3, 143
Travel  85, 98, 140, 148
Treaties  33, 36
Trials  33
Trollope, A.  128
Tropics  67, 141

## Index of Subjects and Personal Names

'Twain, M.'  129
Type and typography  3, 4, 5
  composition  5
  founding  3

Ulrich, C. F.  4, 177
Underbrink, R. L.  7
Unemployment insurance  39
Unesco  vii, xv, xvii, 182
United Nations  27
Universities  41
Upholstery  80

Values, theory of  9, 29
Van Duzer, H. S.  128
Van Patten, N.  102
Vance, L. E.  85
Varet, G.  10
Varnishes  5
Vascular plants  60, 61
Vaughan, F. M. McA. Clifford  33
Vaughan, H.  129
Vehicles  71
Ver Nooy, W.  108
Vertical file material  171
Verwey, G.  25
Veterinary medicine  68, 69, 74
Vicaire, G.  157–8, 171
Viking art  79
Vocal music  88, 89, 90, 91–3
Vollmer, H.  76
Vosburgh, M. E.  5
Voyages  64, 140, 141, 148

Wade, A.  130
Walford, A. J.  ix, 7, 162
Walker, E. P.  62
Walker, J. E.  v
Walpole, H.  129
Walton, I.  129
Ward, W. S.  176
Watches  80
Water  56
Watt, R.  159, 168

Wealth  31
Webb, A. D.  24
Webb, S.  182–3
Weed, K. K.  176
Weeds  61
Welding  70
Welfare  23, 38–9
Wells, C.  129
Wells, G. H.  127, 129
Wells, H. G.  129
Wells, J. E.  104, 112
West, C. J.  54
West Indies  28
Western Hemisphere  26
Westminster Assembly  14
Whitaker, H.  141
Whitaker, J.  168, 169
White, C. M.  21–2
White, G.  129
White, J. G.  43
Whitford, R. H.  52
Whitley, W. T.  18
Whitman, W.  129
Whitmore, J. B.  153
Whitney, J. P.  144
Whittier, J. G.  129
Wilde, O.  129
Wildlife  73
Williams, A. W.  119
Williams, Dr D.  14
Williams, J. B.  29, 149
Williams, S. H.  118
Williams, S. T.  122
Williamson, H.  130
Wilson, G. F.  122
Winchell, C. M.  7, 24, 161, 162
Winfield, P. H.  31
Wing, D.  167, 168
Wise, T. J.  8, 119, 123, 125, 126, 127, 128, 130
Wissowa, G.  139
Witchcraft  12, 43
Women in aeronautics  72
Wood, B.  116
Wood, C. A.  63
Wood, E. S.  63
Wood engraving  3

Woodbridge, H. C. 124
Woods, F. 118
Woodward, G. L. 109, 167
Woodworking 80
Woolf, C. 120
Wordsworth, W. 130
World War I 26
World War II 26
Worthington, G. 126
Wright, A. 102
Wright, J. K. 140
Wright, L. H. 113
Writers 85, 100, 104, 114-30

Writing 3
Wyatt, H. V. 58
Wycliffe, W. 104
Wyman, C. W. H. 3

Yeats, W. B. 130

Zaunmüller, W. 100
Zeitlinger, H. 51
Zischka, G. A. 7
Zoology 46, 58, 61-4, 74